Singers and the Song

Singers
and the Song

Gene Lees

OXFORD UNIVERSITY PRESS
New York   Oxford

Oxford University Press

Oxford   New York   Toronto
Delhi   Bombay   Calcutta   Madras   Karachi
Petaling Jaya   Singapore   Hong Kong   Tokyo
Nairobi   Dar es Salaam   Cape Town
Melbourne   Auckland

and associated companies in
Berlin   Ibadan

Copyright © 1987 by Gene Lees

First published in 1987 by Oxford University Press, Inc.,
200 Madison Avenue, New York, New York 10016

First issued as an Oxford University Press paperback, 1989

Oxford is a registered trademark of Oxford University Press

Library of Congress Cataloging-in-Publication Data
Lees, Gene.
Singers and the song.
1. Music, Popular (Songs, etc.)—United States—
History and criticism.   2. Singers—United States.
I. Title.
ML3477.L43   1987   784.5′00973   86-33233
ISBN 0-19-504293-X
ISBN 0-19-506087-3 (PBK.)

Since this page cannot legibly accommodate the copyright notices
of the songs that appear in this book, the facing page will constitute
an extension of the copyright page.

2 4 6 8 10 9 7 5 3 1

Printed in the United States of America

To Francy, Sahib, and Gigi

Foreword

These brilliant essays are as difficult to describe, and certainly to pigeonhole, as the restless original mind that produced them. The author calls this "a collection about singers by a writer who is a singer," but that is a little like calling *Moby Dick* a book about a whale hunt. This is about Americans. Gene Lees knows that the best of American music, jazz—and even the worst of Top Forty and disco—tells us who we are, where we came from and where we're going. He knows that if you made a thorough study of American classics like Armstrong's *West End Blues*, Ellington's *Ko-Ko*, Parker-Gillespie's *Shaw 'Nuff*, if you knew everything that went into the making of such miracles of brevity and everything that leaked out of them into the mainstream of our culture, you would arrive at a clearer understanding of contemporary America than you'd get from any number of sociology courses.

All the essays in this book, and the companion volume on instrumentalists that will follow it, first appeared in the *Jazzletter*, a remarkable journal published, edited, circulated by mail, and largely written by Gene Lees. Accepting no ads and meeting few deadlines, the *Jazzletter* has a thousand-odd subscribers who include the cream of jazz musicians (Dizzy Gillespie, John Lewis, Artie Shaw, Gil Evans), film composers (Henry Mancini, Johnny Mandel), film-makers, critics, singers, music educators, and magazine editors, in addition to Gene Kelly, Dudley Moore, and Steve Allen who bought about three dozen subscriptions to send to his friends. Only I. F. Stone's *Newsletter* compares with it.

This stubborn little publication tapped into an underground of holdouts against the Mickjaggerization of America, odd folk who knew that Jerome Kern was as great a songwriter as Franz Schubert, who warmed to Baryshnikov when he said it was Fred Astaire's dancing that lured him to America, who care what happened to singers like Dick Haymes, and who prefer the folklore of jazz musicians to the gossip of fan magazines.

The *Jazzletter*'s creator is a combination of music critic, classical as well as jazz, linguist, translator, and biographer. Critics are not supposed to bare their vulnerable throats by going on the road and recording as singers, but Lees was a singer before he became a critic, and a lyricist whose words to Jobim's *Quiet Nights of Quiet Stars* and Bill Evans' *Waltz for Debby* have been recorded by every vocalist of stature from Tony Bennett to Ella Fitzgerald. So when Lees writes about Sinatra, he not only tells us he's great, he clarifies why in a way that no one else ever has. "Anybody who thinks Sinatra was just the boy next door," Lees says, "has a plentiful lack of knowledge of the art he brought to such perfection." His letters, which many people keep, are, like his conversation, full of surprises. For example: "Among singers, we all know how good Perry Como really is. I've never encountered a critic who knew it."

The *Jazzletter* came into being in 1981. Lees had just published a radically new rhyming dictionary, based, he says, on the patterns of French rhyming dictionaries. He had wearied of writing of all kinds, lyrics included, except for a prodigious correspondence with his close friend Julius La Rosa, a highly articulate man whom Lees considers one of the best singers in the business. He sensed after a time that he didn't hate writing but only writing brief pieces on complex matters to fit the space restrictions inevitable in publications such as *Saturday Review, Stereo Review, High Fidelity,* and *Down Beat.* "Without knowing it," he says, "I needed a larger form and was finding it in my correspondence with Julie. I can't tell you how much he had to do with my return to writing."

One day Lees sent a letter to his legion of musician and singer friends to ask whether they would be interested in a music newsletter, if he were to start one. A week later his mailbox was full of subscription checks.

From the beginning, the *Jazzletter* was not restricted to jazz, any more than this book is restricted to American singers. It is not so much about jazz musicians as *for* jazz musicians, reflecting the richness and variety of their interests and of those who are drawn to this music. Lees is not given to picking over the dried bones of jazz musicology but offers fresh nourishment about Edith Piaf, of whom Americans know little, and the late film composer Hugo Friedhofer, of whom we know nothing. When Friedhofer died, his friends asked Lees to handle the press. Lees telephoned the *New York Times* to give the paper the information for an obituary. He found that the people on the arts-and-entertainment desk had never heard of this revered patriarch of film scoring. The *Times* printed not one line about the passing of this historic figure. "That did it," Lees says. "I said to myself, 'We cannot continue at the mercy of amateurs promoted from the city desk. We have to have a publication of our own.' Hugo's death was the proximate cause of the *Jazzletter*."

In the extraordinary *Pavilion in the Rain,* Lees destroyed the persistent myth that the Big Band Era was killed off by bebop and television, showing with the meticulous care of the newspaper reporter he once was that the primary cause was the systematic dismantling of the public transit system. This essay has gained currency among university educators. *Pavilion in the Rain*—and for that matter, the entire book—should be assigned reading in colleges as an exquisite remembrance of that vital time "when so much popular music was good and so much good music was popular." One is tempted to quote its magical opening paragraph, evocative of Fitzgerald, but I leave you to discover it for yourself.

The essays in this book are not idly strung together but carefully selected to be read in sequence, beginning with *William and Harold and How to Write Lyrics,* one of the most original and readable things on the roots and development of the English language yet to see print, and ending with the awesome four-part *A Journey to Cologne* wherein the universality of jazz binds together the youthful poems of Pope John Paul II as adapted by Lees for a suite of songs sung by Sarah Vaughan and performed by an exalted conclave of American expatriate and European musicians, assembled by a visionary Italian ringmaster and conducted by the Argentinian Lalo Schifrin in one of the most-bombed cities of World War II. This great essay is best read in conjunction with hearing the record album that resulted from the project, although it stands perfectly well on its own.

The conflicting themes of war and creation run through the entire collection, coming together at last in *A Journey to Cologne,* which in passing unfolds the wit, sensitivity, and gruelling anxieties of its author. It is an apt climax to this magnificent book.

—Grover Sales

Grover Sales teaches jazz history at San Francisco State and Stanford universities and is the author of Jazz: America's Classical Music.

Contents

Singers and the Song

The minstrel boy to the war is gone,
  In the ranks of death you'll find him;
His father's sword he has girded on,
  And his wild harp slung behind him.

—Thomas Moore

William and Harold and How to Write Lyrics

In the autumn of 911, the Frankish king Charles III, known as Charles the Simple, unable to halt the bloody Viking incursions on his northwestern coast—indeed, the longships had gone up the Seine as far as Paris—made the best of a bad situation by coming to an agreement with the marauders. This was the so-called treaty of St. Clair-sur-Epte. Charles allowed them to settle permanently in an area to which in due course they lent their name. They were, in their own language, *nortmanni*, northmen. A little over a thousand years later some of their far-distant descendants would come from places as yet not dreamed of, such as Quebec and Winnipeg, Wichita and Chicago, Rimouski and Hoboken and San Diego, to land once more on these shores, young men bearing names derived from the *nortmanni,* such as Beaudry and Dupuis, Plumber and Draper, and Fitzgerald. They called the beaches here by new and alien names—Utah and Omaha, Sword and Gold—and many of them would die in the surf or flinging their grappling hooks up the cliffs or climbing the ropes with rifles on their backs, die in their struggle to come home to their ancestral Normandy.

In return for his undoubtedly grudging generosity, Charles got an agreement from the *nortmanni,* whose leaders became the dukes of Normandy: they were to keep the other Vikings off his neck, support his monarchy, and speak the language of the coun-

try, which was already recognizable as French, a dialect of the soldier Latin left behind by the long-vanished Roman garrisons. He
thereby initiated the chain of historical events that determined
how people who speak English as their primary language actually
think, tell jokes, express anger, make love, and write songs.

Charles the Simple might be called the grandfather or possibly the midwife of the English language. But whatever we call him,
had he not allowed the Vikings to settle in Normandy, the Franco-
Germanic hybrid we call English would not exist.

The Normans were a ruthless, energetic, bellicose people with
a taste and a talent for power. One of their dukes had by his mistress a son, a boy who was called William the Bastard. This is not
a flattering name, and so after he defeated the army of King Harold near Hastings in September of 1066 and had himself crowned
King of England, he saw to it that he was henceforth known as
William the Conqueror. This is called public relations.

Conquerors are notably disinclined to learn the language of
their subjects. We may surmise that this is because they are so busy
with more important things, such as appropriating land, giving
themselves titles, selecting the best of the local girls, and dispen-
sing justice to those who object. In time the conqueror's language
is perceived as that of the successful—the rich and the powerful
who evolve into an emplaced aristocracy. To this day names like
Beaumont and Clairmont and those with the prefix "de" seem to
people who speak English to have more class than those of Anglo-
Saxon origin. Traces of the social strata extant under the Normans
are preserved in surnames. Those of craftsmen are English, for
example Baker, Fisher, Hedger, Shepherd, Shoemaker, Wain-
wright, Weaver, Webber. But those of skilled artisans are
French—Carpenter, Draper, Mason, Plumber, Tailor. And of
course Irish names beginning with Fitz, corrupted from *fils de*, son
of, are all Norman French.

Legal proceedings were conducted in French. This continued
until the Plague killed so many people that there were not enough
French-speaking judges to go around and English at last became
the language of the courts. But by then the very vocabulary of the

law was almost entirely French, excepting Latin technical terms such as *sine die* and *nollo contendere,* and thus it remains: *tort, appeal, justice, jurisprudence, arraignment, verdict, illegal.* For nearly three hundred years, until 1362, Parliament (itself a French term) spoke French.

But though the common people learned a certain amount of French, they did not forget their own language, which in our time is referred to inaccurately as Anglo-Saxon. The Angles and Saxons were only two of the Germanic peoples who had brought their languages to England. The Danes had been there, and they left their mark in place names ending in *-by,* such as Rigby. Old Norse also made up part of the language which, by the time Harold caught an arrow at Hastings, was already known as English.

Once the flow of French into English was begun, it never ceased. And whereas the first influence was Norman French, Central French later penetrated the language. Thus we find in English a whole series of separate but related words imported from those two forms of old French—*catch* from Norman French, *chase* from Central French, the *w* of the former replaced by a *g* in the latter: *warden* and *guardian, warranty* and *guarantee, wage* and *gage, reward* and *regard.* Indeed, English preserves many traces of the evolution of the French language that French itself does not. These include any number of words imported twice, both before and after French dropped an *s* and replaced it with a circumflex accent over the vowel—*hostel* and *hotel,* for example.

Because the French were the aristocracy, to this day things in French seem so, well, *chic,* that we continue to import French terminology insatiably, adding to the English vocabulary such words as *couturier, coiffeur, chemise, culotte, chef, maître d'hôtel* (now assimilated to the point of the truncated "mater dee"), *hors d'oeuvre, cuisine, à la mode, à la carte, au gratin, au jus,* and *table d'hôte,* reflecting a profound admiration for French food and fashions. So great was French pioneering in the field of flight that its vocabulary is still extensively French—*aviation, aviator, aileron, fusillage, nacelle, dirigible.*

Latin remained the language of the scholars. For three centuries England's literature was not just bilingual but trilingual. There is a "pop" song of the period that contains these lines in French, English and Latin:

> *Ma très duce et très amé,*
> *night and day for love of thee,*
> *supiro.*

English continued to borrow from Latin words that had already entered it in their French forms, giving us such pairs as *blame* and *blaspheme, chance* and *cadence, count* and *compute, dainty* and *dignity, fealty* and *fidelity, frail* and *fragile, poor* and *pauper, ray* and *radius, spice* and *species, strait* and *strict, sure* and *secure.*

With their pride of language broken, the English became wanton in their importations from other languages, eventually taking in *shampoo, bungalow,* and *pajama* from Hindi, *typhoon* from Chinese, and *tycoon* from Japanese. An enormous amount of Spanish has come into English through the American Southwest, and the process is accelerating.

But of all the languages to which English is indebted for the richness of its vocabulary, none compares to French. Roughly half the language is French or else derives from Latin words that are also used in French. The other half derives from Anglo-Saxon or Old Norse. The result is that English seems to have two words, or more, for almost everything. Those that derive from Anglo-Saxon seem earthier and more immediate than those from French, as in the pairs *freedom-liberty, friendship-amity, hatred-enmity, truth-verity, lying-mendacity, domicile-home.* Consider your own response to those two French words *hostel* and *hotel* and that Anglo-Saxon word *inn.* An inn seems older, more intimate, cozier, than a hotel, with good plain food and a fire. The words for basic things and concepts tend to derive from Ango-Saxon: *heaven, earth, hell, love, hate, life, death, beginning, end, morning, night, day, month, year, heat, cold, way, path, meadow, stream.* But we use French or Latin or sometimes Greek words to cope with and express abstractions. When we use a French word instead of the Anglo-Saxon, it has an effect of intellectuality and detachment. English contains the French word *crépuscule* but it does not have the emotional heat and evocative power of *dusk, twilight, sunset,* and *sundown.*

I have often wondered whether a language shapes the people who speak it or a people develop their language in accord with their own tendencies of temperament. A language is always in harmony with the broad general character of the people. The Spanish language, with its formality, seems like the Spanish people. The German language, with its relentless consistency and inflexible structure, is like the German people in their passion for *Ordnung,* order. And the French language, with its clarity and transparency and lightness, is so like the people who speak it. Only a people who spoke such a tongue could have invented the *soufflé.* Or *meringue.*

In the case of English, one can see various important ways in which the language has shaped the people. Of course, all history shapes us, but English has some peculiar and powerful emotional effects on those who speak it as their native tongue.

Let us return to the Anglo-Saxon peasants laboring in the fields for the Normans. At their work they spoke English. When they surrendered the product of that work to the master, they spoke French. They raised pigs and cows and sheep and lambs, but when they turned the meat over to the Normans it became *porc* or *boeuf* or *mouton* or *veal.* In many French words the *l* has fallen silent, replaced by *u,* which is how *veal* became *veau.* English uses the older form of the French word. A French word containing *u* after another vowel often yields up its meaning if you replace it with *l.* The acute *é* at the start of a French word, like the circumflex in *bâtard,* usually indicates a vanished *s.*

The use of French words instead of the available Anglo-Saxon equivalents is one of the ways reality is masked in the thought processes of English-speaking people. I have yet to encounter a psychiatrist or psychoanalyst who had a grasp of this fact.

The horse escaped double-naming. The only thing you can call horse meat is horse meat. And we won't eat it. But the French, Swiss, and Italians will and do. How would you feel about ordering swine flesh in a restaurant? That is what pork is called in German—*Schweinfleisch.* Would we eat horse if the meat were known as *cheval*? I think we might. Calling it *cheval* would permit us to avoid the awareness of where it came from.

Polite ladies and teachers caution the young not to use certain words because they are "not nice" without having any idea why they are not nice. They are "not nice" for no other reason than that they are, or sound like, or seem like, Anglo-Saxon words, still perceived as the language of the coarse and lowly. For example, to avoid the use of the word *belly,* which derives from Anglo-Saxon *belg,* polite people say *stomach,* which is grossly inaccurate since the stomach is an internal organ of digestion. But *stomach* derives from the French name for that organ, *estomac,* and therefore seems more genteel (from French *gentil,* meaning kind). A promenade seems to have more "class" than a mere walk. And in English the verb *to promenade* carries a connotation of conspicuous display and self-conscious posturing. Nice people don't say sweat, they perspire. An odor *(odeur)* is less offensive than a smell. It is far more elegant to recline than to lie down, to retire rather than to go to bed, to dine than eat.

This psychological bifurcation reaches its extreme in words pertaining to the body. Those Anglo-Saxon words denoting the body and its parts and functions have not only been barred from polite conversation for centuries, they have been literally outlawed until recent times. People could and did go to jail for using them.

The most suppressed word in the English language is a verb for the act essential to the survival of our own and every other species on this fragile sphere. There are more than four billion human beings on it, not to mention dogs, cats, lions, armadillos, dolphins, dugongs, lemurs, ladybugs, and fireflies. And we all got here the same way. The word in question is the only transitive verb we have for this action. And we are not supposed to use it. Mind you, the French cognate for it is used only in a coy and evasive way in slang expressions such as *fous le camp* and *je m'en fous.* The French use their word for *kiss* to replace it and then, having thoroughly confused the issue, use their word for *embrace*—demonstrably something done with *les bras,* the arms—to replace *kiss.* But the French cognate of our condemned word has nowhere near the power of shock of the English, which to the day she died my mother referred to as "That Word." That Word is not, despite a popular theory, an acronym for an old British navy charge, *For Unlawful Carnal Knowledge.* Nor can it be defined as slang. Besides the French cognate, it has another in German, *ficken,* and still others in other languages. It traces back to Sanskrit.

Although French too has its evasions, they are nowhere near as extensive as those of English, and the French do not have the same fear of words that the English do, or the same need to conjure euphemisms from the vocabularies of other languages. The result is that many words that are quite "strong" in English from suppression have become weak from casual use in French. A classic example is *con.* It surely is not necessary to explain the cognate in English. Add the word *pauvre.* When the French call someone a *pauvre con,* the expression not only does not have the force of its English equivalent, it does not even have the same meaning. It means merely poor guy, poor jerk, and there is even a certain compassion in it. A film advertised and exhibited all over Paris was entitled *P'tit Con.* Even today, long after the death of Lenny Bruce, it is difficult to imagine a title utilizing the English cognate on billboards and movie marquees in Canada, Australia, the United States, or England.

The discomfort with Anglo-Saxon words, and even words that sounded as if they might be Anglo-Saxon, lasted so long that eventually any direct mention of the body became difficult if not impossible for many people. In some, even an indirect symbolic allusion became distasteful. During the reign of Queen Victoria, the polite English person would avoid use of the word *leg,* from Old Norse *leggr,* substituting the word *limb,* which is in fact Anglo-Saxon but looks French, perhaps because of a resemblance to *jambe.* This idiocy went so far that gentlefolk would even speak of the "limbs" of a table, and in time came to find even the sight of them so suggestive that they took to hiding them under long tablecloths. One can only shake one's head in wonder at the neurasthenia of people afraid of being turned on by a table.

It is but a short step from finding the word for something dirty to finding the thing itself dirty. The Protestant Reformation did not originate in England, but the structure of the language assuredly made its people particularly susceptible to the Manichaean austerities of the sects we refer to collectively as Protestantism.

Finally, with the rise of Puritanism, at first in England and later in America, certain Anglo-Saxon words were driven altogether underground, and it became illegal to print them. This remained so well into the twentieth century. During the time of its banishment, That Word, as if in retaliation, took on a quality of anger that eventually made it extremely useful in expressing insult or contempt. In French, its cognate can be used for similar purpose but has nowhere near the intensity, because the taboo is lighter.

In any culture, there is a strong relationship between taboo and humor. What one should not talk about is precisely what is funny to talk about since it surprises, and surprise is a critical element in causing laughter. Religious jokes seem to be fairly common in many Spanish-speaking countries, sexual jokes less so. The latter are probably the predominant form of joking in English, because of the capacity of both the subject and the Anglo-Saxon vocabulary for it to induce shock. The two are inextricably linked, which one can see by taking any such joke and replacing its Anglo-Saxon terms with French or Latin synonyms.

If Anglo-Saxon provides the vocabulary with which we express anger and induce laughter, it is also the vocabulary that induces sexual arousal, as an examination of a piece of contemporary pornography reveals. And it is also the most effective vocabulary to use in poetry or lyrics. It is then, at any level and for any purpose, the most emotional part of the language. We use the French half of our language to express our abstract thoughts, the Anglo-Saxon for our most concrete feelings.

Editors and teachers commonly urge writers and students to use small words, as if there were some special virtue in their length alone. The reason these words are so effective is not that they are

small but that they are Anglo-Saxon. Lo these nine centuries after
William the Conqueror crossed the Channel and left poor Harold,
as an old Lancashire-accent music-hall rhyme puts it, "with an eye
full of arrow, on 'is 'orse with 'is 'awk in 'is 'and," the old language
still has an extraordinary hold over us.

It has been said that we whose primary language is English
speak Anglo-Saxon until the age of three and then begin learning
French. Ever afterwards we will by some deep intuition use the old
language for matters of the heart and things of the earth and
things close to home, and French to soar into imaginative abstraction. A child first learns words like *hand, foot, arm, leg, mouth,
smoke, burn, feel, touch, rain, sun, moon, sleep, wake, love, fish, kiss,
sky, stars.*

Cole Porter uses French to light and sardonic effect in such
songs as *I've Got You Under My Skin,* urging the recipient of the
attentions to use her mentality and wake up to reality. But when
he wants to evoke strong images and emotions, he turns to Anglo-
Saxon, as in his magnificent song *In the Still of the Night,* using such
words as *flight* and *thoughts* (with their vanished *gh* gutturals), *gaze*
and *stray.*

Johnny Mercer, the archetype of the modern troubadour and
perhaps the best lyricist in the whole field of American song, does
the same thing constantly.

Mercer's work unceasingly illustrates a principle stated by T.
S. Eliot: that poetry can communicate before it is even understood. It is haunting because of the evocative power of the language he uses and the resultant instantaneous imagery.

Yet for all this vividness of imagery, English has drawbacks as
a language in which to write lyrics. For one thing it is poor in
rhyme. There are only four words in English that rhyme with
love—*above, dove, glove, and shove,* with *of* forming, at least in
North American usage, a fifth. (In proper British English, *of*
rhymes with *suave.*) Since the overwhelming majority of our songs
are love songs, this presents a problem, and leads to endlessly
recurring references to the stars or moon or sky above and to
things one is dreaming of. In French, however, there are fifty-one

rhymes that I know of for *amour,* including the words for *suburb, deaf, day, work, drum, tower,* and *around.* Thus it would be child's play in French to knock out a quatrain or two about being deaf to all else when I come home after a long day's work with a heart beating like a drum to my true love in our ivory tower in our suburb, all of it in rhyme. Try it in English.

The rhythmic character of the French language further enriches its rhymes. There are scores of words that rhyme with *nuage,* meaning cloud, including *verbiage, mariage, visage, voyage, pillage, cage, bandage, village, plumage,* and *image.* All these words exist in both languages. They rhyme in French but not in English. The stress in French is even, balanced, which tends to determine the character of French music. Consider the music of Debussy, so like the French language in its elegant equanimity. Because of this balance, all the aforementioned words can function as one-syllable or masculine rhymes: mari*age,* pil*lage,* ban*dage.* But English is a strongly stressed language, and most of those words have what is called a feminine stress, with emphasis on the penultimate syllable. Thus in English only two words on that list rhyme with each other, *pillage* and *village.*

Rhyming in French has been further expanded by the gradual dropping of terminal consonants. Going back to the words that rhyme with *amour,* we find that it is correct to use *faubourg,* meaning suburb, because the final g is silent, or *sourd,* meaning deaf, because the d is silent. Furthermore, you can rhyme singular words with plurals in French because the s is mute except before a vowel, in which case you should not be at a rhyme point anyway.

Finally, the option of putting the adjective before or after a noun further opens up the rhyming of French. To be sure, whether you put it before or after the noun subtly and sometimes profoundly alters the meaning. But this alternative has almost disappeared from English. At one time it was quite acceptable to put the adjective after the noun, particularly in poetry, and the practice was unobjectionable as recently as the 1930s, when Oscar Hammerstein could without qualm write of building a home "on a hilltop high."

But I would hesitate to do that today. For better or worse, lyrics have tended toward the natural sequence of normal speech, and in English the now almost infrangible rule is that the adjective precedes the noun.

Some years ago in Paris, I told Charles Aznavour that I envied him and other French lyricists the richness of the language's rhyming. "It's true," he said, "but in practice we end up using the same rhymes over and over again, just as you do in English. It is what comes before them that gives a lyric freshness." This is quite correct. It takes dogged patience to find a new approach to an old rhyme.

Another advantage of French over English is the device of liaison, the technique of linking syllables in a fluid manner. You pronounce *très* as *treh* (but not *tray*!), as in *très tard* (very late), but *très agréable* as *treh zagrayabl*. In either instance, the flow of sound is elegant and smooth. This and other rules of pronunciation render almost non-existent the collisions of consonants that the better lyricists in English, such as Mercer and Alan Jay Lerner, seek so consciously and constantly to avoid. And that avoidance further restricts the writer's choice of words.

For all these reasons, French flows better, and it is my impression that the devices of the language's pronunciation make it possible to sing it faster than English. The magnificent songs of Charles Trenet have, sad to say, fallen from fashion. Back in the 1930s, the years between the wars, as the French think of them, when Jerome Kern, Harold Arlen, Howard Dietz and Arthur Schwartz, Irving Berlin, and Cole Porter were at the peak of their productivity in America, Trenet in France turned out a body of songs (both lyrics and music) that are among the best of this century, including *La Mer,* which has a magnificent lyric, a hymn to the sea that was turned in an American incarnation into the pedestrian love song *Beyond the Sea.* Another of his songs, *Que reste-t'il de nos amours?* (What's left of our loves?) fared rather better as *I Wish You Love,* although the English lyric has little to do with the original. In any case, I don't think certain of Trenet's songs—songs such as *Je chante, Pigeon vole,* and *Fleur bleue*—could have been sung as fast as he was wont to do them had their lyrics been in English.

Much of the better American popular music created before the rise of rock and roll is being seen as an art music, and perhaps rightly so. During the period between 1900 and 1955—when, as Alec Wilder said, the amateurs took over—these two languages, French and English, produced an astonishing body of exquisite songs. No other language, not Italian, not German, not Portuguese, not Spanish, raised the popular song to such heights. Support for this view comes from colleagues in other countries in explaining their fascination with American songs. The brilliant Portuguese lyrics that played as important a role in the *bossa nova* movement as the music itself, the work of such poetic writers as Newton Mendonça and Vinicius de Moraes, were something new to Brazil, and in part inspired by the work of such Americans as Cole Porter. In the case of de Moraes, there was undoubtedly a French influence as well, since he had lived in Paris and spoke French.

What American songs and French songs of that golden age had in common was excellence. In style, subject matter, and content, however, they were quite different. Most of the best American songs came out of musical theater and, to a lesser extent, movies. The songs were at first little interpolations into negligible stories, but later, as musical comedy became more sophisticated in structure and content, each song was expected to advance the drama or illuminate the characters and situations. The composers usually tried to design several of the songs in a play so that they could stand on their own, be recorded and played on the radio. This ambivalent function was never more brilliantly fulfilled than by Lerner and Loewe in *My Fair Lady* and by Frank Loesser in *Guys and Dolls*.

The great French songs came from a different tradition, one growing out of the old music halls and for which there has never really been an American equivalent. This is the individual song written for an individual singer—Mistinguette, Maurice Chevalier, Edith Piaf, Jean Sablon, Juliette Greco, Charles Trenet, Gilbert

Bécaud, Charles Aznavour, Yves Montand, and the Belgian Jacques Brel. Sometimes the performers were, as in the cases of Bécaud, Brel, Trenet, and Aznavour, themselves the composers of their material. But sometimes, as in the instances of Chevalier and Piaf, the singer was dependent on the output of certain favored composers, with whom they would often work in close collaboration. Piaf's songs were *designed* for her. They were not songs she picked up from song-pluggers or musical comedies.

Because these songs were meant to be heard in recitals, referred to as *tours de chant* (one-man or one-woman shows that far predate the *Evening with So-and-so* format that emerged later in the United States), they had to have a powerful and unique dramatic character, each of them a free-standing entity, a sort of short story in a setting of rhyme and music. Thus while the best American songs were fragments of dramatic monologue, often written in the second person and addressed to some unseen "you," the French song might be a first-person narrative, or, not infrequently, an observation in the third person. This use of the third person, which one encounters in Hoagy Carmichael's *The Lamplighter's Serenade* and Mercer's humorous *The Girlfriend of the Whirling Dervish,* is comparatively rare in American popular music. Usually the narrator of the song is himself or herself a participant in the tale. The strong tradition of the objective external observer, which you find in some of the wonderful French lyrics of Boris Vian and in Piaf songs such as *Les Forains,* hardly exists in American popular music, except, interestingly, country-and-western music.

The American song tended to be 32 bars long, with an AABA or ABAB melodic structure. The French song was much more likely to be long form, to accommodate the subject material. The chanson evolved into a complex tale-unto-itself, such as Brel's *Zangra,* often exploring complex and difficult subjects, as opposed to the almost incessant love songs of the United States. Not that the French don't love love songs. But the character of them is very different and the view of the subject has always inclined to be more realistic, a consequence of the comparative lack of taboo about language.

Much country-and-western music is commercial trash, but some of the songs—those of Mickey Newberry among them—are excellent indeed, every bit as good as what the Nashville people call "uptown music." Good country-and-western songs not infrequently explore subject matter much like what you encounter in French chansons. In the 1940s, Edith Piaf recorded *Jean et Martine,* which is about the worried wife of a truck driver waiting for him to come home. There is a country-and-western song on the same subject. The important difference between them is that in the latter song, the wife prays, God intercedes, and the husband comes safely home through the storm. In the Piaf song he is killed. The American song caters to the religious primitives who form so large a part of the country-and-western audience, but it also illustrates the sentimentality of much American popular art, movies included, in its maudlin happy ending.

If Trenet's songs were exuberant celebrations of life, alternated with occasional wistful and gentle explorations of sadder subjects, Piaf's songs were almost universally tragic, and unblinkingly objective. She was singing her tough narratives about prostitutes when Cole Porter's comparatively pallid *Love for Sale* was barred from American and Canadian radio stations.

In older American movies, women manage the miracle of becoming mothers with no detectable abdominal enlargement. Florescence apparently occurs by parthenogenesis, although sometimes it seems to be the consequence of kissing, and the condition is announced without use of the word *pregnant,* the husband saying something like, "You mean . . . you mean we're going to . . . to have a . . . " to which the lady may reply with shyly-lowered eyes, "Yes, dear." It seems unlikely that this bowdlerization of movies did anything to protect the morals of children, most of whom were bright enough to notice for themselves the changes that overtook a woman who really was, in one of the euphemisms of the time, in a family way. What is more, farm children even knew how she got that way.

It is the lack of suppression either of language or fact in French movies, novels, plays, and songs that doubtless inspired the strange British and American belief that the French are a "sexy" people, casual in dalliance. A people who had to cover the legs of tables and even put frilly ruffles on the legs of pianos were bound to find any people sexy. The French happened to be the closest— and reading the works of Zola and Hugo while Victoria was imposing her vision of virtue on England and, later, lamenting her Albert to Disraeli. No wonder her son Edward was always popping off to France.

The strange vision of love that never seems to have a physical fulfillment, embodied in the songs and movies of a recent American yesteryear, goes far back in history to the Manichaean heresy that is also the root of Protestantism. Manichaeus was born in Persia in 215 or 216, the son of a father who belonged to a sect that believed in sexual abstinence. After the dreams and visitations from angels that customarily attend religious conversions, Manichaeus formed his own sect and set forth a cosmogony whose complexity is exceeded only by its lack of accord with reality. In its essentials, it was a dualism, good versus evil, light at war with darkness.

The Manichaean religion died out in China around the fourteenth century, but its influence is still with us, because it affected Aurelius Augustinus, who was born in Roman Africa in 354 and is known to us now as St. Augustine of Hippo. Augustine is considered the greatest thinker of Christian antiquity. Significantly, he was a Manichaean for nine years before his conversion to Christianity. Augustine's views were so uncompromisingly severe that he made even other churchmen uncomfortable, and one of them accused him of lapsing into Manichaeism. Augustine believed that mankind is involved in Adam's guilt and punishment through dependency on the sexual passion for reproduction. Retaining the Manichaean hostility to sex, he saw spirit as good, matter as bad. Therefore physical life is bad. And the act that makes life is particularly evil. It apparently did not occur to him to blame God for setting things up that way, nor did it to those whom he influenced, including Calvin, Janssen, and the New England Puritans. In a park near downtown Geneva, Switzerland, the city of Calvin's birth, there is a row of heroic statues celebrating Calvin and his disciples. And there, larger than life, stands Roger Williams.

But there is another way that the Manichaean heresy came to shape our lives. By a direct lineage, it gave rise to a later heresy, that of the Cathars in northern Italy and southern France, which flourished in the twelfth and fourteenth centuries. The Cathars— also known as the Albigenses—continued the doctrine that life was evil. They had a passionate belief in celibacy, did not favor reproduction, and pushed the whole thing to its logical extreme by looking favorably on suicide. Marriage was considered partic- ularly odious, a sort of institutionalized vice. The highest state was that of being "perfect," which one attained through a ceremony called the *consolamentum.* Such were the rigors of this condition, including sexual abstinence, that most believers put it off until they neared the ends of their lives, when they gave up, with appro- priate repentance, that for which they had probably lost the capacity.

The hotbed of this religion was Provence, that haunted and haunting part of southern France whose vision is burned into our minds by Cezanne. And it continued there until it was bloodily eradicated by the church in actions that evolved into the Inquisition.

Now, it was in Provence that our love songs were born.

The vision of romantic love to which most of us in this era are addicted was more or less unknown to the Greeks and Romans. Love was not unknown, as witness the story of Ruth and Naomi, the devotion of Damon and Pythias. Nor was uncontrolled pas- sion, as witness David's deadly compulsion for Bathsheba, the poetry of Sappho, and the dalliances of Greek gods. But a single helpless lifelong devotion was considered an aberration, even per- haps a form of insanity.

The troubadours of Provence changed that.

Scholars debate the meaning of the poetry that these song- writers produced. One author claims that they were "eager to clothe the caprices of their senses with mystical grace." Others have held the opposite, contending that the troubadours were Cathars whose love poems were coded celebrations of their own religious experiences.

It is a poetry that talks of conspiracy and secrecy and guarded nocturnal meetings and fear of discovery and a yearning for some sort of initiation. Into what? Into the perfect state of the Cathar religion?

Whatever the true meaning of the songs of the Provence troubadours, it is wise to remember that they came into being where that intensely anti-sexual religion had flowered. The songs are full of longings for kisses that never come. The passions are never consummated, and this very fruitlessness is idealized. Jauffre Rudel wrote these lines:

> *Car nuls autres joys tan nom play*
> *come jauzimens d'amor de lonh.*

Let us note in passing that the words *joy* and *play* come into English unchanged from that period, while their spellings became *joie* and *plait* in French. The lines translate:

> For no other joys so much me please
> as those of love from afar.

This reminds us immediately of the lyric to *My Silent Love:*

> I reach for you as I reach for a star,
> worshipping you from afar . . .

One of the troubadours wrote of a man who all his life loves a princess he has never met. He meets her in the end only to die in her arms. Was the poet describing the final Cathar initiation at the end of life? Whatever it was, its tradition finds an echo in a Richard Whiting–Leo Robin–Newell Chase song:

> Will I ever find
> the girl in my mind,
> the one who is my ideal?
> Maybe she's a dream

and yet she might be
just around the corner,
waiting for me.

Will I recognize
the light in her eyes,
that no other eyes reveal?
Or will I pass her by
and never even know
that she was my ideal?

This is an idealized and essentially asexual vision of love. Since the only possible excuse for doing "it" was that you were *in love with* the object of your ardor, and the only thing you could do about *that* was to marry her or him, that song actually hints at an entire life lived in celibacy.

The idealized asexual vision of love took its deepest hold not in Catholic France but in largely Protestant America. Protestantism, echoing the anti-sexuality of Manichaeus, took root in England, partly, I suggest, because the suppression of the Anglo-Saxon language eventuated in an array of unconscious assumptions that made her people particularly susceptible to its guilt infliction and denial of the physical self. And the most extreme Puritans emigrated to America. Little wonder, then, that the vision of love first put forth by troubadours of Provence should spring up again west of the Atlantic.

It is impossible to estimate how deeply the songs of the 1930s, '40s, and '50s, saturating the North American society through radio and records and movies to an extent never before possible, influenced the life outlook of the people consuming them. And song after song told them love would solve everything, once you found Mr. or Miss Right.

Love doesn't solve everything, of course. It isn't even a very good cure for loneliness. But generations of Americans grew up with expectations inculcated by an all-pervasive popular music and by movies that ended with a comparatively chaste kiss whose duration was limited by the film industry's censorship system. Because the songs and movies celebrated the heady emotion of *falling* in love, millions of people thought that this temporary exhilaration was love itself and so, when it ended, many of them moved on to the next marriage. And possibly the next, in a process that became so universal that a sociologist named it "sequential polygamy."

That era is ended. Many factors contributed to its fading. Rock-and-roll was a major one. While women's liberation asserted a woman's right to sexual freedon, rock lyrics proclaimed man's right to use these liberated women without gratitude or responsibility or even feeling, and the girls who were its fans became the disposable instruments of male gratification, leading inevitably to a song called *You Don't Have to Tell Me that You Love Me.* Rock-and-roll not only defeminized women. It dehumanized them. Rock music made "groupie" a new word in the English language, although the phenomenon was far from new.

American songs of the first half of the twentieth century gave us a vision of sexless love, rock-and-roll a vision of loveless sex. Meanwhile, the pornographers were destroying the mystery of women even among children browsing at magazine racks.

It was once accurate to say that the French made comedies about sex while the Americans made tragedies about it. But boudoir farce is now common in America. This is due in part to the changed emotional climate of which the freer use of certain Anglo-Saxon words is both a consequence and a cause.

As for English, that hybrid tongue once confined to a small island country, it has become the first true world language. In the number of people who speak it, it is second only to Mandarin Chinese, and to none at all in the area of diffusion. About 300,000,000 people speak English as their first language and another 120,000,000 as their second. Meanwhile French purists in France and Quebec try desperately in an age of international radio and television and air travel to halt the invasion of their language by that self-same English language the Norman French created by imposing their own on a conquered people. French engineers go on talking about *les pipelines* (pronounced peeplean) while fashionable French women praise a new fashion as *très smart.* One might call this Harold's revenge.

    And English is growing not only in the number of persons
who speak it but also in the size of its vocabulary, due partly to its
capacity, far beyond French, to create words from within—*con-
trail*, for example, from condensation trail; *laser* and *scuba*—and
partly to its unhesitating and even eager importation from other
languages, including *discothèque* from French, *marina* and *macho*
from Spanish. An unabridged general dictionary of English now
contains about 500,000 entries. Language experts say that English
dictionaries of 750,000 entries will soon be in use.

    And all this, the songs and the profanity and the neuroses and
this expanding powerful language, because of Charles the Simple.
And his treaty of St. Clair-sur-Epte.

The Sparrow Edith Piaf

Americans never really knew Edith Piaf. When she died, the *New York Times* said in its obituary, "Strangely, Miss Piaf was perhaps best known in the United States for her *La Vie en rose,* a song of happiness and love." There may have been something ironic about it, but there was nothing strange. Her act was bowdlerized and glamorized for her appearances at the Versailles and the Waldorf-Astoria in New York. Her songs about prostitutes and their *marlous,* about the murders that often ended the search for love, were thrown out or cleaned up for Americans raised on a diet of sexless love in songs and happy endings in movies and *Saturday Evening Post* fiction.

To anyone who really knew her work, death added no unexpected dimension to her legend. Death was in her life and in her songs, gritty realistic ballads about the Paris streets and the outcasts who prowled them. Her songs—and her life—were filled with the desperate faces one sees fitfully in the poems of Villon, the novels of Balzac and Hugo, and the erotic fantasies of Jean Genêt.

One of Piaf's classics, *Un Monsieur me suit dans la rue,* is about a little girl who dreams of the day when a man will follow her in the street. When at last one does, he is *"un vieux dégoûtant,"* a disgusting old man. Later another man follows her in the street—

she is now a prostitute. In the final verse her childhood dream is fulfilled for the last time: a sexton follows her coffin.

She sang songs of this kind in the era before rock, when you assuredly did not mention death or prostitution or juvenile sexuality in American songs. *Un Monsieur me suit dans la rue* was about all three. Even today, when rock has become pornographic, a silly satanism fills the grooves of records, and drug use has been chronicled and condoned for more than twenty years in American pops, we hear only a sophomoric rebellion against the Puritan tradition, bad little boys writing bad little words on walls. We hear nothing— nothing whatever—to compare with the songs of Edith Piaf.

Cole Porter dealt with prostitution in *Love for Sale* but not for the mass audience. Porter knew about as much about the harsh life of a whore as Paul Whiteman, by his own honest admission, did about jazz. The song is a soft one, the prostitute's life seen through a misted long lens from the luxurious penthouse apartment on top of the Waldorf-Astoria, where Porter lived in the cushioned comfort of inherited wealth, the same Waldorf where Piaf presented herself with a scrubbed face to the New York chic set. And at that, *Love for Sale* was barred from radio broadcasting for years. *Un Monsieur me suit dans la rue* was never played on American radio either, not even in French.

Through the American misrepresentation of Piaf was to some extent corrected in the early years of the LP by the release on the Angel and Capitol labels of collections of her songs, you still could not get *Un Monsieur me suit dans la rue*. Nor could you get *Paris-Mediterranée,* a song about a girl who meets a man on a train bound for the Riviera and beds with him. On their arrival in the railway station the next morning, she sees him arrested. She shrugs and says, "You just can't trust the people you meet on trains these days."

Her real name was Edith Giovanna Gassion. She was given the name Piaf by the cabaret owner Louis Leplée. It is Parisian slang for sparrow. (Or at least it was in her day; who can keep up with the slang of Paris?) No name ever suited an entertainer better. Her voice was neither pretty nor melodious. It had that rapid French vibrato that is obtained I know not how—or why. (Even housewives sing that way in France.) But that voice was filled with an intense and urgent energy that could not possibly, it seemed, be coming from so tiny a body. She stood four feet eleven inches tall and, when she was in good health, weighed ninety-nine pounds.

In her work she always wore a simple black dress with a sweetheart neckline. As she stood in a stark spotlight, she seemed all head and hands. And the hands were marvelously expressive. They floated disembodied in the air, open and at ease. As a song progressed, they became more agitated. At last, at the peak of a song's drama, they curled into trembling claws, at once imploring and ominous. In the last months of her life, those wonderful hands, gnarled now by arthritis, looked more than ever like talons. But they never lost their eloquence.

Her songs were, in effect, rhymed short stories of pain, irony, and compassion for the human condition. Occasionally the blues and some country-and-western songs give a hint of a similar flavor. But the blues by their very twelve-bar construction are structured for quick aphoristic snapshots of life, not for long-form story-telling. And country-and-western songs, even those that do deal with comparable subject matter, are almost always compromised by sentimentalism or a maudlin self-pity. Nothing in all the songs of the English language approaches the vinegar imagery of the French *chansons réalistes,* in which the narrative has primacy. There is a tunelessness about many of these songs that no doubt derives from the fact that the lyrics were written first. In all history, only a few composers have been capable of creating fluid contoured melodies for existing text. When lyrics are written first, composers almost always come up with melodies that have a slightly stiff and recitative quality. Thus it was with Piaf's songs, but they worked for her to intense dramatic effect. American songs, in the golden age of Kern and Gershwin and Youmans, put a primary emphasis on melody; French songs, at least of the kind Piaf sang, put it on drama, and must be listened to in a different way. (There is another kind of French song that is gloriously melodic.)

Piaf wrote almost nothing. But no singer was ever more truly defined in her songs. The best of them were drawn from her life by the writers who worked with her, such as Raymond Asso, who created the bulk of her early repertoire. *Paris-Mediterranée* is a case in point.

Traveling to Nice with her half-sister Simone Berteaut, Piaf was smitten by a handsome well-dressed man who shared their compartment. She leaned close to him, he took her hand, she put her head on his shoulder. When the man stepped into the corridor for a smoke, Piaf told her sister she was mad for him and would never leave him. At Marseille, the man got off the train to stretch his legs. The girls watched in astonishment from a window as two cops clapped handcuffs on him. The man turned and gave her a last smile before being led away.

Piaf later told the story to Asso, who turned it into *Paris-Mediterranée*.

When Piaf was about sixteen, singing in the streets near Porte des Lilas, she became enamored of a little blond delivery boy and sometime bricklayer named Louis Dupont, known as P'tit Louis. They lived together, along with her sister, in a scabrous hotel in the rue Orfila, where they slept three in a bed. Piaf sang and Louis made his deliveries and on Sundays they went to the films of Tom Mix, Rudolph Valentino, and the little tramp the French call Charlot—Chaplin. She gave birth to a girl she named Marcelle. She soon tired of Louis, resumed her infidelities, and got a job singing in a sailor's suit in a dive called the Juan-les-Pins. Simone was hired as a stripper although she was as flat in front as she was behind, stood only four-feet-eleven, like Edith, and was not yet fifteen. P'tit Louis objected to Edith's working there because she was surrounded by prostitutes. She left him.

Having no need for full-time lodgings, as the two girls now saw things, they moved from one shoddy hotel to another, dragging Marcelle along with them. Piaf had no idea how to wash baby clothes. When Marcelle's got dirty, she and Simone would throw them away and buy new.

Much of the time the baby was left untended at their hotel. One day Edith and Simone returned to find that P'tit Louis had come on his bicycle and taken the child away. When the two girls went to the old hotel in the rue Orfila, he told Edith that she could have her daughter only if she would return to him. She shrugged and walked away. The child had been a nuisance anyway.

A few months later, P'tit Louis sought her out to tell her Marcelle was in hospital with meningitis. She rushed there with Simone. The child died the following morning. Edith was eighteen.

She was ten francs short of the eighty-four she needed for the funeral. She had lived all her life on the edges of prostitution: abandoned by her parents, the Italian street singer who was her mother and a father who was an itinerant street acrobat from Normandy, she had been raised in a bordello by her grandmother, who was its cook. So, after getting drunk on Pernod, she did the natural thing: she accosted a man on the street, the boulevard de la Chappelle. In a hotel room, he asked her why she was doing this and got what must have sounded like one of the tiredest of the hard-luck stories told by whores since time immemorial. Yet the man gave her more than the ten francs and left.

She continued singing in the streets by day, with Simone, two and a half years her junior, collecting the cash, and at the Juan-les-Pins at night, living in a succession of shabby Pigalle hotels. Their friends were pimps, prostitutes, burglars, pickpockets, con men, and hoodlums. Piaf liked tough guys. They were her preferred bed companions. And they protected her when she worked the streets. All her life she had a taste for the company of pimps. It was a bent she shared with Billie Holiday. The difference is that Holiday's early history was totally hidden from the American public; Piaf virtually trumpeted hers.

Americans for years saw Pigalle as a place of naughty fun but the French know it as a sinkhole, the haunt of gangsters and their girls, of weary *putes* and their vicious "protectors". In recent decades it has been repopulated by gangsters from Algeria. It is very easy to get your throat cut in Pigalle.

Piaf fell in love with a pimp named Albert. She refused to whore for him, however, and begged him to let her continue working as a street singer. He at last agreed, providing she handed him thirty francs a day. In due course she broke with Albert, as she did with all her men when boredom set in. Some of her friends gathered to protect her when he came after her. He pulled a gun and demanded that she return to him.

Piaf said—one of the great lines—"Fire, if you're a man!" All ninety-odd pounds of her.

He did, too. But one of her friends struck his arm and the shot only grazed her neck.

Edith—the French pronounce it Ay-deet—took to singing in the area between l'Etoile and La Place des Ternes. She was singing for a small crowd in the rue Troyon one autumn afternoon in 1935 when a well-dressed man stepped forward, gave her ten francs, wrote his name and address on a corner of his newspaper, and told her he owned a cabaret called Cerny's in the rue Pierre-Charron. She auditioned for him the next afternoon. Louis Leplée said he could use her. But that name, he said, her real name, half French and half Italian, Edith Giovanna Gassion, would have to go. He named her *La Môme Piaf. Môme* means brat, urchin, waif, but the connotation is affectionate. Edith Piaf, then, made her nightclub debut as the Waif Sparrow, or the Kid Sparrow.

Louis Leplée was the first person to start teaching her her profession. She and Simone began immediately to call him Papa Louis. He made her learn new songs. He began an advertising campaign for her. He planned every detail of her opening, including the lighting. That first night the place was full of celebrities, including Maurice Chevalier and Mistinguette. Terrified, Piaf began to sing, "C'est nous les mômes, les mômes de la cloche . . . " The audience talked on. And then they began to fall silent. "She's done it!" Louis Leplée cried. She was invited to tables. Gentlemen addressed her as "Mademoiselle." She was astounded. Chevalier praised her.

It was not, however, Chevalier's praise that emplaced Piaf in the national awareness. It was Louis Leplée's murder.

Leplée had become her manager, mentor, and father figure, building her career, arranging for her to perform in galas as well as his club. Under his direction, she got her first record contract, cutting *L'Etranger* for Polydor. One night, with a record date scheduled for nine the following morning, she went on one of her periodic benders with Simone, dragging back to their hotel at eight a.m. Knowing how angry Papa Louis would be, she phoned to tell him she couldn't make the session. The voice on the phone told her to come immediately to his home on the boulevard de la Grande Armée. As she sobered up in the taxi, she began to think it was not Papa Louis who had spoken to her. A crowd stood about in front of his house, into which Piaf was escorted by a cop. During that night four young men had come to Leplée's house, tied up his cleaning woman, and shot him where he lay in his bed. Piaf was arrested as a material witness, which, in view of the company she kept, is hardly surprising. She was soon released for lack of any evidence of complicity in the killing, but not before photographers and newsreel cameraman had made her face famous. (There were several theories about the death, but the case has never been solved.)

Years later a French critic wrote that his first awareness of her had come from a Paramount newsreel in which she was seated on a bench, telling the police, "*Je ne sais rien, je ne sais rien*"—I know nothing. Such was the power of her personality, he wrote, that he was fascinated by her without ever having heard her sing a note. Some people have that kind of presence.

Again, Piaf made use of her life's experience: The song *Browning* that she sang several years later describes a little hole in a man's head and the other little hole, in a gun barrel, out of which comes Madame Death.

After the Leplée affair, Raymond Asso became the next important figure in Piaf's life. She'd met him through Leplée. He was a slim, intelligent man-about-show-biz in his early thirties, and a veteran of the Foreign Legion, which was not without its appeal to Piaf. She had a taste for *Légionnaires* and sailors. Simone said, "It was Leplée who discovered Edith, but it was Asso who made

her." Asso took her as a mistress, then became her manager,
coach, and teacher, an incarnation of the Henry Higgins character
in Shaw's *Pygmalion*. She was barely literate, having had only a year
of school. Asso taught her to sign her autograph without errors;
all her life she did so using phrases he had written out for her to
copy. He pounded a measure of education into her and also
Simone, forcing them to learn such names as Baudelaire.

But he also listened patiently, smoking a pipe, as she told him
her tales of the streets. He decided that she would have to have a
repertoire entirely her own, drawn from her own experience, and
began writing the first of what would be a long list of her most
famous songs, such as *Elle fréquentait la rue Pigalle, Mon Légionnaire, Le Fanion de la Légion, Je n'en connais pas la fin, C'est lui que
mon coeur a choisi, Le Grand Voyage du pauvre nègre,* and *Le Petit
Monsieur triste*—the very core of her early repertoire. It was Asso
who introduced her to Marguerite Monnot, who had written
L'Etranger. Monnot, an extremely well-schooled musician—she'd
made her piano recital debut at the age of three and a half, playing
Mozart, and had been trained by Nadia Boulanger—became his
collaborator of choice and one of the most important composers
in Piaf's life. Asso would write a lyric, Piaf would recite it, and the
dreamy Monnot would go to the piano and start playing, gradually
fitting melody to lyrics. It was a unique professional relationship.

A genuinely tough young man, as well as a refined one, Asso
cleared out the crowd of pimps and hoods who hung around Piaf.
And the minute he thought she was ready, he got her her first
important booking at the A.B.C., the best of the major Paris musical halls, on a bill with Charles Trenet. Asso next introduced her
to Raoul Breton, the music publisher, and his wife, whose support
was critical to the success of a singer in those days. It was Mme
Breton who suggested that she henceforth bill herself Edith Piaf,
not La Môme Piaf. And Piaf worked. She studied Marie Dubas, a
singer she admired all her life—how Dubas walked on a stage and
left it, her gestures, her inflections, the way she sequenced her
songs.

She was a smash at the A.B.C. Raymond Asso had made her truly famous. But her affairs usually lasted about eighteen months, as Simone has noted, and his days as her lover were numbered.

In 1969, six years after Piaf's death and a year after Asso's, Simone Berteaut published a book about her half-sister, titled simply *Piaf.* (They had the same father, Gassion.) It is a remarkable book, both in its unconscious self-portrait of the archetypical gofer, namely herself, and for the insights into Piaf's character. It is one of the finest studies of a singer ever written. It examines the egotism, the compulsion, the hunger, the ingenuous self-involvement—and the drive. It is all the more compelling for being a naive rather than a clinical portrait. And Berteaut hardly even questions her own utter devotion to her half-sister.

She quotes Piaf as saying, "A woman who gets herself dropped is a poor sap. There's no lack of men—the streets are full of them. But you have to find a replacement first, not after. If you wait till after, you're the one who's been cheated on; but before, it's him. And that makes one hell of a difference."

Berteaut says, "Edith always applied this principle with a clear conscience. No man was ever able to make her change. She'd cheat first, and then see what happened. Sometimes she'd tell them; other times she'd just laugh watching them. And if any man thought he'd cheated on her first—boy, was he wrong! She'd already beaten him to the punch. As long as the new guy wasn't ready to shack up with her she didn't say anything; she kept the old one. She had to have a man around the house."

Piaf had the sexual rectitude of a starfish. Of all the famously libidinous show business ladies, not even excluding that English actress long known in Hollywood movie circles as the British Open, Piaf appears to have been the most voracious and the most casual. She must have had thousands of men in her life. Berteaut tells how, when they were living at one Paris location and found themselves without a man of an evening, they would open a window and put themselves on display. When a cop arrived with a complaint, they'd grab him. Both of them. Indeed, although she never says so, Berteaut gives the impression in her book that when a man took on Piaf, he might get two for the price of one. Charles Aznavour called the endless succession of men "Piaf's boys."

Raymond Asso's successor was the singer and later actor Paul Meurisse, an urbane man whose cool polish and perfect manners impressed her. War was pending and ex-Légionnaire Asso had been called back into military service. Born in Dunkerque, son of a bank manager, Paul Meurisse had come to Paris as an insurance investigator who really wanted to be a singer. He'd entered an amateur contest, won it, became a chorus boy, and was singing in cabarets when she met him. Pierre Hiégal, who supervised her recordings for the Polydor label, later wrote, "When one evening Paul said to her, 'Come over to my place for a glass of champagne,' she accepted quite naturally—and stayed two years."

This time, her life's adventures became the material not for a song but for a play. Her new friend Jean Cocteau wrote a one-act drama about Piaf and Paul Meurisse, who fought incessantly and bitterly, which he called *Le Bel Indifférent*. Piaf and Meurisse starred in it, playing characters based on themselves. The success of the play launched Meurisse as an actor.

They continued their battles, offstage as well as on, and finally parted. Singer Tino Rossi tried to effect a reconciliation, but Piaf had decided to make Meurisse jealous. Knowing Meurisse was following her, she met a man in a cafe. Meurisse dragged her home. In the ensuing battle their apartment was wrecked. And Piaf left for good. She was twenty-five.

By now Paris was under German occupation. Piaf and Simone took up residence, along with the secretary she had acquired, in a high-class bordello frequented by Gestapo officers in civvies, out for a little fun between torture sessions at their nearby headquarters, incognito members of the French underground, and big-time gangsters, both French and German. The conquerors were constantly after her to perform for them in Germany. She never did. But she did do performances in various stalags for French soldiers still held by the Germans. During one of these, her secretary, Andrée Bigeard—unbeknownst to her employer an active member of the French underground—told her to ask permission to have her picture taken with the German guards and their French prisoners. Back in Paris, the faces in this photo were carefully blown up and attached to false identity cards and travel documents, which Piaf slipped to the prisoners on a second visit to the camp. Many of them escaped with those documents.

In the spring of 1944, on the advice of one of their pimp friends, Piaf and Simone checked out of their brothel. A few days later the house was closed and its owners jailed.

When the war began to go badly for the Germans the atmosphere in Paris grew grim. Black-bordered posters bearing the names of hostages appeared on walls. From time to time, the Germans would shoot a batch of them, often in the ruined old castle in the Bois de Vincennes. Piaf sang a song called *Où sont tous mes copains?*—Where Are All My Pals?—against the projected backdrop of a French flag. The audience was full of German officers. The next day Occupation authorities told her to take it out of her act. She refused. Her only compromise was to drop the flag from her staging.

Paul Meurisse's successor, aside from the casual lovers, was Henri Contet, of whom she said to Simone, "We've never had a newspaperman; it'll be a change for us." Contet was a writer with *Paris Soir*. Piaf seemed to have an instinct for taking up with men who could educate her, and Contet was no exception. She in turn affected their lives just as deeply. She had made an actor of Meurisse. And now she turned Contet, as she had Raymond Asso, into a lyricist. If Asso had created the body of her first repertoire, Contet—working with Marguerite Monnot—created that of the second, such songs as *Y'a pas d' printemps, Coup de grisou, Monsieur Saint Pierre, Histoire du coeur, Mariage, Le Brun et le blond, Bravo pour le clown,* and the great *Padam . . . padam.* Contet went the way of all her lovers, but, like Asso, continued writing for her.

She had long since lost count of her lovers. At one point she decided to file them by period: the streets; the sailors and colonial troops; the pimps; the flings. She referred to the time of Asso and Meurisse as her professor period. Contet she listed in the brothel period. After Contet, she went into what she called her factory period. She'd made Asso and Contet into famous songwriters. Now she began manufacturing singers.

The first was Yves Montand, a six-foot hundred-and-eighty-pound "dream," as she called him, born in Italy and raised in Marseille. She met him when he was assigned on a bill with her at the Moulin Rouge. She promptly vivisected his act, telling him it was corny and out-of-date, and mocked his Marseille accent. She told him that when he was ready to accept it, she would train him. And train him she did. She developed a new repertoire for him, some of it written by Henri Contet. She taught him gesture and movement, sometimes rehearsing him for fifteen hours at a stretch. In two months, she created the Montand the French public was to know, the dramatic figure in simple brown slacks and shirt. Then she made a movie with him, about a singing star who takes a lover and turns him into a famous singer only to lose him to the stardom she has herself created. Montand was in love with and wanted to marry her, but when his name became as big as her own she threw him out.

She next took an interest not in one but nine singers, Les Compagnons de la Chanson, who had begun singing together in the French resistance. She coached them and took them on tour with her, as she had Montand.

In the mood of francophilia that saturated the United States in the years right after the wear, Piaf acquired an American reputation. In November 1947 she toured the U.S. with Les Compagnons. The tour was a failure for Piaf, although Les Compagnons, whose act was all sweetness and light, with songs such as *Les Trois Cloches,* The Three Bells, went over well. Piaf decided to leave the tour and go home. The critic and composer Virgil Thomson wrote a newspaper column explaining the character of her work, ending it with, "If we allow her to leave on the heels of this undeserved failure, the American public will have given proof of its ignorance and its stupidity." On the strength of that review, she was booked into the Versailles. Charles Boyer, Marlene Dietrich, and Jean Sablon were in the high-society audience that came to cheer her. She had been booked for a week; she stayed twenty-one. She and Dietrich would become close friends.

A few months earlier, toward the end of 1946, when she was thirty-one, she had met, in a Montmartre cafe, Marcel Cerdan, the boxer, born in Casablanca, billed as the Moroccan Bomber, the French contender for the world middleweight championship. Cerdan was a handsome roughneck with a heart of utter simplicity.

Piaf was intensely lonely during the Versailles engagement. Then she got a call from Cerdan, who happened also to be in New York. He took her to dinner, then to Coney Island after midnight. Some of the sports fans in the crowd recognized him; and some people recognized her, begging her to sing *La Vie en rose*, which she did, on the spot, old street singer that she was. She saw Cerdan fight for the first time. And she was in love again. But Cerdan was married. Marriage to Piaf was impossible.

The relationship with Cerdan was unlike any she had known. She had always bought gifts for her men and dressed them. Cerdan would not allow this. He, on the contrary, bought her gifts, a mink coat among them.

Cerdan went into training for his title fight with Tony Zale in New York. Piaf was booked into the Versailles during that time. She arrived early, and Cerdan, against the rules, smuggled her into his training camp at Lake Sheldrake. Despite the supposedly debilitating effects of sex on prizefighters (and tenors), Cerdan, in Madison Square Garden on September 21, 1948, took the title from Zale at the end of the fourth round. A euphoric Piaf left the arena to sing at the Versailles. The crown cheered when she went on, and cheered anew when Cerdan entered.

The next autumn she again played the Versailles. Again Cerdan was to fight in New York: Jake LaMotta had challenged him for the title. Cerdan was to travel by boat, but Piaf phoned to urge him to take a plane instead.

On October 28, 1949, the Air France Constellation in which Cerdan was a passenger plowed into a mountain peak of the Azores. Cerdan died in the crash, along with the brilliant young French violinist Ginette Neveu. Piaf believed she had killed him, and nearly went mad. She entered onto the most bizarre period of her life. After trying to starve herself to death, she induced Simone to obtain a three-legged table with which to conduct seances. The tapping table told her to resume eating. From then on she consulted it daily. What she did not know is that her half-sister was moving the table, which Berteaut revealed in the 1969 book. She constantly asked it for advice, advice that a terrified Berteaut was forced to give.

It was during this period that she discovered Charles Aznavour, singing in the duo of Roche and Aznavour. The other member of the team was Pierre Roche, who later would emigrate to Canada. Piaf was taken by one of the songs they had written, *J'aime Paris au mois de mai,* I Like Paris in the Month of May, a very attractive tune with a charming lyric. Though he was tiny and had a large nose that Piaf immediately criticized (and which later was altered), she thought Aznavour had big talent, and took him into her entourage. He went to live with her at Boulogne, where he slept on a sofa. He became her secretary, chauffeur, handyman, and general factotum.

Berteaut says that Aznavour's relationship with her was purely professional. Aznavour's own attitude to Piaf seems to substantiate this. In any case, her bed would not remain empty for long. In still another nightclub, she met a big, rough looking American, with a pock-marked face, named Eddie Constantine. Constantine's looks, which would stand him in good stead when, later, he became a sort of Humphrey Bogart tough guy in French movies, were at odds with his background.

Born in Los Angeles in 1915 into a family of Austrian opera singers, a prize-winning voice student at the Vienna Conservatory, he had been an L.A. studio singer, doing commercials for cigarettes and chewing gum, a work that he—like so many others before and after him—disliked intensely, as profitable as it was. He went to Paris to take his chances, working for a time as a production singer. Then Piaf found him. The factory began to hum as Piaf relentlessly rehearsed Aznavour and Constantine.

Cerdan remained her great love, no doubt because he had died at the peak of the romance, before she could grow bored with him. This time *le grand amour* could be preserved forever in the shrine of her illusions. Cerdan could never be lined up with her other trophies. Once she had a party for eight of them, all of whom turned up in the blue suits she always bought her men, along with the cigarette lighters and watches.

Piaf flew with Simone to Casablanca, effected a reconciliation with Marinette Cerdan, brought Marinette and Cerdan's children back to live with her at Boulogne, bought Jacques Fath clothes for her lover's widow, and undertook the education of his children.

And then the bad days came. With Aznavour at the wheel, her car went off the road and was destroyed. They were unharmed. Three weeks later, asleep with Aznavour in the back seat of a car driven by the bicycle rider who was her current lover, she was in a second accident. This time she got two broken ribs and a broken arm. The doctors eased her pain with morphine, to which she became almost immediately addicted. She took up with another cyclist, a friend of the first. She began to sentimentalize about her lost child Marcelle. Then came Jacques Pills. (It is pronounced Peelse.)

She'd met him in 1939, an elegant man and a gentleman, the husband of Lucienne Boyer and half of Pills and Tabet, the biggest singing team of the time. He'd seemed beyond her wildest aspirations. Now, all these years later, he brought her a song—his lyrics, music by his accompanist, one Gilbert Bécaud. It was *Je t'ai dans le peau,* I've Got You in the Skin, which as always she made her own, in the process helping launch another singer, Bécaud. As for Pills, it was, once again, love at first sight for Piaf. With Pills, she was convinced, she could kick her morphine habit, a habit Pills didn't even know she had. He thought she was on cortisone. Berteaut recalls her crawling around the floor looking for a lost syringe. And the pushers were both supplying her and blackmailing her. Pills, who long since had been divorced from Boyer, proposed to her.

"This woman," Berteaut wrote, "demolished by drink and beginning to be corroded by drugs, dreamed of a first communion dress like a ten-year-old." In July 1952, Piaf and Pills were married in a civil ceremony in the town hall of the fashionable sixteenth arrondisement. In September, on her fifth trip to the United States, after a fix, she married Pills a second time at the church of St. Vincent de Paul. Marlene Dietrich was her witness. Piaf wore a long dress of pale blue, and in a photo taken as she entered the church escorted by Dietrich, she looks like the radiant child she thought she was. She was thirty-seven. Pills was forty-six.

Pills was soon to learn his bride was both an alcoholic and a drug addict. Three times he put her in a clinic to take the cure. They parted in 1955 but remained close friends.

Her work was deteriorating. Yet she pulled herself together to make a triumphant appearance—her seventh American trip—at Carnegie Hall at a fee of three thousand dollars per night.

She used to speak of "my pals the Americans." But in France she had acquired a reputation for unreliability and bad work. Nonetheless, Bruno Coquatrix, who owned the Olympia theater, decided to take a chance by giving her a one-month engagement. She was a smash. Coquatrix cancelled other contracts to keep her for twelve weeks. Her record sales soared.

She suffered an attack of delerium tremens. Again she was hospitalized. And again she left for the United States, to perform in New York, Los Angeles, Las Vegas, and Chicago. The tour lasted eleven months, and she was paid a higher fee than anyone in American history to that time, excepting Bing Crosby and Frank Sinatra.

In the fall of 1959, on her way to the airport to leave on her ninth tour of the United States, she was in her third automobile accident. Her face was badly cut, but she recovered with little scarring. In February 1960 she collapsed onstage, vomiting blood, at the Waldorf-Astoria and was taken to Columbia Presbyterian Hospital for stomach surgery. Jacques Pills came to her bedside.

A young American fan, a twenty-three-year-old painter named Douglas Davies, sent her flowers. When she left the hospital, she took him back to Paris with her. She collapsed onstage in Stockholm and returned to Paris for more surgery. She broke up with Davies, who—like so many of her lovers—remained her friend. He died in June 1962 in a plane crash near Orly Airport.

Simone Berteaut records that in the twelve years from 1951 to 1963, Piaf survived four automobile accidents, an attempted suicide, four drug cures, one sleep treatment, two attacks of d.t.s, seven surgical operations, three hepatic comas, a spell of insanity, two attacks of bronchial pneumonia and one of pulmonary edema. She had ulcers, arthritis, and jaundice.

She had been blind in childhood. Whether the blindness was hysterical or caused by cataracts, as she believed, is problematical. Considering that she had been hideously neglected and half starved by her mother before being taken to that Normandy bordello, the former seems likely. The nature of the cure further suggests it. The prostitutes were very good to her. They scrubbed and scraped away her encrusted filth. They made rag dolls for her during her blindness. They mothered her. In August 1921, according to her legend, after the ladies of the house had become aware that she could not see, they shut up shop for a day, dressed like housewives, and paraded through the streets to the basilica of Ste Thérèse de Lisieux to burn candles and urge divine intercession for Edith. Four days later she could see. Or so Piaf told Simone, who presumed she must have heard the story from her father, since Edith had been seven at the time of her "miracle."

After that, Louis Gassion took his daughter on the road with him, making her sing in the streets and cafes and teaching her to con money from the gullible. It is hardly a wonder that she hated bathing (when she acquired her luxurious home at Boulogne, she filled the bathtub with goldfish), liked whores and partook of their morality, manipulated people with uncommon skill, was most at home in cabarets and the streets, and sustained a pathetic belief in the supernatural.

The ravages of hard living had taken a toll. Yet she worked in spite of her ill health, touring in France and other countries until one of her periodic collapses would force her to cancel. She had very little money, having given far too much of it to musicians, vagabonds, sycophants, and parasites of various styles and stories.

In the fall of 1962, Piaf opened once more at the Olympia. She was terribly weak by then. A doctor watched from the wings as she tottered toward the microphone, so thin that the cords of her neck and the tendons in her hands stood out conspicuously. Her hair had thinned to a reddish fuzz.

The recording made during that engagement is an incredible testament not only to her talent but to raw courage. There was a new kind of rasp to her voice, the rasp of physical pain. And yet that recording is one of the best she ever made. One of its songs is *Le Billard électrique,* about a boy who plays a pinball machine as he waits in a bar for a girl. The song is rhythmically punctuated by a hysterical *ding! ding!* She had recorded the same song some years before. The early version was great Piaf. The latter is even greater Piaf, for her energy had become demonic. At the end of the song she screams *dinnnng!* The sound is frightening in its intensity.

A male voice is heard in one song on that final album from the Olympia—that of Théo Sarapo, a hairdresser of Greek parentage who was half her age. They had recently been married and she was trying to turn him, like others before him, into a singer. It was as if she could imagine nothing else that one might do with one's life. The French snickered at her and Sarapo, who was seen as a gigolo opportunist. Berteaut says that on the contrary, Sarapo (Piaf gave him the name; it is Greek for *I love you*) loved her desperately and stood to inherit from her only her debts. He came from a comfortable family to whom he very properly introduced Piaf before their marriage. The doctors had told him her life was nearing its end; he married her anyway. Berteaut recalls him hovering by Edith's sickbed, in a house on the Riviera, combing her hair, putting eau de cologne on her face, and washing her hands.

She had had a concerto grosso of illnesses in those last years, but it was cancer that finally killed her at forty-seven. Told she was dying, her close friend Jean Cocteau said, "Piaf had genius. There will never be another Piaf." On October 11, 1963, four hours after he learned she was gone, Cocteau, who had suffered a stroke early in the year, was himself dead of a heart attack. No one doubted that Piaf's death caused his.

The Church at first refused Piaf a religious burial on the grounds that she had lived "in a state of public sin." A few hours later, however, the official position softened, purportedly in consideration of Piaf's deep piety. Her friends no doubt concluded, with French cynicism, that someone had put in the fix.

Mourners at her burial in the cemetery of Père Lachaise included Marlene Dietrich, Gilbert Bécaud, Jacqueline François, the faithful Jacques Pills, and Aznavour, along with a very large crowd of very little people: forty thousand of them, mostly from the working class. As Piaf had requested, the souvenirs she treasured most were buried with her. The inventory: three fluffy toy animals, a green silk cravat, some religious pictures, a plaster statue of Ste Thérèse de Lisieux, whom she believed had restored her sight, a silver medallion of the Virgin, the épaulette of a Légionnaire, a sailor's beret, and a postcard from the chapel of Milly-la-Forêt with a dedication from Cocteau.

Sacha Guitry said, "Her life was so sad it seems almost too beautiful to be true." That's a cute little oxymoron. There is nothing beautiful about arthritis, drug addiction, alcoholism, or cancer. But it is in accord with general view of her life as tragic. I do not share it. Born literally on a sidewalk from a slut of a mother who had no interest in her, this indestructible child of the streets climbed with cunning and courage to the highest levels of the international entertainment world. She had sung for Princess Elizabeth, the soon-to-be Queen of England, who invited her to her table, an honor Piaf could not quite believe. When she was awarded a Grand Prix du Disque in 1952, she was photographed with the *Président de la République* and Nobel-prize-winning novelist Colette. Her friends included the rich, the famous, and the fascinating of two continents, actors, playwrights, composers, poets, and politicians.

Only a few months before her death, she sang from the top of the Eiffel Tower for the world premiere of the movie *The Longest Day*, the film about the bloody but successful Allied landings at

Normandy in 1944. Her audience, gathered for dinner in the gardens of the Palais de Chaillot, included Winston Churchill, General and former President of the United States Dwight D. Eisenhower, Viscount Bernard Law Montgomery of Alamein, Lord Louis Mountbatten and General Omar Bradley, the very architects of Germany's defeat, the King of Morocco, Don Juan of Spain, Queen Sophia of Greece, and movie celebrities such as Elizabeth Taylor, Sophia Loren, Ava Gardner, Robert Wagner, Audrey Hepburn, Curt Jurgens, and Richard Burton, not to mention all the people of Paris who heard that fierce voice ringing out from the sky such of her songs as *Non, je ne regrette rien*—No, I Regret Nothing.

If in the early years she collected lovers who could help her career, she repaid the debt in the later years by gathering around her men she could—and did—help. She earned and threw away fortunes. She had a remarkable ability to get people to do exactly what she wanted, including the half-sister who lived through her. Although she had a dumpy little body, men were mad about her, one after another, and she lived a sex life far beyond the wildest fantasies of any bored housewife. If she burned her candle at both ends, for a long time it burned exceeding bright. Cocteau said she was like "a terrifying little sleepwalker who sings her dreams to the air on the edge of the roof." Ah, but her father was a juggler and acrobat who had taught her the rudiments of his trade; she had a spectacular sense of balance. If the last years were hard, so they are for many people who have known nothing of the heights she attained. And singing your dreams to the air beats life in a Normandy whorehouse.

A year or two after she died, I got a call from Paris from the New York music publisher Howie Richmond. He had published some of the Antonio Carlos Jobim songs I had translated from Portuguese. He asked me if I knew French. "Better than I do Portuguese," I said. Howie said he was planning a one-man Broadway show for Charles Aznavour and wanted to know if I would come to Paris to write English adaptations of the Aznavour songs. I left the next day. The first song I did was *J'aime Paris au mois de mai,* which I called *Paris Is at Her Best in May,* as a sort of brand-x refutation of *April in Paris.* I had no idea at the time that this had been the first of Aznavour's songs to catch Piaf's attention.

Aznavour was playing the Olympia, working on the same stage where Piaf had made that last album. We talked in the dressing room, probably the same one she used—the star's dressing room. At the end of each show he would put a table across the door of that room and sit behind it, signing autographs with a star's conditioned automaticity for the long lines of people who came by and discussing with me the pending New York show. Naturally, during those weeks, I asked about Piaf. There is much about him that is like her. He is tiny, and works in simple attire. The songs he writes are in her tradition, though not as harsh. He has that same quick vibrato.

He told me that Piaf had a rich and raucous sense of humor, that she was always surrounded by friends, and that she would have liked to sing comic songs, had her public been willing to accept her as anything but the tragedienne.

One of the songs that bears her name, he said, is actually his. When he showed it to her, she said, "Charles, that song is me!" She begged him to let her put her name on it as its writer. She said she would make it up to him if he did.

"And did she make it up to you?" I asked.

"Of course," he said. "She gave me my career."

Roses in the Morning
Johnny Mercer

It is often difficult to recall where and when you met someone, but in his case I remember exactly. He was in my opinion the finest lyricist in the English language, an exquisite craftsman and the one with the most personal voice. I had arrived in Los Angeles from New York and called a friend to ask if we might have dinner that evening. She said she had to attend a birthday party for John Williams, then asked, "Would you like to go?"

"Since it's my birthday too," I said, "I'd love to."

It was John's thirty-sixth birthday. I remember that because everybody brought him three dozen of something. Someone brought him thirty-six baby turtles, on whose fate we can only surmise, and someone else gave him thirty-six Black Wing pencils. Black Wings were the pencil of choice of composers in those days. Because of those three dozen Black Wings, I can set the year as 1968, when John Williams turned thirty-six, the date as February 8, and the time at shortly after eight p.m. That is when I met Johnny Mercer.

He was standing with Henry Mancini and a portly man who turned out to be Dave Cavanaugh of Capitol Records. I did not have to ask who he was: I knew that pixie smile from a thousand photographs. When I was in high school, he was a very big singing star, though to the day he died he was never sure of that. He founded Capitol Records during World War II and turned out record after record that a wartime generation of young people found compellingly interesting. You could not get them in Canada and so I would slip across the border to Niagara Falls, New York, to buy them—Mercer's own and those of the stable of fresh talents he assembled for the company—and take them back under the seat of a bus. I was always in fear of being arrested for smuggling and sent to prison forever. I was about fifteen. I dreamed of playing piano like Nat Cole and writing songs like Johnny Mercer.

Hank Mancini introduced us. He said, "Gene's a writer from the East." The East being New York. And Dave Cavanaugh said something kind about my lyrics. I said, "Well, Mr. Mercer, if I know anything about writing lyrics, I learned it from Cole Porter and you and Charles Trenet."

"How'd I get in there between two queens?" he said with a quick smile.

One learns not to embarrass one's heroes with overpraise or dumbstruck attention. After some restrained statement of my admiration for his work, I excused myself and went on about the party, a Hollywood affair of demonstrative embracing, kissed cheeks, gushing compliments, and maneuvering for professional and social advantage.

Two or three days later I got a note from Mercer at my hotel. I couldn't imagine how he'd known where to find me, although the answer turned out to be a simple one: he'd asked Henry Mancini. He said that by coincidence he had, the day after the party, heard a lyric of mine, *Someone to Light Up My Life,* sung by Vic Damone, on his car radio. "That is some elegant lyric," he wrote. "It made me cry. I wish I had written it." Long afterwards, I learned that he treasured a telegram from Cole Porter saying something similar about one of his own lyrics.

Thus began a friendship. Whenever John came to New York or I to Los Angeles, we'd booze and talk shop, sometimes about lyrics, sometimes about the corruption of the music business. "Whatever we do," he said, "the publishers will always be two jumps ahead of us." I was warned against drinking with Mercer, told by various persons that he could become suddenly and sullenly—and articulately—nasty. It was notorious that he would get drunk at parties, turn vicious toward friends and strangers alike, and then, shaken with guilt and hangover the following day, send them roses. He was always cautious with Jo Stafford. She has bearing and presence. Nonetheless, once, at a Capitol Christmas party, John, already well into the wassail, started in on her.

Jo said, "Please, John, I don't want any of your roses in the morning." That stopped him.

Some of the stories were funny but many were not, and some people came away from parties bearing an abiding dislike for Mercer. An executive at RCA Victor in New York, who had idolized him for years, wanted to meet him. A mutual friend introduced them in the Rainbow Room at the top of Rockefeller Center. Alas, he caught Mercer on one of his bad nights, and afterwards said he wished they'd never met because now his illusion was shattered. Carlos Gastel, for many years Nat Cole's manager, once told Mercer off in a bar, saying, "Talent gives you no excuse to insult people." I know two or three people who despised Johnny Mercer. For others, it wasn't that simple. The songwriters Jay Livingston and Ray Evans, while nursing no illusions about him, never let anyone forget that Mercer's recommendation of them for a motion picture assignment he was too busy to take himself launched their professional careers. John was as generous in his praise of good songwriters as he was quietly critical of the shallow practitioners of the craft. As for me, I liked John. A lot. And we got along, perhaps because we shared the lyricist's paranoia, which John once perfectly expressed in a single line: "You get tired of being everybody's lyric boy." He was referring to all the lead sheets and demo tapes sent to you by musicians who think lyrics are dashed off in a moment from ideas picked casually out of the air. Music, as they see it, is the important art. Everybody uses words, don't they? And music may be the more important art—even the most important of them all for, as Walter Pater observed, all the arts crave after the conditions of music. But it isn't the easier art. "I think it takes more talent to write music," John said to me once, "but it takes more courage to write lyrics."

Although John sometimes wrote quickly—*Days of Wine and Roses* was written in five minutes, *Autumn Leaves* in a taxi on the way to Los Angeles airport—he often suffered for a lyric, as every conscientious lyricist does, and the exquisite *Skylark* took him a year. "Sometimes you get lucky," he said. "But not often." Asked what was the hardest part of writing a lyric, he used to say, "Finding the title." And it is.

Once I arrived in California from New York to work on some songs for a film. I rented a furnished apartment in Westwood, installed a telephone, and called John at his home in Bel Air. He was away for a few days at his other home in Palm Springs. He and his wife Ginger also maintained an apartment in New York. I left a message with his answering service and went to work on my lyric assignment. John called a few days later and said in that soft Georgia accent, "Whatcha been doin'?"

"Looking for a rhyme," I said.

"Why didn't you call me?" he said. "I'da laid one on yuh."

"I did call you. You were away, remember?"

He invited me to dinner. I said that until I had this one song solved, I would be unfit company for man or beast. He knew exactly what I was talking about. He told me to call him when the song was finished and we'd go out somewhere.

Perhaps a half hour later I got a call from a Harold's Liquor Store in Westwood, saying they had some Scotch for me. "I didn't order any Scotch," I said.

"Mr. Mercer ordered it for you," the man said. "A case of Glennfiddich." On an earlier trip to California I had spent an evening at John's house, where I tasted Glennfiddich single-malt Scotch for the first time and raved about the flavor. He had remembered.

"*How* much?" I said.

"A case."

"I'm only going to be here a month!"

"Do you come to California often?"

"Fairly."

"Well, we can send you two or three bottles now and you can get the rest whenever you come back."

And so it happened. Every time I came to Los Angeles on a job, I'd call Harold's Liquor Store. I drank John's Glennfiddich on and off for about three years.

And I kept hearing how saber-tongued he could be when he'd been drinking. Finally I asked a mutual friend about it. "It's all true," he said.

"It's never happened to me."

"Your turn will come," he said.

But it never did. Once I saw John starting to get edgy with a waitress at Charlie O's in New York. When she had gone to get us two more drinks, I said, "John, why are you giving her a hard time? She's been perfectly pleasant to us, and you're being a son of a bitch." I figured the friendship might end there and then.

But John looked me evenly in the eye and said, "You're right," and when the girl returned he was cordial to her, and as we left he gave her an enormous tip.

I was always amazed, in the years after our first meeting, how many of my lyrics he had learned. I of course had known hundreds of his all my life. I remember singing them when I was no more than ten as I rode my bicycle to the beach in the spring on grav-elled country roads through fields of apple and peach blossoms in the Niagara Peninsula. I was in love with songs, and undoubtedly I absorbed principles of euphony and articulation from Mercer long before I ever knew him or even imagined that I could know him. One pub-crawling evening we wandered around New York singing fragments of each other's lyrics back and forth, like musicians trading fours.

I loved John's work more than anyone's, more even than Howard Dietz's, Yip Harburg's, or Cole Porter's. I loved it—even before I knew enough about the subject to understand that these were my reasons for loving it—for its perfect literate craftsman-ship and for the powerful vivid use of Anglo-Saxon imagery. And of course for his range.

Every singer knows that the most singable vowels are *oo* and *oh*. In *I Remember You*, John used both sounds, and particularly the *oo*, throughout the song. It is an amazing lyric, so simple that its sophisticated inner craftsmanship could easily escape notice:

> I remember you.
> You're the one who
> made my dreams come true
> a few
> kisses ago.
>
> I remember you.
> You're the one who
> said, "I love you too.
> I do.
> Didn't you know?"
>
> I remember too
> a distant bell
> and stars that fell
> like rain,
> out of the blue.
>
> When my life is through,
> and the angels ask me to recall
> the thrill of them all,
> then I shall tell them
> I remember you.

The bridge begins and ends with the *oo* sound. And it is used as an inner rhyme in *you too*. Very few of the words end with stopped consonants, and those few fall on short passing notes. All the other words end in semivowels and fricatives—*one, dreams, remember*. The liquid semivowel *l*, occurring here as a double *ll*—in Italian, the *ll* is sustained longer than the single *l*—begins in the release and then recurs through the rest of the song: *bell, fell, recall, thrill, all, shall, tell. Shall-tell* is an inner rhyme echoing *bell-fell*, at least in American English. (In England, *shall* would not rhyme with *tell*.)

Another Mercer masterpiece, *I Thought about You*, further illustrates his grasp of the craft:

I took a trip on a train
and I thought about you.
We passed a shadowy lane,
and I thought about you.

Two or three cars
parked under the stars,
a winding stream.
Moon shining down
on some little town.
With each beam,
same old dream.

With every stop that we made,
I thought about you.
And then I pulled down the shade
and I really felt blue.

I peeked through the crack
and looked at the track,
the one going back
to you.

And what did I do?
I thought about you.

Long notes create the rhyme points in songs. Since short syllables should be fitted to short notes and long syllables to long, the rhymes must be long sounds that can be sustained. You can sustain only the vowels, and preferably the long forms of the vowels. Consonants—*b, t, d, g,* for example—cannot be sustained, with the exception of the fricatives *f, s, sh,* and *th.* They can be sustained, but the sounds they make are silly and unattractive. Short vowels as in *bit* and *up* can be sustained but they have a somewhat abrupt sound. One would normally avoid using as a rhyme a word with the kind of abrupt termination you find in *back* or *crack.* There are four consonants that can be sustained to euphonious effect. Known as semivowels, they are *l, m, n,* and *r.* Mercer used open vowels and words ending with the semivowel *l* in *I Remember You.* Words like *train* and *lane, stars* and *cars, stream* and *dream, down* and *town,* containing semivowel endings, are also good rhyme words. Now, notice how Mercer uses the open vowel *oo* and semi-vowels at rhyme points through most of *I Thought about You* and then, toward the end, deliberately brings in the abrupt consonant *k* to evoke the click of a train's wheels. The word *clack* is never even used; yet you hear the clacking in your mind. It is implied by the sound and the rhyme.

"Do you think Johnny was conscious of these things?" his wife Ginger asked me, after he was gone. I am sure he never gave them a thought when he was writing. But he assuredly was aware of them. I know because we occasionally touched on them in conversations. He had an enormous sensitivity to language and the way it works. "We all come from Gilbert," he said to me once, referring to William S. Gilbert. The tradition is rooted in Gilbert. It came to America through the Gilbert and Sullivan operettas and, later, through Wodehouse, who was known in his time not only for his satiric fiction but also for some very good lyrics for music by Friml, Romberg, and Kern.

Aside from its craftsmanship, I love John's writing for its emotional warmth, a warmth always controlled by a fastidious restraint. He never overstated. Everything was subtle: "as if the mayor had offered me the key . . . to Paris."

The vast body of our best song literature came from the Broadway stage roughly between 1920 and 1955, at which time it began the long decline to its present squalor. But Mercer's work, a catalogue of about 1500 songs, was written mostly for movies. He wrote seven Broadway shows: *Walk with Music, St. Louis Woman,* which later toured Europe with an all-black cast under the title *Free and Easy, Texas Li'l Darling, Top Banana, Li'l Abner,* and *Foxy.* But he wrote lyrics, and occasionally music as well, for nearly thirty movies, and maybe more, including *Hollywood Hotel, Cowboy from Brooklyn* (for which he wrote *I'm an Old Cowhand*), *Going Places, Naughty but Nice, Blues in the Night* (which originally had a quite different title; the producers changed it when they heard Mercer's lyric), *The Fleet's In, You Were Never Lovelier* (which score, written in collaboration with Jerome Kern, produced *Dearly Beloved* and the splendid *I'm Old Fashioned*), *Star Spangled Rhythm* (which gave us the haunting *That Old Black Magic*), *The Harvey Girls, Out of This World, The Belle of New York, Seven Brides for Seven Brothers, Daddy Long Legs, Merry Andrew, Breakfast at Tiffany's* (which produced *Moon River*), and *Days of Wine and Roses.*

Johnny Mercer was born in Savannah, Georgia, November 18, 1909, and never severed his ties to that city. He was a Scot by ancestry and had cousins in Scotland. He was the son of a successful real estate man and the grandson of a colonel who served under Robert E. Lee. Harold Arlen's nickname for John was "the colonel."

The South virtually exudes poetry, or at least it used to. Heavily populated by the Irish, who have been called a word-drunk people, and by Scots, who rival them in a passion for imagery, the South has a language to which the black population has also made a substantial contribution. Mercer grew up surrounded by black people, at ease in the rhythms of their speech. Of all the awards he got in his life, he was proudest of one he received in 1944: a black boys' club in Chicago voted him the outstanding young Negro singer of the year.

Whatever the historical reasons for it, southern literature—as represented by Thomas Wolfe, William Faulkner, Carson McCullers, and many with Celtic names—is memorable for rich poetry, and southerners, black and white alike, have a taste for arresting imagery to express their visions of ideas and events. They seem unself-conscious about it, not afraid of appearing "literary" or "poetic," as one would be in the stiff-jawed industrial North or the taciturn farm valleys of Vermont. And all Mercer's lyrics, at least in the use of language, were deeply southern, though not in ways that limited them. Rather, they were southern in ways that made Mercer's diction free and flashing and open: "The clouds were like an alabaster palace."

The Mercer family had a summer home at Vernon View, twelve miles out of Savannah. The attic of John's mind was crowded with images of unpaved roads covered in crushed oyster

shells and winding through trees hung with Spanish moss, of aza-
leas and marsh grasses and inlets of the sea, of kerosene lamps
seen through the mosquito netting that hung around beds. The
family was well-to-do, and surrounded by colored servants with
whose children he played marbles or one-o-cat—softball. They
spoke Gullah, a dialect so dense that it almost isn't English, and
John understood it. He was steeped in their music, lullabies and
work songs and that of their Sunday church services. He sang in
the Christ Church from the age of six until he was seventeen,
amused relatives by singing such party songs as *The Goat that
Flagged the Train,* sang in quartets songs like *You Tell Me Your
Dream,* collected records, knew all the Harry Lauder numbers by
heart, and about the age of fifteen wrote a song called *Sister Susie,
Strut Your Stuff* in the style of many songs in fashion at that time.
He listened to Louis Armstrong, Bessie Smith, Red Nichols, Bix
Beiderbecke, and Frank Trumbauer.

Mercer's songs tend to fall into four primary groups: his train
songs, like *I Thought About You, Laura,* and *On the Atchison, Topeka
and the Santa Fe;* his French songs, such as *Autumn Leaves, Once
Upon a Summertime,* and *When the World Was Young,* which captures
to a striking degree a French viewpoint, although John spoke
hardly a word of French; his bird songs, such as *Bob White, Mister
Meadlowlark,* and *Skylark,* one of his most exquisite lyrics; and his
southern songs, such as *Lazybones, Blues in the Night, Ac-Cent-Tchu-
Ate the Positive,* and *Any Place I Hang My Hat Is Home.* There is a
recurring theme of aging and time past, which begins cheerfully
in *You Must Have Been a Beautiful Baby* and evolves sadly into *The
Summer Wind, The Days of Wine and Roses,* and the aforementioned
When the World Was Young, which people often call *Ah, the Apple
Trees,* one of the most poignant brief phrases in all his songs.

Mercer's politics seemed vague, but they were of conservative
bent. He believed in the American system but he wasn't happy
about the surburban sprawl that was occurring, and as time went
on he struck me as troubled by the social inequalities of the coun-

try. Certainly he was saddened about the deterioration of the environment.

Johnny seemed to feel that he had never really made it on Broadway. He may have been right. Some of his shows were successes but none was a really substantial hit. The reason perhaps was in John. In writing lyrics for the stage, one must become the characters whose words you are creating; like an actor, you must take on other identities, think and thus write in the tone and style of those characters. And John was always John, at once country boy and cosmopolite, southerner and American, American and internationalist. Therefore he was truly in his element in films, where a personal style has often been valued more than a general flexibility, whether in songwriters, directors, or actors. He remained a Georgian, remembering the littoral wetlands and the clouds of pink flamingoes and terns and gulls that used to be there, and the quick slithering alligators. "Now it's all freeways," he said with simple sadness one night.

John was an odd sort of duck, cantankerous and kind, humorous and morose, a compound of compassionate poeticism and personal bitterness. Very Celtic. The bitterness never colored his work; you will find no trace of it in his lyrics, although there is often a sardonic self-mockery, as in the lines "When an irresistible force, such as you, meets an old immovable object like me. . . . " The music to that song was Mercer's. So was that of *Dream.*

"He never had any musical training," his wife said to me once, "and he was hesitant." That is unfortunate. Frank Loesser, another brilliant lyricist spawned by Hollywood, never had any training either, but he wrote wonderful melodies. So, occasionally, did John.

John said once, "I tried to be a singer and failed. I tried to be an actor and failed. So I just naturally fell into lyric writing." But he hadn't failed as a singer. Perhaps because he founded Capitol Records—with Glenn Wallichs and fellow songwriter Buddy De Sylva—and thus recorded for his own company, he may have felt he had not made it fair and square. But I loved his singing, which had great humor, and a lot of people did.

Hilaire Belloc wrote, "It is the best of all trades, to make songs, and the second best to sing them." A small framed copy of that quotation hung on the wall of John's studio, fifty yards or so behind his house, snuggled in a canyon's foliage in Bel Air, next to a golf course on which deer sometimes wander. But he never really saw it that way. In his heart he felt it was best to sing songs.

One afternoon when John and I were roaming around New York, I had an urge to get one of our conversations on tape. I called the Canadian Broadcasting Corporation and asked for use of their Manhattan studio. John and I went up to the office on Fifth Avenue, sat down at a table covered in pooltable green felt, forgot the microphone, and talked. A radio broadcast was edited out of that tape. It was lost for years and then turned up again. Hearing it was eerie, as if John were alive again.

"Have you ever figured out what makes us write songs?" I asked him. "Both of us—all of us."

"I don't know," he said. "I think it comes from a creative urge when you're little. Of course I was always stuck on music. I gravitated to songs because I loved music so much. I would like to have been an advertising man, I think I wanted to be a cartoonist, I was an actor. But all the time I was listening to songs, buying songs, writing songs. And I think that's what I was really cut out to do."

John believed that in most instances, the melody of a song should be written before the lyric. My own experience confirms him on this. Only a very few composers in history, Richard Rodgers among them, have been able to lift words off a page and make them sing. Given finished lyrics, composers often come up with melodies that are a little wooden, a little academic, tending to *recitativo*. They do not seem to be as sensitive to the music in speech as lyricists are to the speech in music. "I've lost a lot of good lyrics by turning them over to composers," John said.

That afternoon in New York he said, "A tune writer has to know how to build up a lyric so that the laughs come through, and the lyric writer has to know how to baby that tune, when he gets a good one, to search and search till he gets the right lyric to it. You can ruin great ideas if they're written improperly. I find that there's a very strange alchemy about working too little or too much on a tune. Sometimes if you work too much and you're *too* careful, you lose the whole thing. But if you get a fine fire going at the beginning, and you control it, you can rewrite enough without rewriting too much. That's the best way to write, I find."

"What do you think of contemporary lyrics, as a whole?" The year, I think was 1970.

"I think in the main what we're going through right now is a lot of drivel. A lot of people who can't write are trying to write. And I think those who do write well are basing most of their stuff on a modern-day kind of hobo philosophy. It's a futility because of the war in Viet Nam and because of crime and violence and everything. And it's built on an Elizabethan structure, and hill music, which is also based on Elizabethan structure. And so a lot of these kids who are writing, like Simon and Garfunkel and Jimmy Webb and Johnny Hartford and the kids down in Nashville, take the guitar and try to philosophize to a hillbilly tune with chords that come from 'way 'way ago. That's the general picture. Of course, there are many exceptions, including a guy like Alan Jay Lerner. I think Webb is a superior writer—I didn't mean to classify him with the others. And Burt Bacharach is trying very hard to be different, too hard as far as I'm concerned, although I think he's gifted. I don't know. What do you think?"

"I pretty much agree. I like Webb's things too. *By the Time I Get to Phoenix* is a very good song. Why don't you record again?"

"I'd like to. I'm singing really not too badly, so they say. I think my voice is deeper. I think I know better how to sing in tune than I used to. I don't think anybody cares, that's the main thing."

"I think there would be considerable interest. You always did your humorous things. You never recorded your ballads. Why?"

"I can't sing well enough."

"I don't agree."

"I could try it now. I think I'm a little better than I used to be."

Some time after that, John recorded two excellent albums for the Pye label in London. Whether my urging had anything to do with it or not, I do not know, but he recorded some of his ballads, such as *The Summer Wind,* to poignant effect.

"I don't think," I said, "that I've ever heard a song of yours that didn't have a payoff in the last line."

"Well, I think that's kind of the way you approach writing; if you're brought up in that school, you don't even *begin* a song if you haven't got an ending of some kind."

"Have you ever started out when you didn't know what the ending was going to be?" I said, and we both laughed.

"Yeah, I *have*. Sometimes I *wound up* without having an ending!"

"That's a desperate feeling!"

"It is!"

"And particularly when you've got some good lines in there and you don't want to lose 'em, but you have to top 'em."

"That's right," John said, and we laughed some more.

"Let me ask you about a couple of people you've worked with. One is Jerome Kern."

"Well, Mr. Kern was kind of the dean. He was the professor emeritus. He was the head man. And everybody respected him and admired him because his tunes were so really far above the others. He was new and yet he was classical in feeling. He had great melodic invention, he had great harmonic things. So he was at home with the professional composer. They respected him above all, he taught all of them something. The lyric writers liked him—if they could ever write with him. Strangely enough, he wrote with about ten or fifteen lyric writers, more than people think he did, although of course his biggest collaborator was Hammerstein."

"Well, there was Harbach, and Ira Gershwin, and Wodehouse, and yourself . . . "

"Well I wrote one picture with him, and Dorothy Fields may have written two or three. He was a fascinating guy. He was small. He wore glasses. He had a prominent nose and a very quick, alert mind. He was terribly curious. Berlin has the same kind of mind. Porter too, although Porter's mind was a little more sophisticated, more effete. Kern was terribly interested in anything that went on around him. He loved to play Indications, he loved to play Scrabble. If you brought him a brand new game, he'd be like a child about it. He'd want to play that for a week. He'd give parties and they'd play these games. He collected first editions and had a fabulous library which he sold for I think about a million dollars. He also had a coin collection which he sold for a lot of money. He was interested in everything all the time. He interested himself in the book and in your lyrics and the costumes and the choreography just as much as he did in any other part of the show. And because he was good, he had a kind of conceit about him. But he also, like most men of that much stature, had a kind of modesty about him too. I liked him very much."

"Was he easy to work with or hard?"

"He was hard to work with because his standards were high. With me, it was nothing at all, it was really fun, it was an enjoyable job. Of course, I didn't work that long with him. I didn't have a fight with him. If I'd had to write six or seven shows with him and he'd thrown his weight around, I guess he could have been a son of a bitch. But he wasn't."

"How about Harold Arlen?"

"Harold Arlen is a *genius*. I don't know what to say about him, except he doesn't write enough. He's been bothered by illnesses and the various mundane things of this world. But it he were writing like he wrote twenty years ago, I don't think you could catch up to his catalogue. I think he's been inactive so long that people have sort of forgotten about him. He's wonderful. I think he'd *like* to write. I think he probably *needs* to write, for his spirit, for his heart. He's a very tender, very sensitive man, and he writes so beautifully. It's easy for him. It sounds terribly inventive to us, terribly difficult, what he does, but not to him. It's like turning on a tap. It just flows out of him. We did two shows together, *St. Louis Woman* and *Saratoga,* which is kind of a quiet score. Not many people know it and not many people have heard it. Maybe that's because it isn't too good. It wasn't a hit. We did about ten movies at Paramount. The songs that came out of them were songs like *Out of this World, Old Black Magic, Ac-Cen-Tchu-Ate, Come Rain or Come Shine.* We had a lot of songs that are people's favorites that you don't hear much, like *Hit the Road to Dreamland, This Time the Dream's on Me. Blues in the Night* is probably our best-known song."

We talked about *Days of Wine and Roses,* written with Henry Mancini for the film of that name. The title comes from Dowson: "The days of wine and roses, they are not long . . . " Mercer's remarkable lyric consists of only two sentences. In them he expresses the startled sadness of everyone's eventual dawning perception that time has slipped irretrievably away and some things have been lost forever, including the joy of naive discovery, and that one has begun to grow old. It is a brilliant lyric, a jewel of the form. In a way it is typically Mercer. Paul Weston told me, "John was worried about time and his age when he was twenty-eight." Once John and I were walking down a street when two truly beautiful girls passed us, going in the opposite direction. John and I both looked over our shoulders to watch them walking into their future and our past, chatting happily and oblivious of the darkness ahead. John said, "I'm still looking but they're no longer looking back." *Days of Wine and Roses* expresses John's haunted preoccupation with time. It could be argued that the modern era of lyric writing dates from that song—in English, at least; the French have been writing songs in this manner for eighty years or more, Charles Trenet being one of their best.

"You think so?" John said. "You see a thing in that song that I don't know if I see."

"A quality of abstraction."

"Yeah," he said. "Well, I'm not so sure it's purposeful on my part. I don't know whether when Dali painted his pictures, he did it purposefully or he just said, 'I've just got to say something I feel here, and this is the best way to say it.' I'm not sure it was all that intended."

"Oh, I'm not saying that it is or has to be intended. I'm just saying that things you wrote there and ways you wrote there would not have been acceptable or understandable to the public of the 1930s."

"Well, I'll tell you, maybe I give them more credit. Irving Berlin said a long time ago, 'Johnny gives everybody credit for knowing what he's talking about.' You don't write down to the ten-cent-store girl or anybody else. I don't. You certainly don't. And when I try to be literate, I just assume they know what I'm talking about. When I try to do what we're talking about right now, to get images—we did it in *Charade*. In the middle part, where it goes, *in the darkened wings, the music box played on,* I assumed they know what I'm talking about. I can't stop to say, 'You know, there's really not a music box, it's really the orchestra.' You take that to Andy Williams, who's really a fine, intelligent cat, and he says, 'There's always something in these songs I don't understand. But I'm gonna sing it anyway.'"

I took a photo of John that day. After he was dead, Ginger told me it was one of the few pictures of himself he ever liked. Maybe I caught him the way he saw himself. Or maybe, and this is more important, I saw him the way he saw himself; or better yet, that he let me see himself as he was. The relationship was that of two professional lyricists who enjoyed talking about the work to someone else who understood the mechanics of the craft. Somehow the ease of the relationship is in that photo, it is in the eyes, and in the slight gentle smile. There is kindness in those eyes, and laughter, and sadness. It's John, at least the John Mercer I knew.

As the day faded into what the Brazilians call—magnificent term!—*tardinha,* the little afternoon, John and I went somewhere and had a few Glennfiddichs and then dinner, and when we emerged into the streets it was late sunset. White windows shone on the faces of buildings that stood like black cardboard against a rose-colored sky, and high above those deep streets the purple clouds looked solid, carved, sculpted. We took a cab and suffered minor spinal traumae as we bumped over the pot-holes to some club in lower Manhattan where Jimmy Rowles, with whom John had written several songs, was working. I think Jimmy Rowles was Johnny's favorite pianist. Certainly he was one of his favorites.

It is more than difficult to evaluate Johnny Mercer's effect and influence on the American culture. It is impossible. John infiltrated our minds, a benign alien who captured our very processes of thought. Those who grew up when Mercer was at his most active had an advantage over the young of today. We absorbed into memory lyrics by Lorenz Hart and Howard Deitz and Tom Adair and Mercer, those magnificently literate men who gave us, in collaboration with some very gifted composers, the common, everyday, garden-variety popular songs of the period. One assimilated from them one's sense of the English language. They were glorifying and elevating it, not in inaccessible works of High Culture but in popular music that you heard every day on the radio. And Mercer was the best of them all. Today we hear illiteracy rampant in popular music and in television commercials, since those who now write advertising copy grew up on the Beatles and Elvis Presley and thus have been conditioned to the defective and inarticulate use of the English language.

John heard and used the American vernacular with great sensitivity and skill. He was remarkably in tune with it, using it as it evolved in such songs as *Jeepers Creepers* and *Ac-Cent-Tchu-Ate the Positive*, and he sometimes hastened that evolution by popularizing words and phrases. *Ac-cent-Tchu-Ate the Positive* became a phrase of American English, complete with black Baptist rhythmic emphasis. And *latch onto*, which was jazz slang when Mercer used it in that song, turned up by the late 1950s in a *New York Times* editorial.

Mercer chronicled his time in songs. He noted the urbanization of America in *I'm an Old Cowhand*, with lines such as "I ride the range in a Ford V-8." He made fun of the affectations of his adopted home in *Hooray for Hollywood* "where you're terrific if you're even good." When the war came, he made humor of the

training of the soldiers in *G.I. Jive*. And more seriously, as they
began to move out to the blood baths of Normandy and Iwo Jima,
he caught the anguish of those last moments of young couples in:

> This will be my shining hour,
> calm and happy and bright.
> In my dreams, your face will flower
> through the darkness of the night.

And when that night was over, and the survivors came home,
Mercer threw them a party in the song *In the Cool Cool Cool of the
Evening*. ("If I ain't in the clink, and there's something to drink,
you can tell 'em I'll be there.") Later, in a song written with pianist
and singer Blossom Dearie, he made witty fun of the cold-war
paranoia inspired by the FBI and CIA:

> Everywhere you go,
> I think you oughta know,
> I'm shadowing you.
> Turn around and find
> I'm half a step behind.
> I'm shadowing you.
>
> In Venice,
> I'll be a menace
> in your Italian hotel.
> In Paris,
> I shall embarrass
> you on the rue d'la Chappelle.

His lyrics were only part of his influence on America and on
twentieth-century music. Mercer was one of the three founders
and the first president of Capitol Records, a company which had
overwhelming influence for the good in the 1940s and, later, a
comparable influence for the degradation of music.

The label was founded in 1942, during the darkest days of the
war, when the Germans were winning everywhere and the U.S.
Navy's Pacific fleet had been almost competely destroyed at Pearl
Harbor. The sources of shellac in the South Pacific had been cut
off by the Japanese conquests. Where Capitol got its shellac was

for a long time a mystery. The answer is this: Mercer signed to the label a young man who led a dreadful band—and whose father owned a warehouse full of shellac in San Diego.

Capitol was off and running, an innovative and tremendously creative company that gave a great lift to American music. If it had a weakness, it was that its president, Johnny Mercer, had no interest whatever in the business end of the company. He was interested only in the music. Once, during the company's early days, when its headquarters consisted of one small room over a store on Vine Street in Hollywood, Mercer and Paul Weston were listening to some of their newly recorded material. Co-founder Glenn Wallichs was on the telephone. Mercer liked to listen to music loud. Finally Wallichs said, "Johnny, would you turn that down? I'm on long distance, trying to line up a distributor in Pittsburgh."

"Ah, to hell with that," Mercer said. "Let's listen to the music."

Variety predicted that Capitol would fail in the face of competition from the big three, Columbia, RCA Victor, and Decca. But it did not fail, and demonstrated that good popular music could succeed with the people if only they could be exposed to it. Capitol was to prove to be, in its early years, the most creative and innovative of all the large record companies, one of which it rapidly became, spreading its influence in American music to an extent that is beyond estimate. Without it, we might never have had the Stan Kenton band, all the recordings of Nat Cole, the consequent dissemination of Cole's influence as a pianist on Oscar Peterson and Bill Evans and all those whose work flows from them, the brilliant recordings of Peggy Lee, those of Andy Russell and Jo Stafford and Margaret Whiting, the second career of Frank Sinatra, and so much more.

Mercer operated from a philosophy that is strange by today's standards. He believed that you should not release a record unless you liked it. The idea of making a record for purely commercial reasons was beyond his comprehension, and the concept of regularly scheduled releases was alien to him. And the label—silver lettering and a picture of the capitol dome in Washington, D.C., against a simple black background—was generating excitement throughout America. There was something new going on, and the young people knew it.

Although it has become fashionable to denigrate Stan Kenton in recent years—and his excesses justify it—it should not be forgotten that the band in its early days was really startling. The good instrumentals from big bands usually came out on the B sides of more commercial pop records. The Kenton band was noted from the beginning for its instrumentals. Such records as *Artistry in Rhythm, Eager Beaver, Artistry in Bolero,* and *Opus in Pastels* constituted the underscore music of a generation growing up in the middle and late 1940s. Nor is it true that Kenton made *no* contribution. He introduced an enriched harmonic pallette, a powerful use of brass, an expanded application of players' technical resources, and a sort of dramatic approach to orchestral jazz that have been imitated ever since, sometimes by musicians who would deny Kenton any influence whatever.

Kenton was the most powerful force in the development of the stage-band movement in colleges and universities, which has had both good and bad effects on American music. It has undoubtedly raised the level of American and ultimately world musicianship. Kenton did that, and Mercer in collaboration with Paul Weston gave Kenton his chance.

Purely as a pianist, Nat Cole was one of the most important influences in jazz. Under Mercer's control, Capitol pushed a jazz pianist as a pop artist. But Nat was also a superb singer, with impeccable time and bounce. That whispered throaty sound, coupled with his cultivated enunciation, influenced other singers, and some of them quite far away. Nat was visiting Germany when he went one evening to a restaurant where a blond singer and pianist was doing Nat's material and imitating him perfectly. Amused and pleased, Nat attempted to pay his compliments. The German did not recognize him. And he spoke not a word of English. Nat realized that the slavish imitation was entirely phonetic.

Nat's influence extended far beyond voice, since he was the first to recognize and hire Nelson Riddle as a vocal arranger.

Would Sinatra's second career have taken off without Nelson Riddle—and if Capitol had not signed him after his original label, Columbia, dropped him?

Would Jo Stafford have become a star if Mercer had not founded Capitol?

It has been said that an institution is the lengthened shadow of one man. It is impossible to measure the length of Mercer's shadow, given the influence of his lyrics and the way Capitol Records shifted the course of American music.

Mercer's lack of interest in business was the company's fatal flaw.

Mickey Goldsen, who was head of publishing at Capitol for some years, recalls a disagreement he once had with a songwriter wanting yet another advance on his songs. When Mickey refused him, the man went to Glenn Wallichs and intimated that Goldsen was cheating him. Wallichs was disturbed. He and his associates prided themselves on Capitol's honesty, which alone made it a novelty in the record business, and he summoned Goldsen to his office to say that he was hurting the company's reputation. Goldsen flared. He shouted, "It's in the newspapers that Buddy De Sylva's got his secretary knocked up, and Johnny Mercer's in the nearest bar insulting everybody, and *I'm* hurting the company's reputation?"

Others were brought in to fill the deficiency caused by Mercer's indifference to business, including Jim Conkling, who had been a college classmate of Paul Weston's. But Mercer was never comfortable with the company's size and success.

In time De Sylva took sick and wanted to sell Capitol. Mercer was a holdout. But finally, he and Wallichs and De Sylva sold the company to Electrical and Musical Industries (EMI) of England. And the standards of Capitol Records fell when it was guided not by Mercer's philosophy of excellence but by corporate principles of avarice. Gone were the sense of cultural responsibility and the passion for innovation and music.

Nat Cole's sales had helped build Capitol. In the 1960s Nat made a telephone call to the company. The switchboard operator said, "Capitol Records, home of the Beatles." Nat slammed the receiver down in anger. Tony Bennett, who had a deep belief in the psychosomatic source of illness long before the fashion of holistic medicine, has always insisted that Capitol's shabby treatment of Nat in the later years was the source of his cancer.

Mercer got a similar shock when he paid a visit to the Capitol Tower, that odd building—designed to look like a stack of records—that he and Wallichs and De Sylva had built. A receptionist asked his name. John gave it.

"Who?" she said.

He repeated it.

"And may I ask what this is concerning?" she inquired.

John was as disturbed by that incident as Nat Cole was by the phone call.

"We never should have sold the company," he said to me on several occasions. And he was right.

In the last years, he and Ginger traveled a lot. Their trips were always by train or boat. He hated flying. He worked in London with André Previn on a musical that never made it to Broadway. One day, trying to get on the back step of a bus, he lost his equilibrium and fell, giving his head a severe crack on the pavement.

He began work on his memoirs. John was the only one I ever knew who wrote lyrics on a typewriter. He had learned to type when he worked in his father's office during his adolescence, and he typed neatly and well on a machine with a cursive font that I always instantly recognized on an arriving envelope. He would sit there at his typewriter, alone in that studio, trying to preserve in words the days when he went to New York with a little theater group, then, later, obtained small roles in other plays; about an early and encouraging encounter with Eddie Cantor; about turning away from acting toward writing and meeting Ginger when she was a dancer with *Garrick Gaieties;* about writing with Harold Arlen and Hoagy Carmichael and Kern.

After he was gone, Ginger asked me to look at the manuscript and possibly edit it, which I did. There wasn't enough there to publish, and all sorts of important things—the time he saved a drowning man in the Malibu surf, for example—weren't even mentioned. The document wasn't so much an autobiography as a melancholy musing on time gone by. He wrote of entertaining troops in California during the war. He said that they discovered California on their way to the South Pacific, and after the war came back to it with their brides and had their children and turned Los Angeles and the San Fernando Valley into the smog-choked sprawl that it is. He regretted the passing of Georgia wetlands.

"I am over sixty years old now," he wrote. "And when just the other day I heard Richard Frederick and Anna Moffo do a medley from *Show Boat,* Jerry Kern's wonderful melodies, I pulled over to the side of the road, parked, and cried like a young boy.

"I sit here in California, writing these reminiscences in a heavy rain, thinking of the fires and mud slides, and it does seem as if the magic sunny land I knew has been 'struck', like the movie sets it built, and has disappeared overnight, all its geniis gone back into bottles, leaving skyscrapers where the orange blossoms used to scent the wind."

John had a talent for darkness, and the manuscript reminded me of one of his most vivid lyrics, written when the young men were coming back from the war to discover everything changed:

> When an early autumn walks the land
> and chills the breeze
> and touches with her hand
> the summer trees,
> perhaps you'll understand
> what memories I own.
>
> There's a dance pavilion in the rain,
> all shuttered down . . .

I learned from, of all people, Harold of Harold's Liquor Store in Westwood that John was ill. I dropped in one day to buy some Glennfiddich, the supply of which John had provided me having long since gone. I asked Harold if he had talked to John lately and he said that John, under doctor's orders, was on the wagon. I was disturbed more than amazed by this news. John's concern for his own drinking is manifest in some of the songs, including *Drinking Again, I Wonder What Became of Me,* and *One for My Baby (and One More for the Road)*. I called him and paid a visit to him and Ginger. We talked for a while, pleasantly enough, and he confirmed that he had stopped drinking. What I did not know then was that he had a brain tumor. What I do not know to this day is whether he knew it. This was the cause of his disequilibrium.

I did not see him for several months. Then Tony Bennett and Lena Horne performed in concert at the Shubert Theater in Century City. Afterwards there was a reception for friends and for people in the profession. I saw John and Ginger. There was little chance to talk, but I said, "How y' feeling, John?"

"All right," he said, "except that I keep falling down a lot." He had once joked to me that he had had a lot of practice falling off bar stools, and I thought he meant he was drinking again, as in the song. Later, as the party was ending, John and Ginger walked ahead of me toward the door. Suddenly he fell. Ginger was helping him up. I was in a dilemma. Should I help? If he had been drinking, would he and Ginger be embarrassed by my intrusion? In the end I did nothing. He hadn't been drinking, of course. I know only that he fell that night and I didn't help him. It was the last time I ever saw him. It still bothers me a little.

The word went out that John was in the hospital. I called his house but got no answer. I called Henry Mancini, who said he had been unable to learn anything. Nor had Johnny Mandel, with whom John had written *Emily*. A strange silence surrounded him—at his own wish, as we found out later. When it became clear that John's illness was terminal, Ginger took him home. That studio in which he had written so many songs—and on whose wall hung a list of his failed projects, such was his masochism—was converted into a hospital room, with nurses attending him day and night. At the end, this master of words was unable to speak. And he died there in his studio, next to the golf course of the Bel Air Country Club where the deer come, in June 1976. He was sixty-seven.

In the weeks after that, I discussed Johnny with any number of his friends. No one was able to explain John, not his talent, not his anger, not his melancholy. Ginger was never able to explain him, and she was married to him from the time in 1931 when he was trying to get established on the New York stage and she took sewing jobs to keep them going.

Mercer's best epitaph is the lyric to *One for My Baby*. The song is much like a French song in that it is a sort of short story, a slice-of-life portrait of a drinker, in which the character goes through a common progression from stoicism to self-pity to aggression to exhausted depression, and the song might justly be considered autobiographical, one of Mercer's deft sketches of himself.

> You'd never know it,
> but buddy, I'm a kind of poet,
> and I've gotta lotta things to say.
> And when I'm gloomy,
> you've simply gotta listen to me,
> until it's talked away.

> Well that's how it goes,
> and Joe, I know you're gettin' anxious to close.
> So thanks for the cheer.
> I hope you didn't mind my bending your ear . . .

No, John, we didn't mind at all.

Pavilion in the Rain

I

On warm summer nights, in that epoch between the wars and before air conditioning, the doors and wide wooden shutters would be open, and the music would drift out of the pavilion over the converging crowds of excited young people, through the parking lot glistening with cars, through the trees, and over the lake— or the river, or the sea. Sometimes Japanese lanterns hung in the trees, like moons caught in the branches, and sometimes little boys too hung there, observing the general excitment and sharing the sense of an event. And the visit of one of the big bands was indeed an event.

The sound of the saxophones, a sweet and often insipid yellow when only four of them were used, turned to a woody umber when, later, the baritone was added. The sound of three trombones in harmony had a regal grandeur. Four trumpets could sound like flame, yet in ballads could be damped by harmon mutes to a citric distant loneliness. Collectively, these elements made up the sound of a big band.

It is one that will not go away. The recordings made then are constantly reissued and purchased in great quantities. *Time* Magazine re-creates in stereo the arrangements of that vanished era, while the *Reader's Digest* and the Book-of-the-Month Club continue to reissue many of the originals. Throughout the United States and Canada, college and high school students gather themselves into that basic formation—now expanded to five trumpets, four trombones, five saxes doubling woodwinds, piano, bass, drums, and maybe guitar and French horns too—to make their own music in that style. By some estimates there are as many as thirty thousand of these bands. The sound has gone around the world, and you will hear it on variety shows of Moscow television—a little clumsy, to be sure, but informed with earnest intention.

Why? Why does this sound haunt our culture?

For one thing, it was deeply romantic. In 1983 the Bureau of the Census reported that people over sixty-five for the first time in American history outnumbered adolescents. More than a quarter of the population was over fifty. These people remembered that era. They once courted to it. With the mean age of the population about thirty, it could be said that half the population of the North American continent was sired out of the moods and marriages and affairs inspired by that music.

It was also a dramatic sound, which is why it has remained in uninterrupted use in film and television underscoring since Henry Mancini, Johnny Mandel, and a few other composers, who had themselves been nurtured and trained in big bands, began to convince producers of its effectiveness toward the end of the 1950s.

The era that gave birth to that sound, and which that sound dramatized, defies—like all historical periods—tidy definition. It begins more or less in the early 1930s but its elements were in place by the 1920s. It ends in the late 1940s although four of its principal leaders, Count Basie, Duke Ellington, Woody Herman, and Stan Kenton were out there traveling, leading their bands, in the 1970s, and Basie and Herman went on into the 1980s. For the most part, however, the tradition had to be carried on by what came to be known as rehearsal bands and a few that came together more or less regularly to record and make brief tours, such as the Rob McConnell band in Canada and, in Europe, the Clarke-

Boland big band led by the late American drummer Kenny Clarke and the Belgian composer Francy Boland.

In broad essentials, however, it was an era of about fifteen years, compared with the rock era that has now persisted for thirty. It was an era when a lot of popular music was good and a lot of good music was popular. This fact has led many of those who grew up in that time to sentimentalize it, which requires forgetting that the music was not all unalloyed gold. If it was the age of Ellington, Basie, Herman, Kenton, Goodman, Krupa, the Dorseys, Chick Webb, Glen Gray, Jimmie Lunceford, Lionel Hampton, Earl Hines, Erskine Hawkins, Lucky Millinder, Will Bradley, Freddie Slack, Bobby Sherwood, Boyd Raeburn, Charlie Barnet, Claude Thornhill, Elliot Lawrence, Glenn Miller, Alvino Rey, Artie Shaw, Teddy Powell, and Sonny Dunham, it was also the era of Kay Kyser, Shep Fields, Sammy Kaye, Blue Barron, Art Kassel, Tommy Tucker (for whom Gerry Mulligan briefly wrote), Orrin Tucker, Wayne King, Freddy Martin, Clyde McCoy, Richard Himber, and others in that vastly successful group known to the fans of more fastidious preferences as the Mickey Mouse or ricky-tick bands. To these hipper fans, the giant in this latter category was Guy Lombardo, who was regularly voted King of Corn in the annual *Down Beat* poll of its readers. They harbored a peculiar hatred of Lombardo, as if his existence somehow posed a threat to the music they admired. The threat was elsewhere.

There are those who think Glenn Miller belonged in this category, thanks in part to the band's use of clarinet lead on the saxophone section, a much-vaunted sound that was cloying in persistent use. Jo Stafford, who in the early 1940s sang with the Tommy Dorsey band, a collection of rugged individualists with a fierce collective pride, said years later, a little hesitantly, as if confessing to an American heresy, "You know, in the Dorsey band, we thought Glenn Miller was . . . kind of corny." But Miller, like John Lennon, has been canonized, and one does not question the status of icons.

The Miller band could play ensemble jazz of a kind, recorded some good instrumentals, and claimed Bobby Hackett, who played guitar in the rhythm section and soloed on cornet, in its personnel.

Hackett lent a certain Bixian beauty to the interlude of *A String of Pearls,* written by an Artie Shaw alumnus named Jerry Gray after Shaw broke up his band and joined the U.S. Navy early in the war. In time Miller too would join up.

The classification of these bands was neither easy nor clear, since some of the dance bands, such as that of Charlie Spivak, embodied a decent level of taste. All the jazz bands played for dancers; and some of the most commercial dance bands occasionally put out something that resembled jazz. Kay Kyser, whose arrangements were a cut above those of most Mickey bands (no doubt because George Duning, later a film composer, wrote some of them), now and then startled audiences with some ensemble swing. It was even rumored that the Sammy Kaye band, in many ways the corniest of them all ("And now this lovely refrain sung by . . ."), could do it. The best of the bands, however, the elite of them, leaned strongly into jazz. Their captious members wanted to lean even further into it and played dance music only as a concession to the exigencies of continued employment. The best of these best—a group that included Basie, Ellington, Shaw, Herman, Tommy Dorsey, and the brilliant but short-lived Jimmie Lunceford orchestra—played excellent jazz, framing the work of some highly individual soloists in ensemble structures of remarkable discipline and power. To hear one of these bands straining the walls of some arena or theater or pavilion, without all the paraphernalia of modern amplification, was one of the great thrills in music.

The tributaries of this vast river of superior popular music arose in the 1920s, although its instrumentation grew out of the marching bands of New Orleans. The instruments were those that could be played while walking and were loud enough to be heard in the open air.

By the 1920s, bands were sitting down, playing for dancers. Benny Carter recalls that when he was in the Charlie Johnson band in that period, its instrumentation was three trumpets, two trombones, three saxophones—two altos and a tenor—and four rhythm, including tuba bass. Not until the bands forgot their ambulatory origins entirely did the string bass, a more flexible instrument than the tuba and certainly a more pulsating one, become the rhythmic and harmonic footing on which all bands to this day have built their walls of sound.

The leading figures in this evolution were Duke Ellington and the arranger and composer Don Redman. Redman worked out the organization of trumpets, trombones, and saxophones into choirs working over the rhythm section. Ellington, who even then was using baritone saxophone to add color and fortify the bottom of the orchestra, was moving in a somewhat different direction. Whereas Redman, whose thinking affected Fletcher Henderson and, through Henderson, other writers, maintained the identity of the sections, using them antiphonally, Ellington was using his instruments in unusual combinations, mixing them up through the sections, as it were. Ellington was becoming more and more adventurous in explorations of harmony, influenced in part by the French impressionists. Eventually he voiced the band to produce strange, almost disembodied, and highly idiosyncratic sounds.

The practices of these two men, modified and transmuted to be sure, have dominated serious non-classical orchestral writing in America and much of the world ever since. It is startling to consider that Don Redman may have been the most influential composer of the twentieth century, when most people have never heard of him, including some of the arrangers and composers who daily use the orchestral tools he bequeathed to them.

Benny Carter, who joined the band of Henderson's brother Horace in 1926, said that Fletcher Henderson's arrangments, written for his own band but copied and given to his brother's band, were his first real encounter with the Redman-Henderson mode of writing. When Fletcher Henderson's band folded, Benny Goodman too acquired some of its arrangements and hired Henderson to write more. When Goodman became a success, other musicians formed bands on his model or steered existing bands in the direction pointed by Henderson. A few looked to Ellington for inspiration, particularly Charlie Barnet and, less obviously, Claude Thornhill, who altered the color of big-band sound, partly by adding French horn, partly by hiring Gil Evans, whom he had known in the Skinnay Ennis band.

The repertoire of the bands was hybrid, drawn from the movies, the blues, Broadway, and even grand opera. The instrumentals were usually original compositions by members of the band or staff arrangers, such as Goodman's *Six Flats Unfurnished* by Richard Maltby.

Most of the bands carried singers, the "boy singer" and "girl singer," as they were coyly called, such as Frank Sinatra and Jo Stafford with the Tommy Dorsey band and Sarah Vaughan and Billy Eckstine with Earl Hines. And many of them had vocal groups, such as the Modernaires with Miller and the Pied Pipers with Tommy Dorsey. Artie Shaw carried only a girl singer, resented even having to do that, and made no secret of his contempt for dancers. The music comprised fast or medium-fast instrumentals and slow vocal performances of songs written mostly by Jewish composers and lyricists. In the big band era, the two most important streams of American non-classical music fused—the black and the Jewish.

The Big Band Era was also the Age of the Movies. Movies came into their own with the addition of sound in 1929. The bands were already taking the form they would have through the 1930s and 1940s. The band era and the movie era coincided, and they died together in the late 1940s, for related reasons. But while they lasted, they profoundly affected America's way of thinking and living.

Because of what were deemed sexual excesses in the movies in the 1920s and then scandals in the film industry, the motion picture studios set up a system of self-censorship. The movies made under that restraint presented a false picture of life.

You might never have known from the movies of the 1930s that there was anybody but Anglo-Saxons in the United States. The late Lenny Bruce, in his routine *How the Negro and the Jew Got into Show Business,* said that, since the Jews controlled the business, including the movies, the bad guys in pictures were never Jewish. But then the good guys never were either. There were no Jews at all—or Italians or Poles or Lithuanians—in most movies, although during World War II some of the minor characters in assaults on Iwo Jima or other far-off places might be named Kowalsky, Shapiro, or Corelli. However, the nice boy, who showed his buddies the photo of his young wife and who you knew was going to get nailed by a sniper, was named Walker or Bridges or something like that, and he was probably blond. The principals in pictures were always Caucasians, and usually Anglo-Saxon, although John Ford and Leo McCarey got away with reminding us that there were a few Irish in America too. What we got was a Jewish vision of what WASP life must or should be like, and it had the curious effect of influencing to the point of distortion the mores of the very WASP culture it so inaccurately portrayed. The average WASP adolescent was baffled by that unperturbed world so insouciantly inhabited by Donald O'Connor, Peggy Ryan, Gloria Jean, Mickey Rooney, Jane Powell, and Jane Withers, and felt only the more an outsider for his or her incapacity to emulate their paradigm of youthful happiness.

Only rarely was the hero of a movie (and *never* the heroine) romantically involved with someone of another race, and if he was, the affair ended unhappily. If the girl was Oriental, she died at the end.

No marriage in a movie ended in divorce. A couple always resolved their problems in the last reel. No man ever slept with his wife. Married couples occupied twin beds, even though twin beds were rare in real life and every child in America knew his mother and father reposed together in the night.

There were two kinds of girls in the movies, nice girls and bad girls. Nice girls always won in the end, bad girls always lost out, although life offered evidence to the contrary. A girl from the home town was always more deserving than the girl from New York.

Bad girls were played by Lynn Bari. Nice girls were played by Joan Leslie. Also by Joan Caulfield, Priscilla Lane, and Bonita Granville. Very rarely a film came to grips with moral subtleties. In *King's Row,* Ann Sheridan had the sympathy of the audience, although it became clear that the girl of the working class she played, Randy Monahan (Irish, right?), was not really bad, just sort of . . . well, y'know, defiant.

All nice girls were chaste. In the end, when the problems of the plot had been resolved, the boy saw the light and married the nice girl. Marriage solved everything: that was the goal of life and all striving, true love the sustenance of a fulfilled destiny. Shortly after the final fadeout, the girl lost her virginity, but only, one presumed, after due process of law and ceremony.

The songs of the time reinforced the view of life presented by the movies. Jo Stafford sang, "A heart that's true, there are such things." Helen Forrest sang, "I never thought it could be but there you were, in love with me." Sarah Vaughan sang, "Then you and I came wandering by, and lost in a sigh were we." Love was a fragile thing attainable, if at all, only by the pure of heart, yet without which life wasn't worth living, and the loss of which was the ultimate personal disaster. "I'll never smile again . . ." Only occasionally, as in Bob Russell's lyric to *Do Nothing till You Hear from Me,* which deplores the pain caused by gossip, did popular music deal with something like reality. In his excellent—and overlooked—lyric to Carl Fisher's tune *We'll Be Together Again,* Frankie Laine touched the ground with "Don't let the blues make you bad."

The big band leaders were big stars, and the movies were quick to conscript them into service—white ones, anyway. Artie Shaw appeared with his band in *Second Chorus.* Tommy Dorsey's band was in *Ship Ahoy,* the Glenn Miller band performed in *Orchestra Wives* and *Sun Valley Serenade,* while Harry James turned up in *Swingtime in the Rockies.* In such films, the band would break out its instruments and start blowing with little or no provocation, even on buses and trains. If there were some Negro porters standing by, they would turn out to be as talented as the Ink Spots or the Mills Brothers, and they would join in, in perfect impromptu harmony. In real life, the musicians on band buses were more likely to be found sleeping, drinking, smoking joints, or groping the girl singer as meager consolations for the monotony of the road.

In *Sun Valley Serenade,* such was the supposed *joie de* musical *vivre* of the Miller band that they played in open sleighs passing though the snowy countryside. How the brass and saxes could hear the rhythm section, how the musicians kept their hands warm enough to play, and how the instruments remained in tune in the cold were questions left to the nigglers in the audience.

Growing up in this false picture of life and love generated by popular music and the movies, the young people of the era were naively unprepared for life. It was acccepted that only virgins were nice girls, even by the boys striving assiduously to reduce their numbers. When the libido did its programmed thing, girls (and some boys) persuaded themselves the feeling had to be love, and not infrequently rushed into inappropriate marriages that ended in divorce. Even then they rarely awoke to the possibility that their ideal of life might not be in harmony with reality. Instead they concluded that *this* marriage just wasn't "it," the great love that solves everything, as in the songs and movies, and went on to the next.

The few realistic songs that were written were not widely heard. For radio, which was exercising an increasing hegemony over music, was deeply if unofficially censored.

The era of the big bands and grand movies was also the era of the Broadway musical, and since its audience was limited to a well-to-do stratum of society, freed by its money from such inconveniences as the consequences of inadvertent maternity, stage composers and lyricists had considerably more latitude than those working in movies or Tin Pan Alley.

The musical was passing through its own golden age. Evolving from the plotless meringue of the 1920s into integrated well-structured near-operas, musicals were often urbane and wry and occasionally realistic works of art, such as *Pal Joey, Carousel,* and *The Most Happy Fella.* But Broadway produced a special and better brand of popular music. For the most part the songs heard on the radio were in keeping with the everything's-lovely-and-Andy-

Hardy-Goes-to-College image of life presented by the movies. There were no whores in western movies, only dance-hall girls. In *By the Mississinewa,* Cole Porter managed to touch on miscegenation, lesbianism, fellatio, cunnilingus, and troilism, but the song, needless to say, was never heard outside the Broadway musical for which it was written. Lorenz Hart wrote *Bewitched, Bothered and Bewildered* for *Pal Joey.* The line "until I could sleep where I shouldn't sleep" was altered in the out-of-show version to "till love came and told me I shouldn't sleep," which doesn't even make sense.

Occasionally somebody wrote a "naughty" song such as the sophomorically smirking *She Had to Go and Lose It at the Astor,* at the end of which it turns out that all she'd lost was her sable cape. But then for a movie called *The Shocking Miss Pilgrim,* Ira Gershwin put words to one of his late brother George's unpublished melodies and called the song *Aren't You Kind of Glad We Did?* Gene Krupa recorded it with a vocal by Buddy Stewart. In its time, the record was amazing. It really was dealing with sex, albeit with charm and a little humor.

A few years later, in the movie *Broken Arrow,* James Stewart marries the Indian girl. To be sure, the girl dies in the end—but at the hands of white racists. The viewpoint of the film is firmly on the side of the Indians and the marriage, and the picture was an important departure. Then Aldo Ray married a Japanese girl in *Three Stripes in the Sun,* which wasn't a tragedy but a comedy of manners, and Otto Preminger released *The Moon Is Blue,* a comedy so ordinary that the public might not have noticed it had the Motion Picture Code seal of approval not been withheld because its dialogue contained the words "virgin" and "seduce."

Songwriters pressed against the censorship of the radio stations and networks—who were themselves under constraints from the Federal Communications Commission—and occasionally slipped something suggestive past the watchdogs, such as *(I'd Like to Get You on) A Slow Boat to China.* Among those in the profession, a fondly remembered act of rebellion was by the late Alec Wilder, who wrote a sweet little song fully in accord with the mores of the time. There was nothing wrong with the words. The problem was with the title. It was called *If You See Kay*. It was broadcast a number of times before some network executive got the point and bounced it off the air.

By the 1980s, when the American population had progressed far toward the universal drug use and casual coupling foreseen by Aldous Huxley in *Brave New World,* and porn video and "marital aids" approximated the feelies he described, it was difficult to remember how constricting the moral tone of that time really was, and how much people suffered because of their hormones. Certainly it was not the Big Band Era of later false memory. The serious musical experiments of the bands usually turned up in instrumentals on the B sides of more commercial songs. If it was the era of Herman's *Your Father's Mustache,* it was also that of *Cruising Down the River, The Hut-Sut Song, Mairzy Doats,* and *Chaballa Chaballa.* (*Papa Loves Mambo* and *How Much Is that Doggie in the Window?* came a little later.) If it was—and it was—the golden age of American song, awash in melodies of Kern, Gershwin, Porter, Arlen, it was at the same time an era of trivial, preposterous, and idiotic songs.

And in the end, the adventurous and exuberant experimentalism of the bands would lose its constituency as radio and the record industry proved that Gresham's law operates in esthetics as well as economics.

Seeking a wider pallette of colors, at least five of the bands— those of Artie Shaw, Tommy Dorsey, Gene Krupa, Harry James, and Stan Kenton—tried using string sections. The effect left much to be desired. A full symphony orchestra requires up to sixty strings to balance its comparatively sedate brass and woodwind sections. Jazz brass is much louder. Yet for reasons of economics, the bands could not employ large string sections. Dorsey carried thirteen players. At its worst, the effect was ludicrous—watching Gene Krupa's fiddles saw away inaudibly, for example.

The main direction of this music's evolution was harmonic. For years the thinking of the arrangers had been well in advance of that of the players. In the 1940s, big band harmony became much more complex and "dissonant." Experiments with polytonality were under way. Stan Kenton pushed his band toward the symphonic, sometimes to laudable effect, sometimes not. Other bands, including those of Woody Herman, Stan Kenton, and Claude Thornhill, and the postwar Artie Shaw band, partook of the bebop revolution. The famous soaring trumpet passage in *Caldonia* is a transcribed Dizzy Gillespie solo, while the sax passage in *I've Got News for You* is a transcription of a Charlie Parker solo on *Dark Shadows*. Herman was one of Gillespie's early admirers, and Dizzy did some writing for that band.

But that era, when hundreds of bands criss-crossed America and hundreds more played in their immediate regions, was over. Like so many epochs in art, it attained some of its finest moments just before it ended. While the prewar records in this idiom today seem thin and archaic, partly, to be sure, because of primitive recording, the best of the band records made after 1945 retain their freshness and vitality. They do not sound callow; the music has attained its maturity. The rhythm sections have adapted to the newer music, and their motion is strong, fluid, and natural. The arrangers, from Redman through Henderson, Sy Oliver, Pete Rugulo, Ralph Burns, Ernie Wilkins, Eddie Sauter, and more—with Duke Ellington, Billy Strayhorn, Gil Evans, and Gerry Mulligan off in a slightly different direction—explored the first important new orchestral formation since the symphony orchestra took shape in the time of C.P.E. Bach and caused the spore-burst of brilliant music that we think of as the Big Band Era.

II

What happened to them? Why did the big bands fade away?

Aside from the yearning for lost youth that doubtless comes to everyone but the most convinced reincarnationist, the lament for that era carries an assumption that there was something inevitable about it, ordained by deity or at least guaranteed as part of the American birthright. But the bands were born and flourished in a confluence of social conditions and dwindled out when those conditions changed.

One author of the era was Irving Berlin, whose name we seldom encounter in jazz histories, except perhaps in a cavil that *Alexander's Ragtime Band* was not a rag. So it wasn't. But it was important to the development of what we came to call jazz in that, first, the song, published in 1911, initiated the fascination with the duple meter that became known as the fox trot, and, second it freed American music from thralldom to Viennese operetta (imported or domestic) on the one hand and ersatz Irish balladry (such as *When Irish Eyes Are Smiling, Mother Machree,* and *Ireland Is Ireland to Me,* all by Ernest R. Ball, who was born in Cleveland) on the other. After Berlin's rise to success, American popular music took on its own character and color, which he in part determined, as Don Redman would a few years later.

Two more names one will not encounter in conventional jazz histories are Vernon and Irene Castle, the popular dance team whose example set off a craze for ballroom dancing in the United States. Between 1912 and 1914, the Castles campaigned to refine the barn dance, cakewalk, two-step, Boston, and turkey trot. One consequence was the Castle Walk, a new style that utilized a naturalistic walking motion as its foundation and made it possible for every left-footed clunk in the country to make at least a pass at dancing. The early fox trot also evolved from these experiments, and its popularity influenced the character of the emerging American music. By 1927 the Lindy Hop, named for the new hero Charles Lindbergh, had arrived. And the Lindy led to the phenomenon called jitterbugging, whose better practitioners took dancing to virtuosic levels of acrobatic ingenuity. And this opened the way for bands to play fast instrumentals. Dancers provided the foundation of employment for the bands. This fact is central to any understanding of the era.

Finally, there were the Toonerville Trolleys.

The Toonerville Trolley was the name of a syndicated newspaper cartoon that expressed a sort of nostalgia even then for a more bucolic America. All over the United States and Canada, electric railways linked cities to smaller surrounding communities that often were the loci of amusement parks in which there usually were dance pavilions. E. L. Doctorow, in his novel *Ragtime,* has one of his characters travel from New York to Boston by going from one electric railway to another. It was possible. Robert Offergeld, the classical music critic and historian, who grew up in eastern Michigan, recalls the line that linked Saginaw, Bay City, and Traverse City. "They were wonderful," he said of the big old trolley cars. "You could hear the whine of them coming well in advance. They used to do about 60 miles an hour, rocking along the tracks, and they'd scare you half to death. And they took you to those little places by the shore, and girls wore boaters. I learned to dance after a ride on one of those trolleys. There was always a candy vendor, and a pavilion, and it was all rather sweet and innocent."

"The biggest system of them all," said David Raksin, who teaches both composition and urban affairs at the University of Southern California, "was in Los Angeles—the Big Red Cars. They linked Hollywood to Santa Monica and Chatsworth. In fact, they ran all the way out to Mount Lowe." It was indeed the biggest. The Big Red Cars, the popular name for a system owned by the Southern Pacific Railroad, along with a smaller system known as the Yellow Cars (the Los Angeles Railway Company), covered a thousand miles of track. Together they constituted possibly the finest public transit system in the United States.

The amusement parks with their dance pavilions would not have come into being without the urban and interurban railways. And those pavilions formed a series of links in the chain of locations along which the bands traveled. They also provided employment for countless musicians in the local or regional groups known as territory bands.

These factors—a taste for a more American music initiated by Berlin, a penchant for dancing inspired by the Castles, a style of dancing that was appropriate to fast instrumentals and therefore encouraged their composition, and a chain of dance pavilions and ballrooms that had grown up along the urban and interurban railways—were all there when in the early 1920s a final, critical, catalytic ingredient was added to the mix: radio, and most importantly, network radio.

The record companies, which were thriving when the new medium came into being, were fearful that "free" music would cut into their sales. Therefore they would not allow their product to be played "on the air." Record labels bore the motto *Not licensed for radio broadcast.* The broadcasters ignored it. A number of artists, including Fred Waring, Walter O'Keefe, Donald Voorhees, Lawrence Tibbett, and Paul Whiteman, sued various broadcasting corporations to halt the playing of their records on radio. Finally, in 1940, the U.S. Supreme Court ended these actions by refusing to review a decision against Whiteman and his record label, RCA Victor, by the Second Circuit Court of Appeals in a suit Whiteman had brought against WBO Broadcasting Company, owners of WNEW in New York City. Judge Learned Hand had written the decision, in spite of the fact that he was an opponent of "judge-made law." Revealing ignorance of the essential nature of artistic copyright, Hand wrote, "Copyright in any form, whether statutory or in common law, is a monopoly. It consists only in the power to prevent others from reproducing the copyright work. WBO Broadcasting has never invaded any such right." The premise is false, the deduction wrong. To play a record on the radio is in and of itself to reproduce the music. One way or another, it is done for profit. And the so-called automatic license provision of American law makes it all but impossible to "prevent others from reproducing" one's compositions. Hand's ruling has had lasting and terribly damaging social and esthetic consequences.

American copyright law has always been weak. Until the twentieth century, the United States was a net importer of music. And business interests wanted then, as they do now, to get everything they could for as little as possible, the ultimate of course being nothing. This resulted in the theft—in effect—of Gilbert and Sullivan operettas by American producers, who presented them without paying the authors. Gilbert, himself a lawyer and former magistrate, and Sullivan had no recourse to American courts, which did not recognize foreign copyright claims. This is why in 1885 they premiered *The Mikado* simultaneously in London and New York. It was a way to establish American protection for the work.

Hand's ruling was in keeping with that American tradition of weak copyright. Subsequently, unable to bar records from the air, the record industry reversed itself and strove to get them exposed on radio, soliciting that exposure to the extent of the institutionalized corruption of disk jockeys, program directors, and music librarians with payola ranging in form from cash to drugs to airline tickets to romantic places.

Nearly all of the program content of American radio is recorded music. But in the early days, and before Judge Hand established the curious legal principle that one industry had the right to live off another, radio had to generate a good deal of its own material, partly due to pressures from the American Federation of Musicians. Even small stations in small towns employed musicians and singers. Radio drew into service artists from other fields, from *Grand Ol' Opry* and grand opera (making household names of such singers as John Charles Thomas, Vivian della Chiessa, Helen Jepson, Lawrence Tibbett, and James Melton), as well as from the nation's symphony orchestras (making Arturo Toscanini, Howard Barlow, and Leopold Stokowski known to laymen everywhere). That public taste is not inherently as bad as the apologists for the record and broadcasting industry would have you believe is illuminated by the fact—by who and what did become popular when a wide range of music was given exposure.

It was not coincidence that between 1928 and 1948 a "golden age" occurred not only in big-band popular music but in moviemaking and theater, and for that matter in the novel as well. These years were the youth of the new communications, communications beyond print. The conglomerates had not yet taken over and debased them. The broadcasting industry's pioneers, particularly William S. Paley of CBS and David Sarnoff of NBC, presented material of a high order along with more obviously popular entertainment. It would be naive to ascribe noble motive to them. They programmed music and people who were esteemed and famous, which happened to include Toscanini. Whatever their motives, broadcasting in its early days substantially fulfilled its potential as the most powerful educational facility ever invented, and it offered a cultural education that all the schools and universities of America combined could not equal. It not only made "culture" available, it made it attractive. The result was a ferment, a leavening of the general public mind that no system of imposed formal education could achieve. Radio caused an epidemic of excellence in America. Later, in symbiosis with the record industry, it would debase American taste to an extent inconceivable in the early 1940s.

Live music of high quality, performed by superior bands and singers, was ubiquitous in radio. Every comedy show had its own orchestra. Bob Hope's program featured the Skinnay Ennis orchestra, whose members included Claude Thornhill and Gil Evans, making the band significant in the evolution of jazz to an extent impossible to estimate. Ennis was later replaced by Les Brown. Phil Harris's band was heard on Jack Benny's show, the Billy Mills orchestra on *Fibber McGee and Molly,* and that of Ozzie Nelson on the Red Skelton show. Fred Allen's *Town Hall Tonight* featured one of the best vocal groups of the time, the five DeMarco Sisters. Bing Crosby was the star of *The Kraft Music Hall,* which for two years presented the Jimmy Dorsey band, later replaced by one led by John Scott Trotter, and a vocal group called The Music Maids. Guest performers included Jack Teagarden, Joe Sullivan, Joe Venuti, and Louis Armstrong. Dinah Shore was heard with Paul Lavalle and the Chamber Music Society of Lower Basin Street. Raymond Scott performed regularly on radio.

Johnny Mercer, Jo Stafford, Benny Goodman, Paul Weston, Woody Herman, Glenn Miller, and Harry James were heard on regular broadcasts. So were John Kirby and Maxine Sullivan, whose show had a long run. Mildred Bailey had a show. Both shows regularly presented black artists such as Coleman Hawkins and Teddy Wilson. Those local shows that did play records might follow Woody Herman's *Wildroot* or Ellington's *Take the A Train* with Freddy Martin or Henry Busse.

It was a glorious and indiscriminate melange in which jazz and classical and country music were mixed on the same station or network, so that it was impossible not to know what the full range of America's music was, no matter what one's personal and primary preference might be. A Count Basie fan was also aware of Spade Cooley and his Western Swing. Those who have grown up on format radio—all rock, all jazz, all Beautiful Music (which it rarely is)—cannot imagine what network radio was like. In the compartmentalization of broadcasting that has since occurred, it is difficult for a rock fan to discover Mahler or Thelonious Monk. In those days one's awareness was expanded without one's knowing it. Expansion of one's cultural knowledge and taste today takes determination and effort.

Historical speculations over the rise of the big bands tend to slight the influence of radio broadcasting—and the fact that this was also a golden age in popular music, theater, and movies. Although broadcasting's purpose was to make money for its proprietors, the unprincipled avarice that became the industry's distinguishing characteristic after the 1940s was not yet obvious. Radio created the public taste that embraced Cole Porter, George Gershwin, Duke Ellington, and Harold Arlen, instead of the musical primitives who came to dominate American popular music from the 1950s onward.

The Swing Era is by custom dated from the sudden fame of the Benny Goodman band. Goodman did nothing first. The style and instrumentation derived from the work of Don Redman and Fletcher Henderson. Henderson had failed as a bandleader, and had Goodman not hired him as arranger and taken up some of his previous writing, such masterpieces from the Henderson pencil as his scoring of Morton's *King Porter Stomp* might be lost to us. Some jazzmen were working in the dance bands. Whiteman had popularized the *idea* of the big jazz band, whether or not his band achieved anything approaching swing. Everything was in place when Goodman's band, on the verge of failure, arrived at the Palomar Ballroom in Los Angeles in August 1935.

One of the reasons for the band's explosive success at the Palomar was the three-hour time difference between the east and west coasts. The Goodman band's broadcasts in the East were heard late at night, when most easterners, and certainly those who had to get up for school or college in the morning, were asleep. But they were broadcast on network at a much earlier hour in the West, and by the time they reached the Palomar, young Californians had become excited about their "swing" music.

Word of the band's west-coast success made show business headlines, the band then made a series of coast-to-coast (as they were called in that age before Comsat) broadcasts from the Palomar Ballroom, and the "swing era" began. Goodman went on to play for eight straight months at the Congress Hotel in Chicago, his home town, broadcasting the while for Elgin watches. And soon the booking agencies were signing up every leader in sight who could front a band that purported to swing.

It was not lost on the advertising agencies and their clients that the young people had a new fad. A great deal can be learned from considering who sponsored what in the next few years. In the 1980s, the tobacco companies denied that they were trying to addict the young through their advertising. The denials rang rather hollow when that is precisely what they did in the 1930s and 1940s.

Kool cigarettes presented Tommy Dorsey on radio. Artie Shaw was presented by Old Golds. Chesterfield sponsored Glenn Miller. *The Camel Caravan* featured Benny Goodman. The master of ceremonies of that program was Johnny Mercer, who each night would improvise blues lyrics from the newspaper handed to him just before the show went on the air. (Clifton Fadiman and Robert Benchley were regulars on the show. Perhaps the measure of the network radio compared with network television can be taken in the fact that Fadiman, Oscar Levant, Franklin P. Adams, and Goodman Ace were radio stars.) Lucky Strike sponsored *Your Hit Parade* as well as *Kay Kyser's Kollege of Musical Knowledge.* In fact, the campaign to turn young people into cigarette smokers dates from 1928, when George Washington Hill, the legendarily tyrannical president of the American Tobacco Company, decided to sponsor the Lucky Strike Dance Orchestra under the leadership of B. A. Rolfe.

Further support for a thesis that the tobacco companies and their advertising agencies consciously sought out the impressionable young is found in the character of the few other products that sponsored the bands. They were all "youth" products. Wildroot Cream Oil presented Woody Herman, Fitch's Dandruff Remover Shampoo *The Fitch Bandwagon,* and Coca-Cola *Spotlight Bands.* Products consumed primarily by adults presented more sedate music, mostly what is called light classical, Strauss and Waldteufel waltzes, the *Oberon* overture, Massenet's *Elegy,* Smetana's *The Moldau,* some Grieg, Tchaikovsky's *None but the Lonely Heart,* that sort of thing.

This flood of live, free, non-recorded music was augmented by the "remote" broadcasts from hotels, ballrooms, and pavilions, which were critical to building the reputations of bands. The four networks—NBC's Red and Blue Networks, CBS, and Mutual—all did them, and did them every night.

It would be remiss to omit mention that the networks did not pay for these remote broadcasts. The musicians were paid by the ballroom or hotel or pavilion where a band was appearing. Furthermore, the ballroom operator sometimes paid for the network's engineer and sometimes even for the installation of the line. The networks' attitude was that the operator would make back his money through the increased attendance this "free" publicity would generate. Radio, then, was already manifesting the extortionist philosophy that remains one of the distinguishing characteristics of American commercial broadcasting. It continued into the age of television. Guests on "talk shows" are minimally paid on the grounds that the publicity of an appearance will bring about bigger nightclub salaries, larger sales of one's book, bigger receipts in concerts. This outlook caused a famous confrontation between Frank Sinatra and the late Ed Sullivan. When the film *Can Can* was about to be released, Sullivan wanted to present clips from the picture framed by walk-on appearances by its stars, including Sinatra. Sinatra refused to appear on Sullivan's show on grounds that Sullivan and his network would be getting expensive entertainment for almost nothing. Sullivan denounced Sinatra, and Sinatra took out a trade-paper ad saying, "Dear Ed: You're sick. Frank Sinatra. P.S. Sick, sick, sick." Sinatra was in the right. The attitude that the publicity of broadcast exposure is far more valuable than the entertainment the artist provides—and that someone else unspecified has the onus of paying the artist—is the key to American broadcasting.

There was, then, in the late 1930s and early 1940s, an extraordinary amount of broadcasting devoted to the big bands. And these were live, not recorded, performances. The bands were not dependent on records for exposure; they achieved it directly through radio; record sales were only a secondary source of revenue for them. So much a part of American life did the bands become that probably no one noticed that their very existence hung on the whims of the broadcasters.

During this period the Broadway musical was evolving and expanding in terms of both dramatic content and musical worth. Broadway had attracted such composers as Irving Berlin, George Gershwin, Cole Porter, Frank Loesser, Vincent Youmanns, Richard Rodgers, Jerome Kern, Harold Arlen, and Arthur Schwartz, and such lyricists as Dorothy Fields, P. G. Wodehouse, Johnny Mercer, E. Y. Harburg, Howard Dietz, Lorenz Hart, Ira Gershwin, and Oscar Hammerstein II, as well as Porter, Loesser, and Berlin, who wrote both words and music. These were the people who produced the Broadway scores that became the mother lode for the Hit Parade of the day. The bandleaders in large measure determined what songs would be exposed on the radio, and they had a taste for the better material. With that era's young people absorbing and memorizing well-made songs, it is little wonder that they are today so often much more literate and better-spoken than their children and grandchildren.

With a superb musical theater as a source of popular music, with other excellent songs, such as those of Harry Warren, coming out of the movies, with other writers like Richard Whiting, Duke

Ellington, Hoagy Carmichael, and Matt Dennis adding to the flow of material, American popular music attained a stature it had not had before and almost certainly never will again.

And then the music business suffered a series of blows.

One of these was the World War II 20 percent entertainment tax. And of course a large part of the audience for the music, the young men who used Wildroot and Fitch's and smoked Luckies, was overseas in military service, along with some of the best musicians and bandleaders.

Another blow, in the view of many people, was the activation in 1941 of Broadcast Music Incorporated (BMI), a new licensing organization owned by the broadcasters. The American Society of Composers, Authors and Publishers had demanded a substantial increase in the fees radio paid for the use of songs by ASCAP composers. The stations refused to pay it. ASCAP forbade the radio performance of its music—the entire modern American repertoire. The stations had to play music that was in the public domain. Under the copyright law of the time, this meant music more than 56 years old. For a brief time, as a result, Stephen Foster's *Jeannie with the Light Brown Hair* made the Hit Parade. The broadcasting industry had in 1939 set up its own performing rights society, financed by the sale of stock to broadcasters. This corporation sought out songwriters not affiliated with ASCAP. They were not hard to find, since ASCAP showed a distinct bias toward the Broadway composer who had since its founding dominated it. It was necessary to have five songs published before you could get into ASCAP, and movie composers were not admitted at all. When ASCAP pulled its music off the air, BMI became an active entity. ASCAP lost $300,000 a month and finally surrendered to the broadcasters. It not only did not get a fee increase, it meekly accepted a reduction in fees from five to 2.5 percent.

BMI's critics have argued that the corporation materially contributed to the decline of American popular music, but that theory is no more credible than the contention that bebop killed the big bands. BMI did indeed build a large pool of musical flotsam, but no radio station had to play it. More complex and compelling forces caused the end of the Big Band Era. If a demon be needed, James Caesar Petrillo was type-cast for the part. It is not that his cause was unjust but that his strategy was suicidal.

A self-important, obstreperous, tyrannical little man, James Caesar Petrillo was president of the American Federation of Musicians and perhaps the best-known labor leader in America after John L. Lewis of the United Mine Workers. Petrillo commissioned Ben Selvin to determine if the play of records on radio and jukeboxes was costing musicians jobs. Selvin, a bandleader who had conducted recording orchestras under innumerable pseudonyms, had worked for the radio networks, and had been a recording executive, read his report to the AFM convention of 1941. He said that the record industry made work for musicians and was paying them millions of dollars. He said it would be "unwise, if at all possible, to curtail the industry when such large amounts are spent on musicians. There are remedies for the unemployment caused by the mechanization of music, but a knockout blow, which could not be delivered, is not the answer." The delegates give him a standing ovation. The membership, including all the major bandleaders, agreed with him.

But Petrillo ignored him and the obvious wishes of his own membership, not to mention Learned Hand's ominous ruling. He demanded that the record companies refuse to allow records to be played on radio stations and jukeboxes. In an astounding act of intransigence, he ordered musicians to stop recording. They did so on August 1, 1942. But the singers did not.

Singers were not required to be members of the AFM and indeed were not accepted as members, no doubt in reflection of the instrumentalist's condescension toward them. And so young vocalists who for the most part had been trained in bands began recording with choral groups. These soupy loo-loo-looing accompaniments were triumphs of banality, but the records helped thrust into fame such singers as Dick Haymes, Perry Como, and Nat Cole—and most significantly, Frank Sinatra.

Twenty years earlier, audiences had been wary of singers with bands. One of the first band singers was Morton Downey. Paul

Whiteman signed him to a contract in 1921 but was so doubtful about featuring him with his band that he put him with farm-team orchestras for two years, finally presenting him with his main band in 1923, and then only infrequently. And Whiteman thought it necessary to put an instrument in Downey's hands to justify his presence on the bandstand, at first a saxophone and later, for whatever strange reason, a French horn, neither of which Downey could play. But Downey made several successful records with Whiteman and then, portentously enough, left to become successful on his own. Later, Bing Crosby too left Whiteman and repeated the pattern.

The singers held secondary positions in the bands, sometimes barely suffered by the musicians and leaders. The pattern of recording usually entailed an instrumental chorus followed by a vocal chorus and perhaps a half chorus of instrumental going out. But then some of the leaders, including Tommy Dorsey and Harry James, began to build up the role of the singers. "With myself and Frank and the Pied Pipers and Connie Haines," Jo Stafford said, "Tommy really created what amounted to production numbers." Asked what had killed the big bands, her husband, Paul Weston, who had been one of Dorsey's arrangers, unhesitatingly replied, "The singers." Alvino Rey gave the same answer to the question.

The seeds of the bands' destruction, then, had been within them since Whiteman hired Downey. Vocal records—by Crosby, Downey, Buddy Clark, Lanny Ross, Gene Austin, Kate Smith, Russ Colombo, and others—had existed side by side with band records, a popular music for listening as opposed to the music for dancing of the bands. Petrillo's recording ban did the same thing to the singers that atomic radiation does to the creatures in cheap sci-fi movies. It made them grow big.

Petrillo's ban continued through 1943, despite efforts of the War Labor Board and finally a direct appeal from President Franklin D. Roosevelt to end it. Petrillo scorned the president as he had scorned his membership. The first company to come to terms was Decca, which signed a contract with the AFM in September 1943. Johnny Mercer's fledgling Capitol followed a month later. Columbia and RCA Victor held out until November 1944.

What Petrillo got out of the strike was a form of tax on record dates, paid by the record companies, which went into a trust fund to pay for free concerts throughout America. In effect, the work of the best professional musicians was taxed to subsidize the mediocre. This was resented by many professionals, among them the late Stan Kenton, who tried in vain a few years later to establish an exclusively professional musicians' union. Ultimately Petrillo destroyed thousands of jobs for musicians. Having engineered a disaster, he behaved like the true politician in proclaiming the settlement "the greatest victory for labor in the history of the labor movement."

By the early 1940s the audience was becoming divided into two factions, those who came to dance and those who came to listen. Wherever one of the jazz-inflected bands appeared, a mass of young people would be seen dancing at the rear of the floor while a smaller group pressed close to the bandstand and stood in rapt attention, preoccupied with the skills of the players. To the latter, every side man—Ray Nance, Tricky Sam Nanton, Johnny Hodges, Joe Thomas, Arnett Cobb, Cat Anderson, Mel Powell, Charlie Kennedy, Charlie Christian, Buck Clayton, Don Byas, Lester Young, Ziggy Elman, Corky Corcoran, Willie Smith, Bill Harris, Zoot Sims, Pete Candoli—was a star. That crowd at the front was the constituency for jazz as a concert music, and some bands came more and more to cater to it. The instrumentalists wanted the music to go in that direction and so did some of the bandleaders, particularly Stan Kenton. Musicians repeated with glee a story about a Kenton trombonist who, asked by someone from the audience, "Why don't you play something we can dance to?" replied, "Why don't you dance something we can play to?" If you want to name a point when the era ended, that may be it.

Paul Weston said the beginning of the end came with a shift in tempos. Earlier arrangements had been designed for dancing, with even the ballads moving along on a comparatively brisk one-and-three beat. "Then the ballads became slower to accommodate the singers," he said. "And the instrumentals became faster to show off the soloists."

"The bands became mere accompaniment to the singers," Alvino Rey said. "And then there was the Kenton phenomenon. Stan Kenton's was not a dance band, except in the early days. When we tried to be more like it, people said, 'Why aren't you like your old self?' The bands became too symphonic. Too many chords. I was one of the worst offenders, because I loved all that stuff. And then, once the remotes went off the air, we had a real problem. Records couldn't build a band the way all those live broadcasts did."

A few people have tried to argue that bebop killed the big bands. But this hypothesis is patently absurd. "It's ridiculous," Gerry Mulligan said. "If anything, bebop came along and revived the musicality of the bands."

Nobody forced people to listen to the few bands who embraced bebop. The alternatives were always there, and it certainly didn't kill Guy Lombardo's band. Benny Goodman never liked and didn't play bebop, and his band went out of business. Woody Herman did like and did play it, and his band was one of the few to survive the era, continuing right into the 1980s. Indeed, the four bands that outlived the era—Kenton, Basie, Ellington and Herman—all embraced or at least accepted the practices of bebop. If bebop was all that inaccessible, the boppers should have slipped away into a seemly unemployment while the more conventional groups continued on, awash in public adoration. It didn't happen that way, and, although he led small groups, Dizzy Gillespie, one of the fountainheads of bebop, turned out to be the most enduring and revered jazz star after Louis Armstrong.

A change was occurring in the audience. Returning from military service, the young men who with their girls had been the natural constituents for the bands were preoccupied with something else, namely, breeding and feeding fans for the Beatles, Bob Dylan, and Mick Jagger. TV would prove appealing to people with problems in finding baby-sitters. And since the birthrate fell during the Depression, the next generation of young people was a smaller one. Meanwhile, the public transportation system, so important to the outlying amusement parks and dance pavilions, was falling apart—or rather was being systematically dismembered.

Harry Chandler, owner of the *Los Angeles Times* and of vast real estate holdings in and around the city, was on the board of the Goodyear Tire and Rubber Company. He had interests in road construction companies and substantial investments in the Southern California Rock and Gravel Company and Consolidated Rock Products, as well as several oil companies. Chandler and his family stood to make money on everything related to automobiles and highways. The *Los Angeles Times* became for all practical purposes a publicity organ of the automobile interests, including the California Automobile Club—itself a lobby for those interests—of which he was a charter member and director for more than thirty years. "At a tremendous rate," a *Times* article happily stated at one point, "the wild virgin areas of Southern California are being broken down to the uses of progress and yielding up their beauties to the motoring public."

In the 1920s, socialists and "progressives" tried to stop the deterioration of L.A.'s rail system by having it taken over by the city. The *Times* opposed this movement, using the usual tactic of painting its proponents Red. In 1936 a group of corporations that included General Motors, Standard (Oil) of California, Firestone Tire and Rubber Company, B. F. Phillips Petroleum, and Mack Manufacturing, maker of Mack trucks, organized a company called National City Lines. Its purpose was to buy up street railways throughout America and convert them to bus lines. National City Lines would then buy buses and oil and gasoline and tires from the parent companies. In 1937 the Southern California Auto Club called for the elimination of the interurban railway lines and their replacement by buses and automobiles. National City Lines, through an affiliate, began buying up the Los Angeles railway system. It removed cars from operation, forcing people to longer and longer waits for them. Then the company obtained permission to tear up the track, with the help of some of its own agents in the Public Utilities Commission.

The railway unions fought to impede this wrecking process, backed, interestingly enough, by the Hearst-owned *Herald-Express,* which had a large working-class readership. Finally, in 1947, after ten years and not until the damage was irreversible, the United States Justice Department brought an antitrust suit against National City Lines and its owners, whose executives in due course were convicted. They were fined one dollar.

The L.A. *Times* continued its assaults on rapid transit systems, and in 1963, the last of the Big Red Cars was taken out of service. By then the *Times* had taken up the cause of smog abatement.

In the 1940s few young people had automobiles or the immediate hope of owning them, which is why Ford, Cities Service petroleum products, Texaco, and General Motors slanted their radio programs toward those older people who did. The young were largely dependent, except for occasions when it was possible to borrow the family car, on tramways to get them to the pavilions and ballrooms. It is impossible, then, to estimate the effect on the band business of the dismantling of the urban and interurban railways, and in any case it cannot be extricated from the other major changes that were occurring.

In consequence of the rise of television, the great radio networks were also being dismantled. (In theory they still exist, but they are little more than a string of news outlets.) Within five years of the incipient proliferation of television, both baseball and movie attendance had declined drastically, the latter to the point where the National Association of Theater Owners was concerned whether "hardtop" theaters, as they were known in the trade— those with roofs on them—could survive. The drive-ins were doing well as the campaign to force people into cars succeeded and young people acquired jalopies and hot rods. The drive-ins were, besides, great places to grope a girl, eliminating the preliminary folderol of dancing that went with big bands. Ministers of the gospel railed against "passion pits" and were mocked for doing so, but in fact the drive-ins did contribute to the loosening of restrictions and inhibitions and led us toward our present age of casual and perfunctory encounter. Many hard-top theaters went out of business, and their premises were converted to other uses. Suddenly one viewed the curious spectacle of supermarkets with marquees, on which were emblazoned not the names of movie stars but the price of lamb chops.

The peak business year for the motion picture industry in the U.S. was 1946, when box office grosses reached $1,692,000,000. That was the year the soldiers came home and took their girls to the movies. The large-scale production of TV receivers got under way in 1947—and motion picture grosses dropped immediately by a hundred million dollars. From there on, attendance at the movies and other out-of-home entertainments declined steadily. Not until 1974 did the movie industry exceed its 1946 box-office take, and when it did so it was in watered dollars. In 1946, ninety million movie tickets were sold per week in the United States; in the early 1980s, the figure was twenty million a week and dropping, although the population of the country had nearly doubled.

The tendency of the public to stay home and watch the glass box was not the end of television's mischief. Caught up in the profitability of TV, which revealed an astonishing capacity to move merchandise, the networks let national radio fall into desuetude. Gone were *The Fitch Bandwagon* and all the rest. Gone were the remotes from the Palomar, the Trianon, and Frank Dailey's Meadowbrook. And local stations, no longer able to depend on high-quality programs piped from New York, Chicago, and Los Angeles, perforce relied more and more on records. In turn the music industry, unable to look to network radio for exposure, and largely ignored by television on the grounds that music wasn't "visual" enough, became dependent on the airplay of records by local stations. The disk jockey became a crucial link in the sales chain of the music business.

Some of the disk jockeys—including Dave Garroway in Chicago, Fred Robbins, Symphony Sid Torrin, and Martin Block in New York, Ed (Jack the Bellboy) Mackenzie in Detroit, Jimmy Lyons and Al (Jazzbo) Collins in San Francisco, Al Jarvis and Gene

Norman in Los Angeles, Sid Mark in Philadelphia, Felix Grant in Washington, Dick Martin in New Orleans, and Phil McKellar in Windsor, Ontario (whose clear-channel station reached much of North America)—fought a rearguard action for good music, jazz in particular. But station management wasn't interested in music. It was interested in cost-per-thousand—the advertiser's cost of reaching a thousand persons.

To a commercial radio station, it is of priority importance to reach the widest possible audience, for the sake of higher advertising rates. To do that, American stations in the early 1950s began emphasizing music that was the equivalent of dimestore prints of mountain stags in polychrome sunsets. This was the early phase of the musical decline, characterized by *Music Music Music, You You You, Wanted, The Wheel of Fortune, The Tennessee Waltz,* and the like, which led down to Bill Haley and the Comets, Elvis Presley, and the dark at the bottom of the stairs. The decline began in the late 1940s, accelerated in the 1950s, and took the great plunge when Todd Storz dreamed up his "jukebox of the air."

Storz, of the New Orleans-based Storz broadcasting stations, observed that the same songs were played over and over on jukeboxes. He reasoned that the radio public would similarly take to a restricted list of hit songs constantly repeated. Their selection would not be according to such vague standards as esthetic worth but to a strict commercial criterion—popularity, as determined by such supposedly objective indicators as the charts published by *Billboard*. The Storz format proved successful and soon was emulated by stations throughout the United States. They played music from lists limited to forty songs, around the clock, seven days a week. Thus Top Forty radio was born. In later years, some stations tightened the playlist to fifteen.

By 1970, computerized "jukeboxes of the air" had come into existence—stations programmed by companies such as Drake-Chenault. A visit to such a station could be unsettling. Banks of tape machines sat there, still. Suddenly one machine would start up, following the command of a computer, and play a song over the air, although in the station itself there might be only an antiseptic silence. Then it would stop and another machine would start. One spool would contain current "hot" tunes, another a collection of "golden oldies." Some songs were described as they began to play, others were "back-announced," all according to commands from the computer, which also ordered the play of commercials and even the recorded on-the-hour news required by the Federal Communications Commission.

Who killed the big bands? A good case can be made against a group of people that includes James Caesar Petrillo, Todd Storz, Learned Hand, Harry Chandler and all his heirs and minions, and the heads of General Motors, Firestone, B. F. Phillips, Standard of California (which means the Rockefellers), and the Mack Truck company, as well as a forgotten functionary who thought up the wartime entertainment tax, which lingered on into the 1950s, still harming American music.

Los Angeles has the worst public transport of any major city on the North American continent, along with the coagulated freeways and all too visible air that GM and Standard and the Chandlers forced on it. A stretch of rail runs beside Santa Monica Boulevard from the Hollywood line on through Beverly Hills almost to the San Diego Freeway, where it trails out. It is a vestige of the Red Cars. Elsewhere in America, you will find odd lyrical memories of the Toonerville trolley: level straight strips of land sentried by maples or cottonwoods or sycamores, grown deep in grass and milkweed and Queen Anne's lace. The steel rails are for the most part vanished, long since torn up and melted for scrap, remembered by creosoted wooden ties. Sometimes, though, you will find the rails themselves, rusting among the wildflowers.

Whether consciously or not, Johnny Mercer caught the end of an era in his lyric for *Early Autumn:*

> There's a dance pavilion in the rain,
> all shuttered down . . .

The Sinatra Effect

When Frank Sinatra's career took off in the early 1940s, journalists rushed to their telephones and then to their typewriters to pose the wrong questions and come up with the wrong answers. Girls were "swooning" at his performances. What was the cause of this mysterious phenomenon?

There were two causes. The first was hunger. Some of the girls had waited so long in theater lines to see him that they fainted. The second was George Evans, Sinatra's press agent, who knew an angle when he saw one and paid a few more girls to fake it.

But what caused this flocking? The journalists went to psychologists and psychiatrists for explanations, and came away with a few, all of them silly. His thin face and slender frame, barely hanging on the microphone, touched the maternal instincts of the girls. Maternal indeed. Or it was the war: Sinatra was a surrogate for the boy-next-door who was away in service.

The journalists and psychologists alike revealed an ignorance of history. The Sinatra effect was by no means unprecedented, and in fact suggested a question I have not yet seen answered, or for that matter even seriously addressed.

This kind of sexual flocking had occurred around many male performers, including Franz Liszt, who plucked a large bouquet of his era's fairest flowers. So too Louis Moreau Gottschalk. It happened around Offenbach. When he arrived in Boston, aristocratic ladies unhitched his horses and pulled his carriage through the streets by hand. No doubt it happened around Spohr. Certainly in Italy, many of the great castrati were adored by quantities of women. When Henry Pleasants said so in a piece about the castrati published in *Stereo Review*, several readers wrote to argue that affairs were impossible for the castrated male. Henry replied that while castration assured sterility, it did not necessarily confer indifference, or even, for that matter, impotence.

It seems that a man, even an ugly one, need only become famous to have women fling themselves at him, particularly if he achieves his high visibility as an entertainer. Let us not even bother with the more obvious cases like Elvis Presley and the Beatles. One would be naive to think that, for example, Toscanini suffered from a dearth of opportunities. And in each instance, the phenomenon erodes the image of the male as the sexual aggressor, the female as the reluctant recipient of his brutish attentions. For there is nowhere in history a comparable example of men flocking in a sort of collective self-humiliation around a famous female entertainer—not Lily Langtry, not Sarah Bernhardt, not Marilyn Monroe, not Olivia Newton-John. But we know how women behaved toward Errol Flynn and John Barrymore, and there is no reason to assume Henry Irving or David Garrick experienced anything very different. A man, if he has the opportunity and that bent of temperament, may try to add a famous beauty to his trophy collection, but he will not stand in a screaming crowd of men clamoring for their idol, and given a choice of an anonymous but beauteous barmaid or a homely movie star, he will almost invariably choose the former. So fully if silently does society recognize this difference in behavior that a man who follows a famous woman and tries to break into her hotel room will end up in jail or a psychiatric ward, while a girl who similarly tracks a public idol will be dismissed more or less lightly as more or less normal.

Whatever the reasons for this mass self-debasement of

women, the fact is that it happened far more to Sinatra than to Dick Haymes, Perry Como, Nat Cole, Andy Russell, or any other of the singers coming up at the time. And of course it did not happen at all to the "girl singers" such as Peggy Lee and Doris Day. Sinatra was The Man, for a whole generation of young people, for the boys as well as the girls. Indeed, the theory that he was merely a surrogate for the absent servicemen overlooked his popularity with a good many of those self-same servicemen.

He said for the boys what they wanted to say. He said to the girls what they wanted to hear. The body of excellent songs that had come into existence in the United States at last found a singer worthy of them. He was the best singer we had ever heard. He was one of the best singers in history. And we knew it. He was our poet laureate.

One of the writers at the time said, with more than a touch of condescension, that Sinatra sang those love songs as if he believed them. But of course. That was the secret. And far from manifesting a callow gullibility on Sinatra's part, this was a striking advance in the art of singing. Sinatra was to American song what Montgomery Clift was to American acting.

As for that forgotten writer's contempt for mere love songs, he apparently did not understand that there are only two things worth writing about, sex and death. The vast bulk of our literature, whether noble or trivial, is about either or both of these subjects. A suspense thriller is about the avoidance of death, the survival of the individual. A love story is (secretly) about the survival of the species. When the hero destroys the villain and saves the heroine, he has achieved the survival, for the nonce, of the individual, and when he takes her in his arms in the fadeout, you know they are about to make their own modest contribution to the survival of the species. Essentially, then, all literature is about survival. Almost all of our stories and songs are about love, the highest exaltation we know excepting that achieved by some people through religion, and even then the terminology of romantic love is often used in the effort to describe the experience.

Sinatra sang the American love song with an overwhelming persuasive immediacy. Julius LaRosa says, "He was able to turn a thirty-two bar song into a three-act play."

Remembering her days with the Pied Pipers and Tommy Dorsey, Jo Stafford says, "Frank joined the band while we were playing a theater in Milwaukee. The Pipers were . . . well, we thought we were pretty good. We were a little clique unto ourselves. Frank was very thin in those days, almost fragile looking. When he stepped up to the microphone, we all smirked and looked at each other, watiting to see what he could do. The first song he did was *Stardust*.

"I know it sounds like something out of a B movie, but it's true: before he'd sung four bars, we knew. We knew he was going to be a great star."

That was early in 1940. The style was not even fully formed. Sinatra had just come up from the Harry James band, at that time much less successful than the Dorsey band. But he had already recorded with James, and in an early Columbia side, *All or Nothing at All,* one of the characteristics of his work is already in evidence: his exquisite enunciation. His vowels are almost Oxonian. The title line comes out almost ohllll or nothing at ohlllll . . .

And there is something else very interesting about the way he treats those words. When you sing a long note, it is the vowel you sustain, almost always. Certain of the consonants, voiced or voiceless, cannot be sustained: *b* and its voiceless counterpart *p; d,* and *t; g* and k. You cannot sing thattttt. It is impossible. You must sing thaaaaat. Or cuuuuup. Or taaaaake. But certain other consonants, voiced and unvoiced—*v* and *f,* z, and s—can be sustained, being fricatives, although I find the effect unattrative. You cannot sustain the semivowels *w* and *y.* But there are four semivowels that can be sustained: *m, n, l,* and *r.* Now, just as Spanish has long and short forms of the letter *r*—a double *rr,* as in perro, is rolled—correct Italian enunciation requires that you slightly sustain all double consonants. And Sinatra has always recognized this principle, whether because of his Italian background or not. You hear it when he extends the *l* in *Allll or Nothing at Alllll.*

Early recording was entirely acoustic. With the development of electrical recording, a new technique was called for, but few people grasped this. Bing Crosby understood it to an extent. He appreciated that it was unnecessary to shout into the microphone. What he did not appreciate was the dramatic possibilities opened up by the microphone and the constantly improving techniques of recording.

Of its very nature, singing through a good sound system or for recording should be as different from vaudeville belting as film acting is from stage acting. One can convey on film with a lift of an eyebrow what might require a conspicuous change of voice or tone or volume or some expansive gesture on a stage. And something similar is true of singing into a sensitive microphone.

Sinatra understood this. It seems that the comprehension came to him gradually: his evolution is clear in his recorded work.

Sinatra has on occasion said that he learned a great deal from listening to Tommy Dorsey play trombone night after night on the bandstand. Indeed, one of the myths about his work in the early days was that he learned an Indian trick of breathing in through his nose while continuing to sing. Whatever the athletic skills of the American Indians, none of them ever achieved this physiological impossibility, and neither did Sinatra. In brass and woodwind playing there is a technique in which the cheeks are filled with air to maintain pressure in the embouchure while the player inhales through the nose. Clark Terry can do this seemingly endlessly. But only a few players have mastered this technique, and Tommy Dorsey was not one of them. He did, however, have remarkable breath control, and his slow deliberate release of air to support long lyrical melodic lines was indeed instructive to Sinatra and still is worth any singer's attention. Dorsey would use this control to tie the end of one phrase into the start of the next. Sinatra learned to do the same. This is evident in their 1941 recording of *Without a Song*. Since Dorsey's trombone solo precedes the vocal, the record provides an opportunity to observe how Sinatra was learning from Dorsey, and how far he had come since *All or Nothing at All*. At the end of the bridge, Sinatra goes up to a mezzo-forte high note to crest the phrase "as long as a song is strung in my SOUL!" But he does not breathe then, as most singers would. He drops easily to a soft "I'll never know . . ." This linking of phrases between the inner units, learned from Dorsey, gave Sinatra's work a kind of seamlessness.

The next time he sings "I'll never know," he hits an A on the word "know" before falling to G, the proper note for the word. This kind of glissando drove the adolescent girls wild. When George Evans had built a general national hysteria, Sinatra had only to sing one of these falls in a theater and the next four bars were drowned in a sea of shrieking. This was in fact merely another device derived from Dorsey, and natural to the trombone.

Sinatra's voice at that time was a pure sweet tenor. A year and a half later, when he recorded *In the Blue of Evening,* he was already losing some of that quality, which owed more to the Irish tradition than the Italian. His singing was acquiring strength. (The entire body of Sinatra's work with Dorsey has been reissued on seven LPs by RCA, ninety-seven songs recorded in thirty-two months.)

If Sinatra had acquired a good deal of his technique from Dorsey, he seems to have drawn some of his conception from Billie Holiday. Indeed, most of the best singers of his generation, including Peggy Lee—his equivalent among women singers for dramatic intensity—seem to have paid at least some attention to Holiday.

Fats Waller is reputed to have said, "Billie sings as if her shoes pinch." Whoever said it, somebody took note of the squeezed quality of her voice. But many informed and sensitive listeners find a deep emotional experience in her work, and there is no questioning her effect on any number of women singers, including Anita O'Day and June Christy, who are her direct stylistic descendants. With a small voice and a tendency to short phrases—in contrast to Sinatra's extremely long ones—she phrases not according to the melodic structure of a song but according to the natural fall of the words. Whether she did this by design or inspired intuition, I do not know. But Sinatra does it by design.

Naturalistic phrasing, however, requires the use of the microphone. Journalists made fun in those early days of Sinatra's way of handling a microphone, his hands around the stand, just under the mike itself. They joked that he was propping himself up with it. They did not understand that he was playing it. He had completely abandoned the previous approach to the microphone, that of standing bravely facing it, using the hands for dramatic emphasis. Sinatra was moving the mike in accordance with what he was singing. And he was the man who developed this technique. In later times, when microphones had been greatly reduced in size, singers would slip them off their stands and walk freely around the stage with them. But those early mikes were bulky and screwed firmly to the tops of the stands. And so Sinatra gripped the stand and drew the microphone toward him or tilted it away according to the force of the note he was putting out at any given moment. He mastered this.

The microphone made possible speech-level singing. It did not make singing unnatural; it restored naturalness to it. But, and this is insufficiently understood, the microphone is treacherous in that it magnifies not only the virtues of a performance but the flaws too. And it is a difficult instrument to use well.

For example, the plosive consonants *p* and *b*, and for that matter *t* and *d*, and sometimes even the aspirated *h*, which pose no problem to anyone singing in an opera house or a bathtub, are booby traps to a singer working close to a mike. Therefore the singer must approach them with caution. Failure to do so results in the phenomenon called popping the mike. You will hear it on many records. Some of the best singers will now and then pop one of those letters in a recording session, rattling the speakers in every living room in which the record is later played. In the entire body of his recorded work, you will not hear Sinatra pop a consonant.

Sinatra's stature as a performer was not fully manifest, however, until he worked outside the context of the Dorsey band. Despite Dorsey's showcasing of singers, Sinatra had been required on the whole to sing at tempos suitable for dancing. Freedom to explore a song as a dramatic miniature did not come until he made four sides for Bluebird on January 19, 1942, eight months before he left the band. These are *The Song Is You, the Lamplighter's Serenade, Night and Day,* and *The Night We Called It a Day.* The choice of composers is interesting: Jerome Kern, Hoagy Carmichael, Cole Porter, and Matt Dennis, for whose work Sinatra would always have an affinity. The Axel Stordahl arrangements were well above the norm of accompaniment in popular music. The string section comprised only four violins and a cello, but Stordahl used them skillfully. These are chamber recordings, really, designed to set off the intimacy Sinatra's work had attained. It is as if he is singing not to a great and anonymous company but to you. With these four sides, Sinatra becomes Sinatra. In later years his work would mellow, deepen, and mature, but the conception and the method were fully developed by then. Sinatra had just turned twenty-six at the time, the bird about to fly. The great shrill mobs of girls were not yet begging him to autograph their underwear, and there is captured in these four songs something "of love and youth and spring" that would never be heard in his work again. They were remarkable recordings when they came out, and they are remarkable now. It is a pity that he and Stordahl did not record two dozen or so songs in that vein at that time.

They would produce a superb string of recordings for Columbia Records, but the orchestras would be larger, the intimacy less, the thinking sophisticated. Sinatra was by then the biggest celebrity in America. Only a few years later, a Gallup poll would reveal that his name was better known than that of President Truman. Newspaper writers were boggled by his earnings—a million dollars a year. The record companies, further impelled by Petrillo's recording ban, rushed to get other band singers into the studios, including Billy Eckstine, inevitably promoted as the Sepia Sinatra, although his style had more in common with his friend from the Earl Hines band, the brilliant Sarah Vaughan; Jo Stafford, who thought of herself as a group singer, had no taste for stardom, and withdrew from it without fanfare in 1959; Doris Day from the Les Brown band; Perry Como (who, as Julius La Rosa says, probably has the most perfect voice placement of all the singers) from Ted Weems; Peggy Lee from Benny Goodman; Andy Russell from the Alvino Rey and early Stan Kenton bands; Kay Starr from Charlie Barnet; and of course Dick Haymes, he of the wondrous richness of sound, who had followed Sinatra through the James and Dorsey bands. David Allyn was an alumnus of the Boyd Raeburn band, a striking baritone with a dark woody timbre, a favorite with musicians, who never got the recognition he deserved. Nobody thought to do anything with Harry Babbitt of the Kay Kyser band, who I thought was one of the best band singers. There was something sunny about his work. Maybe that's what was wrong with it: it said nothing of the dark side of life. One great singer who did not come out of a band was Nat Cole. Cole was one of the most important and influential of all jazz pianists, influential on Oscar Peterson and Bill Evans and through them on many others. That he sang extremely well was discovered almost by accident, and his success as a singer virtually ended his career as a pianist.

Sinatra opened the way for all of them. And he influenced at least two generations of singers, including Vic Damone, Steve Lawrence, Jack Jones, Bobby Darin, Matt Monro, LaRosa, and another underrated singer, the gifted and ill-fated Tommy Leonetti.

But in pioneering a new approach to singing, Sinatra also created a problem. What he did seemed so indisputably right that any other approach to phrasing seemed wrong. If one phrased in the same way, one sounded obviously derivative. But what was the singer to do, not phrase for the meaning of the lyric? Actually, these singers, examined closely, do not sound all that much like Sinatra. Technically, the best male voice of all is that of Vic Damone. The instrument itself, the unbelievably open throat, is gorgeous. One of the best voices belonged to Eddie Fisher. Unfortunately, he never did find out what singing is all about, and his time, or rather lack of it, is legendary among musicians. Steve Lawrence and Jack Jones probably have the firmest musical command, although Jack Jones is inclined to waste a magnificent talent on unworthy songs. LaRosa achieves the greatest unaffected emotional depth. But the voices, in all these cases, bear no resemblance to Sinatra's and all of these people avoid enunciating in his manner.

There is an outstanding exception among the Sinatra derivations, one who doesn't seem to sound like him. Tony Bennett learned his phrasing from Sinatra. But Tony tapped another source of inspiration, which no one seems to have noticed: Louis Armstrong. The clue is in the vibrato. And so Tony gets away with it better than the others. It also helps that his voice is about a fourth or fifth higher than Sinatra's.

Sinatra's work, unlike that of most singers, has distinct phases to it, like the periods in a painter's life.

The first of these is the period with Harry James, which might be called embryonic. Only in retrospect do we find signs of the special. Otherwise he was indistinguishable from any number of capable but bland band singers. Then there is what could be considered the childhood, the period with Dorsey. This is followed by an all-too-brief adolescence, consisting of the four Bluebird sides with Stordahl.

Then comes the young manhood, the period with Columbia, when he turns to Broadway to find songs commensurate with his talent, essaying *Old Man River* (for which he was laughted at, although his reading of it was outstanding) and the *Soliloquy* from *Carousel.* And he is already looking to the past for material: *These Foolish Things, Try a Little Tenderness,* and *When Your Lover Has Gone* were not new even then when he recorded them. This is the first great plateau: *There's No You, What Makes the Sunset?, Mam'selle, Day by Day, If You Are But a Dream, Time after Time, It's the Same Old Dream, Nancy, The Girl that I Marry.* He recorded ballads almost exclusively. When he did tackle brighter tempos, in *Five Minutes More, I Begged Her,* and *Saturday Night Is the Loneliest Night in the Week,* the swing, if any, is rather self-conscious, advanced hardly at all since that dreadful song he recorded with Dorsey, *I'll Take Tallulah.*

And then his career slipped a cog. His record sales petered

out toward the end of the 1940s. He began to have voice problems. Mitch Miller, who was then head of a&r at Columbia and
already committed to the recording by various people, such as Guy
Mitchell, of some appalling trash, was forcing like material on Sinatra. He even made him make a record with Dagmar, that curious
lady famous for a Himalayan bust line. A side man on one of these
painful sessions was a guitarist named Speedy West, who was
known for being able to produce a cluck-cluck-cluckah chicken
sound from his instrument. Despising the tune, his throat both-
ering him, Sinatra struggled through a take. A smiling Mitch
Miller rushed from the booth as if to embrace him—and
embraced Speedy West.

He said later, "At thirty-eight years old, I was a has-been. Sitting by a phone that wouldn't ring. Wondering what happened to
all the friends who grew invisible when the music stopped. Finding
out fast how tough it is to borrow money when you're all washed
up."

Sinatra waited out his contract with Columbia, written off by
the press, struggling with his voice, desperate. Curiously enough,
the only time I ever saw him perform live (other than in the
recording studio) was during that period. He played the Chez
Paree in Montreal. He came onstage full of obvious and visible
anger and anxiety, and sang with a new darkness and depth. It was
shortly after this that he signed a contract with Capitol Records
and made a ten-inch LP with a small orchestra and charts by a
former Charlie Spivak arranger named Nelson Riddle, a discovery
of Nat Cole's. The album, called *Songs for Young Lovers,* tended to
swing lightly. When your voice is not in good shape, and Sinatra's
still wasn't, it is wise to avoid very slow tempos, which require the
long sustention of notes and lines. But the album was shot through
with prismatic new colors. For the first time, his work takes on the
hue of jazz. And the swing is insouciant, unself-conscious: he has
learned to ride a rhythm section. And whatever he had lost in
length of phrase (which later he regained) is more than compen-
sated for by the emotional depth of his readings and the bounce
he brings to the songs.

During the next eight years, he recorded for Capitol twenty hit albums, all ranking among the top twenty, including three at number one and five at number two, and several dozen hit singles such as *The Young at Heart,* and kept up this output when he left Capitol for Reprise, a label Sinatra founded. Sinatra found some very compatible arrangers to work with, including, over the years, Riddle, the brilliant Billy May, Gordon Jenkins, Don Costa, Robert Farnon (for one album only, made in England and never released in America, although it is excellent), Claus Ogerman, Johnny Mandel.

Nelson Riddle once said that the earlier Sinatra, of the Columbia days, sounded like a violin, but the later one, the one who emerged at Capitol, sounded like a viola. That is an apt analogy. The voice had acquired a slightly rougher texture. It had in fact become more Italian. There's no trace of the tenor left, not at least in the voice quality, although his range covered at least two octaves, from F to F.

There is a voice quality that is not limited to Italians but is more common among them than other peoples. It is a gravelly sound that comedians affect when they are aping some archetypal hoodlum. I have often wondered what causes this quality.

"Probably," says Michael Renzi, the pianist, known for his superb work as an accompanist for Peggy Lee, Lena Horne, and Sinatra, who has such a voice, "it's all the shouting and screaming at home when you're a kid." But no. It seems to be a physical characteristic. You hear it in Congressman Peter Rodino, actor Aldo Ray, and many more. Tony Bennett has a touch of it, and so does LaRosa. In women it manifests itself as a rather sexy huskiness. Anne Bancroft and Brenda Vaccaro have such voices. And so, as of the period at Capitol, does Sinatra. His sound acquired tremendous body, and although something has been lost—he never again uses head tone, and certainly not the falsetto that ends *The Song Is You*—he had arrived in the period of his finest work, the artist in perfect control of his material, recording one after another of the greatest American songs, creating albums that are like haunted rooms in a museum. Some of these performances are so definitive that a singer—male, anyway—has to think twice about taking any of them on. No doubt that is why there are not many vocal recordings of *The Young at Heart, The Tender Trap, All the Way, From Here to Eternity.* There may be another reason why so few singers have done *My One and Only Love:* it climbs a twelfth in the first two bars, and there is no way of sneaking up on it.

There is no questioning Sinatra's musicianship. He has never claimed to be a "jazz singer," referring to himself as a saloon singer. But he is a universal favorite of jazz musicians. When Leonard Feather did a poll of musicians for his 1956 *Encyclopedia Yearbook of Jazz,* Sinatra got almost half the votes. Out of a hundred and twenty ballots, Sinatra got fifty-six, Nat Cole thirteen, Billy Eckstine eleven, and Louis Armstrong nine. Among those who named him their all-time favorite singer were Buck Clayton, Nat Cole, Miles Davis, Duke Ellington, Herb Ellis, Tal Farlow, Stan Getz, Benny Goodman, Bill Harris, Bobby Hackett, Carmen McRae, Gerry Mulligan, Sy Oliver, Oscar Peterson, Oscar Pettiford, Bud Powell, André Previn, Jimmy Raney, Howard Roberts, Horace Silver, Billy Taylor, Cal Tjader, and Lester Young.

The late Shelly Manne coached Sinatra for the drum-playing scenes in *The Man with the Golden Arm.* "He had a definite feel for it," Shelly said. "He could have played if he'd wanted to, although whether he'd have been as great a drummer as he is a singer is another question." Woody Herman toured a few years ago with Sinatra. "How was he singing?" I asked Woody later. "Well you know how I feel," Woody said. "He can sing the phone book and I'll like it." In theory Sinatra can't read music. "Well he can't but he can, if you know what I mean," said one arranger who had worked with him. One of Sinatra's early friends was the late Alec Wilder, who wrote the a capella arrangements for the first Sinatra Columbia sides, including *The Music Stopped* and *A Lovely Way to Spend an Evening,* as well as composing such songs as *I'll Be Around* and *While We're Young.* Sinatra heard acetate air checks of two pieces Wilder had written for woodwind octet and string orchestra, learned there were more of them, and determined to see them recorded, which they were, in 1945, with Sinatra conducting:

Theme and Variations, Air for Bassoon, Air for Flute, Air for English Horn, Slow Dance, and *Air for Oboe.* (Ironically, the English horn and oboe soloist was Mitch Miller.) Years later I asked Alec if Sinatra had in fact conducted those pieces. "Yes," Alec said, "he not only conducted, he did them better than anyone else has ever done them, before or since." The pieces, which are exquisite, must be considered experiments in a Third Stream, entailing elements of "jazz" and "classical" music. "He understood something," Alec said, "that is important in those pieces, and that the orchestra itself did not: steady dance tempos."

I watched Sinatra listening closely as Claus Ogerman ran down an arrangement at a recording session. "I think I hear a couple of little strangers in the strings," he said, and Claus corrected them—probably copyist's errors. Composer Lyn Murray recalls watching him over a period of days conduct an orchestra in rehearsal for an engagement in Las Vegas. Lyn said that he expended twenty-one hours rehearsing that orchestra, meticulously preparing every nuance of time and blend and dynamics. "When he was through," Lyn said, "every word of each lyric was laid out like a jewel on black velvet."

I was flabbergasted by the detail work in his reading of the lyric to *This Happy Madness.* The melody is one of Antonio Carlos Jobim's early ones, and the song is, again, very difficult to sing. Indeed, I have never heard anyone else do it. The lyric is mine, and I think I can claim to know what its intent is—what the "undertext," as actors and directors say, is. When the record came out (the song is in an album called *Sinatra and Company*) I sat in open-mouthed amazement as he caught every nuance of the words.

The first half of the release goes:

> I feel that I've gone back to childhood,
> and I'm skipping though the wildwood,
> so excited that I don't know what to do.

I intended the first two lines as a sort of self-mockery, as if the "character" in the song finds himself resorting to an abysmal banality, a dreadful cliche (the reference is to the old song *Childhood in the Wildwood*), and a false rhyme. Sinatra caught this, and sings those first two lines with a hard and self-disgusted edge on his voice. And suddenly in the third line, the voice takes on an infinitely gentle sound, as of total wonder. I couldn't believe it when I heard it. He caught not what the lyric said but what it didn't say.

Asked once by an interviewer what he thought his most important achievement had been, Sinatra said that it was a certain approach to singing that he hoped would endure—or words to that effect. The hope was a vain one. Even as he was turning out his finest work, Elvis Presley was exploding into prominence, and the quality of commercial popular music was plummeting. Those singers who had indeed learned from him were still doing well, but by the 1960s and certainly by the 1970s they were finding it harder and harder to come by record contracts. Eventually all the major singers who grew up in his school would find themselves without major-label recording contracts, and some of the best of them simply vanished. Only Sinatra has sailed on through it all, seemingly safe from the storms of fad. Rock-and-roll did not embrace his naturalism, the effect of a contained and inward drama. As amplification cranked up the volume of guitars and drums to a level dangerous to hearing, the singing became shrill, a distorted and grimmaced music lacking in literacy or subtlety, a hysterical celebration of the mundane that all the press agentry in the world could not disguise. While Sinatra himself retained an audience, packing them in whenever and wherever he chose to go, gradually a great tradition was being forgotten. The fans of Billy Joel and Elvis Costello and David Bowie and Michael Jackson have never heard of Jerome Kern, chances are that few of them had heard of Sinatra, and her fans probably thought that Linda Ronstadt discovered Nelson Riddle—whose pencil was laid aside forever in 1985—when she recorded with him.

What Sinatra's legacy will be we cannot know. But for a time, for a very long time, Frank Sinatra turned the singing of the American song into an art form, and his collected output must be considered a national treasure.

Peg

"When I was small, my mother died," Peggy Lee said. "My father remarried when I was six. She started beating me then and continued to beat me for eleven years, until I left." She said this in the oddest way, her voice detached, as if she were talking about someone else. "I think that is what made me so nonviolent."

"You know, of course," I said, "that the great majority of people who abuse children were themselves abused."

"Yes," she said, "I keep hearing that. But it had the opposite effect on me. I lived my own inward life, and I came to hate violence."

In those few phrases one finds a key to her work—the secret of what makes her one of the greatest singers in the English language, the leading exponent among women of the post-vaudeville naturalistic school of singing with its sense of the improvised, the spontaneous, the conversational. It is the school that began suddenly in the early 1940s, displacing the belting and the Irish-tenor styles exemplified by Al Jolson on the one hand, Kenny Baker on the other. It is a Stanislavskian approach to singing that gives a deep sense of the life behind it and emotion within it, creating the illusion of intimate, unpremeditated self-revealment. It is deceptive in that the skills are hidden. There is no straining. Sweat does not appear on the face, no veins stand out on the brow.

Peggy's voice seems small, slight, fragile. In fact it has great power in reserve, and occasionally, in the early recordings, she turns it on. It is far harder to hit high notes pianissimo than fortissimo, and she does this difficult thing casually, like Perry Como. One day when we were talking on the telephone, I told her I thought no one had achieved this minimalism to the extent she had. You could hear the soft smile in her voice. "Most people don't know how hard that is."

The conventional critical wisdom has always been that Lee is a derivation of Billie Holiday, that she built her style on the earlier singer's. "But I don't think I sound at all like her," Peggy said. "I admired her very much. But Billie sang like this." And she did an eerily accurate imitation of Holiday. Very occasionally in her early records, she'll pronounce a vowel as Holiday would—"kin" for "can," for example. Holiday's vowels are small and closed; Lee's are very open. In her early recordings for Benny Goodman, whose band she joined in 1941, you'll hear touches (but no more) of Holiday. Later they fade away, as her sense of identity grows and she develops her own distinctive lovely enunciation.

She was born Norma Egstrom in Jamestown, North Dakota. She must have been an exquisite child, judging by the beautiful young woman she grew into. She left home as soon as she was able, taking her record collection with her. It included a great many "race records," as they were known in those days. Her listening during that period of her life resulted in her later development of a style that is more attuned to the black experience and vocal style than perhaps that of any other white American singer. And she did this without any affectations of enunciation, and without, indeed, forgoing her own white experience and identity. Her style is a remarkable amalgam, and no doubt it is rooted in her early taste for black singers whose work was unknown to most white Americans of the time.

A friend introduced her to a man named Ken Kennedy, program director of radio station WDAY in Fargo, North Dakota. He auditioned her, liked her voice, and put her on the air within an hour of their meeting. He told her, "We'll have to change your

name. Norma Egstrom just won't do. You look like a Peggy . . .
Peggy, Peggy . . . Lee!"

She sang briefly with a local band in the Minneapolis area,
then got a booking at the Ambassador West Hotel in Chicago,
where Benny Goodman's wife, Alice, happened to hear her. Alice
brought Goodman in to listen shortly after that. Goodman seemed
cold. "I thought he didn't like me," Peggy said. She was rooming
at that time with another singer, née Jane Larrabee, who had
changed her name to Jane Leslie and would later change it again
when she married the noted British-born jazz critic Leonard
Feather. When Peggy returned to their room after some errand
or other, Jane told her Goodman had called. "I didn't believe
her," she says. "But she was insistent, and I called Benny. I joined
the band without even a rehearsal, having to sing everything in
Helen Forrest's keys. Mel Powell was wonderful to me. He helped
me so much."

Goodman was notorious for his coldness and brutal rudeness
to musicians. One can listen between the lines when she talks of
joining the band. Goodman apparently did nothing to make her
comfortable, and Mel Powell, one of the truly great jazz pianists
who later left the jazz world to become a classical composer and
teacher, although he occasionally works with Lee even now,
helped her learn difficult vocal arrangements, and would cue her
for her entrances.

She made a number of recordings with Goodman—*All I Need
Is You, Everything I Love, How Long Has This Been Going On?* among
them. One of the records she carried with her on the band's trav-
els was Lil Green's performance of *Why Don't You Do Right?*
"Benny heard me playing the record in my dressing room," she
said. "He could hardly help it, I was always playing it. Finally he
asked me, 'Would you like to sing that with the band?'" The
record, a huge hit for Goodman and for her, truly launched her.

Heard today, it reveals the first signs of her maturity, her very
personal ability to internalize a song and *act* it. Earlier recordings
sound like apprentice work, but in this one the "character" singing the song seems tough and cynical, two qualities that assuredly

are not part of Peggy Lee's own personality. Some years later (on November 19, 1947), she re-recorded a still better performance of it for Capitol. This time the arranger was Billy May, the conductor Dave Barbour.

She met Barbour, one of the fine jazz guitarists, while she was with Goodman. "She was in love with him," Jane Feather said, "from the moment she met him." Plagued by terrible shyness when she performed, and now deeply happy after a desolate childhood, she left the Goodman band, married Barbour, and retired. They settled in North Hollywood, California, where she gave birth to her only child, her daughter Nicki, now an artist of distinction. (Peggy too is an excellent painter.) Her retirement wouldn't last. Neither would her happiness.

Barbour thought her talent was too important to be abandoned. He said that if she did stay retired, she would some day regret it. In 1944, she was approached by Dave Dexter of Johnny Mercer's fledgling Capitol Records.

The company was about to do an unusual project that would be called *New American Jazz*—an album of four discs by various jazz players. "Albums" consisting of several discs were rare in the jazz field in those days, and the project, when it was completed, would have a considerable impact in the jazz community. Peggy thought, "Well, I could get a baby sitter and go down there and sing." Which is what she did. On January 7, 1944, she sang two songs for the album, a blues called *Ain't Goin' No Place* and the ballad *That Old Feeling*, accompanied by an illustrious group of jazz players: Eddie Miller, tenor saxophone; Barney Bigard, clarinet; Les Robinson, alto; Pete Johnson, piano; Nappy Lamare, guitar; Shorty Sherock, trumpet; Hank Wayland, bass, and Nick Fatool, drums.

For a girl who wanted to retire, the two sides were something of a disaster: they established her as one of the great vocalists in American music. What is more, though nobody noticed it at the time, they hinted at the range of her work: the blues had a toughness, akin to that heard in *Why Don't You Do Right*, while *That Old Feeling* conveyed an impression of a gentle and vulnerable woman badly hurt. Those two sides hinted at the eventual great psychological scope of her work.

No singer, male or female, in American music (and none that I have heard in any other country) has shown the ability to play so many different "characters" in song form as Peggy Lee. Piaf embraced the kind of character songs that appeal to Lee, but her audience would not let her be anything but a tragedienne, for all that she loved laughter. Peggy somehow avoided that trap, and audiences accepted her as a happy character in one song, comedienne in the next, tragedienne in the one after that. To watch her in a concert or nightclub performance proceed through a whole gallery of characters is to take a lesson in acting. It is no accident that she was nominated for an Academy Award for her portrayal of a fading nightclub singer of the 1920s in Jack Webb's picture *Pete Kelly's Blues*. She hoped that this would open the way to a broader career in films, but it never happened, which is one of the disappointments in her otherwise starry career.

Interestingly, Peggy recorded one of Piaf's songs, *My Man*. The music is by Maurice Yvain, the English lyric by Channing Pollock. This is one of the few examples of an English lyric that bears some relationship to a French original. She gives us a vivid picture of a beaten creature who for whatever reason continues to endure life with an abusive man. This performance, recorded in 1958, is one of a series in a gallery of portaits of women.

Her stationery and often her advertising have long borne the inscription Miss Peggy Lee, pointedly asserting identity as a woman. She assuredly is not Ms Peggy Lee. The character in *I'm a Woman*, which she recorded four years later, is not the one we encounter in *My Man*. This is no brow-beaten victim but, on the contrary, a woman boasting of her prowess at the complex of tasks that society imposes on her sex. *Hey Big Spender* vividly conveys the mockery of a hooker putting the mark on a john.

Another song in this gallery is *You Came a Long Way from St. Louis,* by John Benson Brooks and Bob Russell. Again, it portrays a woman skeptical about a man's accomplishments. The lady in the song may be on a higher social plane than the girl in *Why Don't*

You Do Right, but the two have a lot in common in their refusal to be taken in by a man's tall tales and attempts to impress.

Black Coffee, which borders on being an art song, has music by Sonny Burke and a strikingly dark poetic lyric by Paul Francis Webster. It laments the general condition that women—particularly in those pre-lib days—so often faced. This was recorded not for Capitol but for Decca.

Her famous *Lover* was also recorded for Decca. Peggy had an idea for this arrangement, derived from watching galloping horses in a movie. She begged the brass at Capitol to let her record it, but Les Paul had only recently had a hit on the same song so they tried to talk her out of it. Her contract came to an end just at this time, and she was approached by Decca. She told them she would change labels if they would let her record *Lover* the way she wanted to do it. Decca agreed, and Peggy signed. The song was a huge hit, no doubt to Capitol's chagrin, and at the end of the Decca contract she returned to what was really her professional home.

Don't Smoke in Bed, which she recorded in 1969, is the work of Willard Robison, whose songs superbly evoke images of America, including *Old Folks* and *Guess I'll Go Back Home This Summer,* and of troubled family life, such as *A Cottage for Sale. Don't Smoke in Bed* is another portrait of a woman, one who is leaving a man but doing it with heartbreak. Whether Peggy was aware of it or simply chose it because it reflected her feelings on leaving Dave Barbour probably even she couldn't say now. But that echo of her own life certainly is in her choice of this material.

The previous year she had recorded another song on the same theme, *By the Time I Get to Phoneix,* a small masterpiece by Jim Webb. It deals with the fragility of a man's relationship with a girl, his inability to accept the responsibility of it. The meaning is subtly altered when a woman sings it. The moods in the song, the inner attitude, are essentially masculine, and so completely feminine is Peggy that for all the sensitivity of her reading, her performance just didn't work, which is probably why it was not released at the time. *Time-Life* records finally put it out in a 1985 retrospective on her career.

Even as that career soared in the 1940s, her personal life took a tragic turn. Dave Barbour, in the years before he met her, had wrestled with a drinking problem. Now it returned, at times becoming so bad that his life was endangered. She stayed with him, helping him fight it.

She did everything she could to help him. At one time she went on vacation with him to Mexico. "Dave and I were both workaholics," she told me. "We just loved Mexico, and the people we met, and we admired their attitude, the relaxed philosophy and wished we could be more like them. We wrote *Mañana* as a result." Later the song was criticized for being condescending to Mexicans, which, she insisted, was not its intent.

Her aspirations of that period are revealed in still another song she wrote with Barbour, *It's a Good Day,* about clearing out past problems, paying off debts and obligations, getting rid of regrets and making a new start in life. Her lyric expresses what she wanted for her husband, but its optimism proved unjustified. She had begun writing lyrics in the mid-1940s, showing some of her efforts to Johnny Mercer, who gave her encouragement and suggestions, helping her develop into the lyricist who would produce something as skilled as *It's a Good Day.*

It wasn't, however. Barbour went on drinking. "I didn't want to divorce Dave," she told me. "He insisted on it. He made me do it, and it was the hardest thing I ever did in my life." Barbour moved out to Malibu, where she would visit him, to be sure he was eating properly.

She was remarried three times, but never happily and never for long—to actor Brad Dexter, percussionist Jack del Rio, and actor Dewey Martin. "It was always Dave," Jane Feather says.

Once, when I was writing something about Peggy, she said, "Please tell people for the last thirteen years of his life, Dave didn't have a drop to drink. He asked me to marry him again. We were going to be remarried, and he had a physical. His doctor told him he was in excellent condition. Four days later, the aorta burst in his heart, and he died."

All of this life experience turns up in her work. She never overstates a song, never tries to "put it over." The feeling is perceived in flashes, like lightning in a summer cloud. This is the secret of the striking dramatic miniatures of the human and especially woman's condition that make her the extraordinary artist that she is.

Like Sinatra, she has an almost uncanny ability to find and bring out the meaning of a song. Once, in the late 1960s, this ability was brought home to me at the Copacabana in New York. It was the closing night of her engagement. She performed one of my lyrics, *Yesterday I Heard the Rain:*

> Yesterday I heard the rain,
> whispering your name,
> asking where you'd gone.
> It fell softly from the clouds
> on the silent crowds
> as I wandered on.
>
> Out of doorways,
> black umbrellas
> came to pursue me.
> Faceless people,
> as they passed,
> were looking through me.
> No one knew me.
>
> Yesterday I shut my eyes,
> face up to the skies,
> drinking in the rain.
> But your image still was there,
> floating in the air,
> brighter than a flame.
>
> Yesterday I saw a city,
> full of shadows
> without pity,
> and I heard the steady rain
> whispering your name,
> whispering your name.

That song has a meaning few people have ever caught. The phrase "brighter than a flame" refers to the Sacred Heart icon of Catholicism; and the name is the Holy Name. It suggests that without some higher significance, something beyond the short painful life we pass through, life is dark, and the shadows are pitiless. The yearning for a higher meaning is expressed in the constant repetition of the name.

I never expected anyone to take it for anything but a conventional torch song. But that night, Peggy gave it a reading of astonishing religious intensity.

Afterwards, she had her usual closing night party. She introduced me to two of her friends, a monsignor and a younger priest, telling them I had written the lyric to that song.

"Ah," said the monsignor. "Then you can settle an argument I've been having with my friend here. I say that that song is about the loss of God."

I think my mouth fell open. I confirmed that this was indeed its intent and meaning.

And *that* is how deeply Peggy Lee can penetrate into the heart of a song.

Later, when only a few guests remained, and there was music playing on a stereo set, she said, "Do you dance?" Her performance that night had been brilliant, and I think she knew it. Whatever the reason, she was in an almost euphoric mood.

"Not very well," I said.

"Well dance with me anyway," she said.

I did, marveling somewhat that I should be dancing with one of the idols of my adolescence.

"You wrote a column about me a while ago," that soft voice said. I had indeed, expressing my admiration for the subtlety and brilliance of her work.

"Yes, I did," I said, a little apprehensively. You never know, when you write about people, what odd and unexpected little thing may cause offense.

"I read it," she said, "on one of the dark days of my life. I won't even tell you what I was thinking about that day. And then I read that. I can't tell you what it meant to me. I wanted you to know that."

And we danced for a while.

She has that kind of sensitivity. And it's in the songs.

The Last Comeback
Dick Haymes

There is a road up a canyon in Malibu that I never pass without thinking about Dick Haymes. All those canyon roads have a tinge of mystery about them. You wonder what's up there, where they go, and assume there must be something, somebody, or the roads wouldn't be there. The Southern California coast isn't as pretty as its propaganda suggests. Topographically, it is the beginning of Mexico and Central America and the land is burned brown, except for a time in the late winter when it greens up after the long relentless rains that carved out these canyons in the first place.

I went up that canyon—Latigo Canyon—just once, in the spring of 1976, when the tiny pink star flowers are on the jade plants. This is orginally desert country and it has been said that all the flora, even the weeds, are imports, including palms from Florida, the eucalyptus from Australia, the cyprus from the Mediterranean basin, and the various citrus forms from Spain and North Africa. The jade plant, one of the commonest of the naturalized California succulents, is the *Crassula argentea,* and it came here from Argentina. So did Dick Haymes.

He was making the last of his comebacks when I went up into these mountains to meet him. He had returned after ten years in Europe to open in 1975 at the Cocoanut Grove in Hollywood to a house that was packed with his friends. Those who liked him liked him a lot, and one of them prevailed upon me to write something about him for *High Fidelity* magazine to give him a lift, a leg up. I said I'd do it, but I didn't like doing it. It cost me nothing to give him some space in a magazine. But I disliked the fact that he needed the help. I am not one of those who take pleasure in seeing the mighty fallen, and Dick Haymes had been a very big star. He was also a very great singer, which is another thing. I have had uncountable conversations with singers about singers, and Dick Haymes' name would be on the most-admired list of almost every one of them.

I would much rather have been approaching him as a supplicant songwriter with some notes and words on a piece of paper that I wanted him to breathe life into, asking for his help instead of offering him mine. A star is someone who was one when you were young; no one ever achieves that status with you after you pass your middle twenties. And Dick Haymes was a star to me. It was some sort of serious perturbation of the cosmic order that I should, at least for the moment, be in a position of greater power than he. That is what bothered me as I drove up that road that early spring day. I knew by some intuition derived from the very way he sang—the dignity of his work—that he was not a man who would be comfortable in the situation of soliciting publicity. Nor have I ever been comfortable in the role of the one from whom it is solicited.

There's something lousy about being interviewed. You must be cautious, present the best image of yourself that you can, which automatically makes your behavior conscious, self-monitored, and therefore false. I foresaw that we would be wary with each other. And being wary, we would strive not to be wary but to be natural. And there is nothing more artificial than the attempt to be natural. Ah, well. It was not the ideal circumstance in which I would want to meet Dick Haymes, but what the hell, I was there to do a small favor for a man who had given me much pleasure in my life.

I drove up all the convolutions of that long mountain road, watching numbers on mail boxes until I found the one I was looking for. The house was a somewhat rustic place, unprepossessing but with a view to make you gasp. It looked down the wild slopes, hospitable to coyotes, deer, and the occasional mountain lion, to the Pacific Ocean, burning silver-white in the slanting metallic sunlight.

Dick Haymes came out of the house to meet me. He was a tall man, and strikingly attractive. His hair by now was as silver as the sea out there, and it had receded somewhat, but the face was changed remarkably little. Two deep character lines in the cheeks parenthesized a sensitive mouth, but any moviegoer of the 1940s and '50s would have known him instantly. This was indeed the boy I saw in *One Touch of Venus* and *State Fair,* simply older now. He wore khaki shorts and sandals, no shirt, and a gold cross hung from his neck on a fine chain. He greeted me and escorted me into the house. If he was faking naturalism, he was doing it well. Neither one of us wanted to make the other uncomfortable. Everyone who ever knew him makes the point that Dick Haymes was a gentlemen.

Bobby Scott, the composer, who wrote *A Taste of Honey* and *He's Not Heavy, He's My Brother,* among other excellent songs, and who at one time was Haymes' pianist, arranger, and conductor, once described him in an essay as "an encumbered man."

"Sometimes his past," Bobby wrote, "including his marriages, seemed to me to be a giant pull-toy he refused to let go of. There was nothing in a present that I shared for a time with him that he could wrap his fingers around. Dick *had* to pull the weight of that toy.

"I loved Dick. And I liked him, too . . .

"Dick Haymes was a monument to musical good taste. Only on a few occasions did he go for a lower denominator, and those attempts didn't make it. He was a *completed* person early in his career. If he did badly at any time, it was for mechanical reasons alone. His sole intent was to sing beautiful songs beautifully and reflect correctly the strength and genius of the songwriter's design. An excellent writer himself, he knew a great one when he heard it. I meant a great song, not a hit song. Hits rarely are examples of first-class writing, and Dick's sense of what that is was unerring."

Dick introduced me to his wife, Wendy Patricia Smith of Windsor, England, whom he had met eleven years before. She offered me coffee, which I accepted, and then, discreetly, left us. We sat in the living room, whose walls were almost completely of glass, with an awesome view of the ocean far below. I commented on it. Dick said he loved walking in these mountains. I asked him if he ever encountered rattlesnakes. He said, yes, he did, but they're shy, they don't bother you, they just want to get out of your way.

I saw not a trace of bitterness in the man. If there was any in him, he was concealing it. Correction: he was unable entirely to conceal his feeling about his mother, which came out in a muted way. I had heard about it from others. After Dick became famous, they told me, she set up shop as a voice teacher in New York, purporting to be able to impart those secrets she had taught him. And Dick resented it, saying she had taught him nothing. His father was a Scottish mining engineer, whom he adored, the mother an opera singer. He told Bobby Scott he thought she had been unfaithful to his father.

Whether he spoke Spanish, being born in Argentina, I still do not know, but somehow I discovered that he spoke fluent French. At one point his mother ran a couture salon in Paris, so he had spent part of his childhood there. And he attended Loyola College in Montreal, out on the west end of Sherbrooke Street, which has since become part of the great complex of colleges now known as Concordia University. He was thus educated by Jesuits. He told me that he had also gone to school in Switzerland. He was steeped, then, in French culture, and although he looked like and somehow sang like and in movies actually played the nice and unassuming American boy-next-door, he was an international sophisticate of aristocratic tastes.

He gave me the impression that he and his brother Bob, who became a successful songwriter—*That's All* is one of his excellent melodies—were bounced from one private school to another by a

mother who couldn't be bothered with them. I caught a glimpse
of two little boys clinging together for warmth in a very lonely
world.

Haymes apparently intended, like his brother, to be a songwriter, but the voice on the demos he made of his early writings
caught the attention of someone or other in the business, and he
became the band singer with Harry James. He followed Frank Sinatra into that job, and followed him again into the Tommy Dorsey
orchestra, when Sinatra struck out on his own; and then, still
again, followed Sinatra in becoming a single. Sinatra's career
somehow cast a shadow over his.

Bobby Scott said, "He had to shoulder the burden of things
he wasn't even responsible for, such as his good looks. It would
have been all right if he had been handsome and somehow didn't
seem to know it. Then he could have played the game of self-
deprecation to endear himself to the people. Unfortunately he was
bright enough to know how good-looking he was. And worse, he
had that rich baritone voice that affirmed a bigger-than-life mas-
culinity that is sooner than later found repellent by men who are
devoid of it. I remember vividly the impact he had on women in
our audiences—and the reactions of their escorts. It created situations of true danger. . . .

"He was cornered, in every way. Even his own fans somehow
held it against him that he wasn't as famous as Frank Sinatra."

Haymes was very much the figure of his age, the consummate
singer of the best romantic ballads produced by the 1920s, 30s,
and 40s. He was also, like almost every other major singer of that
era, a product and alumnus of the big bands. By the late 1940s,
the careers of all of them were faltering. Perry Como found a
home in the new medium of television. Sinatra established a second career, bigger even than his first. Haymes did not. Why?

The world grew very dangerous after the 1940s. And Sinatra
had a quality of the dangerous about him—the explosive, the
unpredictable. Miles Davis has that quality. So does Marlon
Brando. This makes them compellingly interesting people, quite
aside from considerations of talent. Haymes had that boy-next-

door image, in spite of his background, and he was the perfect singer of those sweet American love songs that seemed to promise an endless unconsummated courtship in accord with the theology and poetry of the Provençal troubadors. That kind of innocence was passé in the raunchy age of Elvis Presley's hips and sneer and rock-and-roll's loveless sex.

Sinatra had learned to swing. Reflecting the changing times, he had gone past *What Makes the Sunset* to a darker kind of love song on the one hand and a casual *Come Fly with Me* kind of week-end-fling sensuality on the other. Even when, later, he purports to look back with profundity, he sees the chicks along the way as nothing more significant than classy vintage wines, as in *It Was a Very Good Year*. More and more Sinatra gave the world the finger, saying he did it *My Way,* and the world bought it—it seemed you needed that kind of resiliency to survive the gathering brutality. Haymes went on singing that he was going to love you *Come Rain or Come Shine,* believing in a *Sure Thing,* treasuring the forever in a world that seemed increasingly ephemeral, protesting *Little White Lies* in a time of massive political deceptions and social fictions, to say nothing of the inexhaustible mendacity of television. In a Charles Manson epoch, Dick Haymes singing *It Might as Well Be Spring* seemed like at best a gentle anachronism.

"He was," Bobby Scott brilliantly observed, "a dinosaur who had lived through an ice age to emerge in a wide-eyed misunderstanding."

It was common knowledge that Dick had got deeply into drinking. I do not know how much he drank. "Fortunately," he told me that afternoon, "I never had that much tolerance for alcohol. I could get falling-down drunk on four drinks. I was rather fortunate in that, unlike friends of mine who can put away a couple of bottles a day. Thus when I stopped, I hadn't done that much physical damage to myself." However, there *were* stories of damage he had done to his body, including his nervous system, and at times he had been unable to remember lyrics.

The reason he went to Europe to live for five years, quite aside from the fact that France and Switzerland were to some extent home to him, was that "I got to the point where I'd loused up my life so much that I thought it was time to leave town. I would not advise people to go away to some distant place to find their heads. But it worked for me. I figured I'd worn out my welcome in the business. And I went away to try to find myself.

"It must have been the right move, because I did, after some more blunders. In 1965, with no problem whatsoever—which is a blessing in itself—I stopped drinking." Behind him there was a well-stocked bar for friends. "I came to a crossroads that gave me a choice of either winding up on skid row or functioning with the gifts with which I've been endowed. Thank God—and I use the name advisedly—I made the right choice."

In the course of that afternoon, I got the impression that Haymes had a mystical religious streak. He was in very good physical condition, being a devotee of yoga. He said he no longer cared in the least about so-called stardom; he simply liked to sing and act. He'd recently done a television role or two, and more roles were pending. He said he had come to the conclusion that the key to it is "dedication with detachment," an interesting phrase that puts one in mind of Huxley's statement that art is created in a condition of relaxed tension. And Haymes said he had come to abhor involvement with one's own ego. On the wall of that living room, burned into a sheet of wood, was the inscription *Keep it simple.*

"Whatever happened in my life, either good or bad," he said, "I find myself directly responsible for. What's past is past; it's a different era. And very possibly I am a different man. There is such a thing as rebirth.

"Strangely enough, after I stopped all this self-destruction, and self-indulgence as well, I reverted for a while to the real young man I used to be. All of a sudden, all of the things I'd loved to do all my life, skin-diving, sailing, skiing, tennis, writing, singing, performing, communicating with people, all came back to me in such a crystal clear concept that I really wondered what the hell I'd been trying to prove. In my case—and everyone has to find his own thing—the problem seemed to be some form of inferiority complex."

Of course. Two little boys in boarding schools, clinging together for warmth. Dick Haymes, meet Peggy Lee and Edith Piaf. Go out and sing for your suppers, kids.

"You see," Dick said, "I love my audience. They are a reflection of me and I am they. There's a communal meditation, if you wish to call it that. People will sometimes ask me after a performance, 'How can you move me so much?' And the truthful answer is that I am you.

"I firmly believe there is a spark of beauty in everyone, and I try to tap it. I try to find it."

By that part of the fading afternoon, we had both forgotten that this was supposed to be an interview. It came time for me to leave. He walked me out to the car. I wished him well, and meant it. I wanted him to make it. I wanted his try at yet another comeback to succeed, wanted it not only because his glorious deep baritone had warmed the American 1940s but because I liked him as a person.

This time the comeback was ended not by drink or his own follies but by cancer.

I drove carefully down that winding road until I reached the comparative safety of the Pacific Coast Highway. And I never pass that canyon mouth without thinking of him.

The Hug
Hugo Friedhofer

David Raksin called that morning, May 17, 1981, and said simply, "Hugo is gone," and my eyes misted, even though we had known he was going to die. He was eighty, he was arthritic, and as his daughter Karyl said later, "he was tired."

Dave asked me to handle the press. I called the *New York Times.* The editor of the Arts and Leisure section had never heard of Hugo Friedhofer, and so the *Times,* which takes a Brahmin pride in being an American historical record, ignored the fall of one of the most important orchestral composers the United States ever produced, even though all his music was designed to enhance the emotional content of movies, some of which did not deserve the dignity of his genius. It is unfortunate that he did not write symphonies, but he didn't, and that's that, and it is some compensation to remember that he was so uncertain of his talent that had he not been given the workaday assignments of movie scoring, he might never have written any music at all.

I got off the phone after that conversation with the *Times* and cursed and said, "Must we be forever at the mercy of amateurs promoted from the city desk?"

I tried to explain my feelings to myself. I loved him like . . . a father? Hardly, Hugo was too childlike for that analogy. Like a brother? No. He was far my superior and senior not only in his knowledge of music but of many things.

Suddenly I understood something I had long felt, in an unformulated way: sex and love have nothing to do with each other. When men love other men, they append "like a brother" or "like a father" to the verb out of their fear of the Big Taboo. And in that moment of grief I knew that I simply loved Hugo Friedhofer. Not as a brother or as a father but as my friend. Just about the last thing he ever said to me, in one of our interminable telephone conversations, was something about "our friendship, which, incidentally, as time goes on, grows increasingly dear to me," following which, embarrassed by his admission of emotion, he changed the subject very swiftly.

In any case, were my inclination towards men, I doubt that Hugo would have been to my taste. He was not tall and slim, and he had a small chin that a thin goatee poorly concealed, a stooped posture ("composer's hump," he called it), and enlarged fingertips stained with nicotine. Men are poorly equipped to judge the looks of other men: they admire the likes of Tyrone Power whom women dismiss as "pretty." But women found Hugo terribly attractive. They say it was his mind that excited them.

And so there he was, my dear friend Hugo, standing there now in sudden memory, gone. This man I loved so much, not just for his talent, although certainly I revelled in his musical genius. I used to phone him whenever I wanted to know something (or had discovered something) about music because, as composer Paul Glass put it, "Hugo always knew." The depth of Paul's loss can be measured in a remark he made to me in a phone conversation from Switzerland that might sound arrogant but which I found touching and lonely and devastated: "Now that Hugo's gone, I may know more about orchestration than any man alive." Paul lost his teacher. So did I.

A footnote to that: Hugo told me he had studied with Paul Glass. Paul told me he had studied with Hugo.

In September, 1981, four months after Hugo died, I went to the Monterey Jazz Festival. Hotel rooms were scarce and so at the suggestion of Hugo's daughter, Karyl Friedhofer Tonge, I stayed with her daughter Jennifer, whose husband, Jeff Pittaway, was then an Army helicopter pilot, at their home in Fort Ord. Jennifer, who was twenty-eight, had hardly known her grandfather. After Hugo married his second wife, Virginia, known as Ginda, pronounced Jinda, Karyl saw him only rarely—"which," she says, "I bitterly resent. I was cut off from him during his most creative years. I didn't really know him until I was in my late thirties. Because of his guilts, he was unable to understand that one can sustain more than one emotional relationship."

And yet Jennifer Pittaway treasured a photo of Hugo in short pants and a wide-brimmed hat, taken when he was two or three. Her own little boy was running around the house, wearing a towel as a cape. "What's his name?" I asked. "Kenny," Jennifer said. "No it's not!" Kenny shouted. "My name's Superman!" I was looking at the photo and then at Kenny and then at the photo again. The boy looked exactly like Hugo at the same age. There is evidence that abilities in athletics and music (which are not dissimilar) may be genetically transmitted, and if I were Jennifer, I thought, I would begin Kenneth Pittaway's musical training now.

Jennifer had joined the Army to go to its language school to learn German, which she by now spoke fluently. She could not afford to go to college to learn it. None of Hugo's descendants gets his royalties. Ginda, from whom he was estranged but never divorced, gets them. And their marriage was childless. Jennifer said that Hugo had called her a warmonger for joining the Army. I hastened to assure her that this was a manifestation of his dark sense of humor or of his willful Taurus (to say nothing of German) consistency: he hated the military.

It was a strange situation. I was explaining him to his own granddaughter.

Jeff was just back from a tiring flight mission and wanted to spend the evening at home with Kenny. So I took Jennifer as my "date" to the festival. As we were progressing in a crowd across the grass of the Monterey fairgrounds, Jennifer said she had always loved the Modern Jazz Quartet. By exquisite coincidence, John Lewis was walking two or three paces ahead of us, unbeknownst to her. I reached out and grasped John's elbow to halt him and I said, with the people flowing around us, "John, I would like you to meet Jennifer Pittaway. Jennifer is Hugo Friedhofer's granddaughter." And John beamed that gentle and shy smile of his through his beard and said, "How do you do. I am honored to meet you," and made a great and elegant fuss of her. Later, backstage, I introduced her to musicians who told her stories about her grandfather, and as we were driving back to Ford Ord she said, "But how do people like John Lewis know my grandfather's music?"

"Jennifer," I said, "everybody in music knows your grandfather's music. And it doesn't matter whether it's classical music or jazz. The name Friedhofer will open just about any door in the musical world for you."

Toward the end of his life, Hugo lived in a two-room apartment on Bronson Avenue in Hollywood. Ginda, who still retained their home on Woodrow Wilson Drive in Los Angeles, lived most of the time in Cuernavaca. Hugo's apartment building surrounds a central courtyard in which there is the usual small Hollywood swimming pool, its bottom painted blue. It is a three-story structure, pleasant enough but slightly gone to seed, of the kind you encounter in Raymond Chandler novels. If you walk along that balcony, around the U shape of the building, you come to the apartment of Jeri Southern, fine pianist and one of the great singers and influences. Jeri was the last love of Hugo's life and, though he was twenty-five years or more her senior, she loved him more than any of us, and took care of him. Jeri remained incommunicado for a week after he died, sitting for long periods in her bedroom staring at the floor. Jeri is more musician than anybody knows. She orchestrated Hugo's last movie.

In those late years I was, aside from Jeri, with whom Hugo had breakfast every morning, one of the few persons who could pry him out of his apartment. "How come," he said to me once on the phone, "you can always lift me out of my depressions?" "Because," I said, in jest, "I am the only one you know who is a worse melancholiac than you are." I used to have lunch with him often but irregularly at Musso and Frank's on Hollywood Boulevard, that great old movie-business restaurant that is now an island of the past in a sea of porno movie houses, hookers, passing police cruisers, tee-shirt shops, and freaks. And when I wanted him to hear some piece of music, I would make a tape of it and drive very slowly and play it on my car stereo. Karyl thinks Hugo always felt guilty about being German because of World Wars I and II. His father, Paul Friedhofer, was a German-American cellist who studied in Germany, where he met Hugo's mother, a singer training at the Dresden Opera. Hugo Wilhelm Friedhofer was born in San Francisco May 3, 1901. He missed the earthquake because his mother, annoyed as she apparently was from time to time with his father, had gone home to Germany, taking her darling with her. Hugo's sister, Louise, became, as he did, a cellist.

Claus Ogerman was coming to Los Angeles from Munich, and he wanted to meet Hugo. Composer after composer wanted to meet him, and since it was known that I knew him, they frequently solicited me to arrange an introduction. "I'm getting tired of being your social secretary," I told him. It was untrue of course. They delighted in what was in his head, and I delighted in opening the door for them to breach his reclusion. His phone no longer rang with job offers. Scores were being written by musicians not even skilled enough to be his students, and in those last years Hugo yearned for an assignment that never came. Anyway, Claus was arriving and Hugo was unfamiliar with his music; therefore I made a tape of Claus's *Three Symphonic Dances* and played it on the way to Musso and Frank's, driving slowly enough to get arrested.

Hugo gave a running analysis of its harmonic structure. But after a while he ceased listening and began to hear the music. Finally he said, "That kraut friend of yours has a melancholy streak."

"That kraut friend of mine?" I said. "What about this kraut friend of mine?" He responded with one of his worst puns, "Two's company, three's a kraut."

Someone once called Hugo "a real giant among film composers," to which he retorted, "No, I'm a fake giant among real pygmies." All the composers in Hollywood should have hated him for that remark, but instead they quoted it with relish, and they still do.

Dave Raksin said that Hugo suffered from "delusions of inadequacy" and that he "persisted in judging his work according to arcane criteria that would, if indiscriminately applied, sink just about everybody in sight." Dave once told Hugo that he had managed to sustain a dark view of nearly everything despite personal successes that might have tempted lesser men toward optimism. And, after he was dead, Dave said, "Sometimes it seemed that the only time life lived up to his expectations was when it disappointed him." But he loved, and very deeply, which is what I suppose I was trying to convey to Jennifer Pittaway. You just had to avoid reminding him of it.

Along with critic Page Cook, I was always fighting for Hugo's recognition, even though he was, as Raksin told him, "complicit in your own ignoring." Once I took him to Musso and Frank's to interview him for an article for the *Los Angeles Times* or the Canadian Broadcasting Corporation or something—Page and I wrote a lot of pieces about him. I am always careful, in interviews, to save my hot questions for the end, so that I don't come away with empty hands if the interviewee gets furious. And so at last I said to him, "How is it that with all those superb film scores behind you and the respect of colleagues around the world, you have all the emotional security of a twenty-two-year-old?"

"Oh, you son of a bitch!" he said. And then, sinking into a pensiveness, he said, "Well, there are among the composers in this town some really fine craftsmen. If you want a certain thing done, you have only to tell them. They have done it before and they can do it again. And I have a very real respect for these men.

"But if you feel about music as I do, you are always working at the outer periphery of your abilities. And that makes you insecure.

"Look," he said as we were finishing our coffee, "I've got my personal estimate of what I know and what I don't know. But I am also acutely conscious of four or five hundred years of musical culture staring over my shoulder, and that makes for a genuine humility. As opposed of course to a false modesty."

He was the gentlest and shyest and, secretly, the most romantic of men, and he literally could not harm a fly. One morning Jeri Southern was killing ants with a sponge on the drainboard of her kitchen sink. Hugo watched in silence with a baleful expression and then said at last, "I hate the part where the Red Cross arrives." Jeri didn't get it for a moment, and then burst out laughing, and later, when he was gone, she suddenly remembered the incident and laughed for the first time in weeks.

Hugo had a steadfast integrity about music and everything else. I do not recall our ever talking about politics, but he recommended that I read the books of Carey McWilliams, which I did. This leads me to believe he was a California socialist, a unique breed with pioneer roots, of the Upton Sinclair stripe. He was German in the thorough discipline of his approach to his music, which was, however, in its airy clarity, rather closer to the French, I thought, than to the German. In personality he was more American than German and more Californian than anything. And he shared with Allyn Ferguson and Jerry Goldsmith a curious distinction: he was one of the very few American film composers actually born in California. Insofar as the politics of Hollywood were concerned, he was a canny observer and trenchant commentator. And I think every composer in the industry not-so-secretly wanted his approval.

Hugo loved words as much as he did music—maybe he thought they were the same thing—and could quote poetry and lyrics endlessly. He could as easily have been a writer as a composer, and his letters are treasures. Indeed it is highly likely that you know some of his poems, for he wrote innumerable limericks, including the very famous one about nymphomaniacal Alice, and sent them on their way to become part of American folklore, authorship unknown. His formal education ended at sixteen when he dropped out of school to become an office boy and study painting at night. But then his interest in music began to predominate, and he studied cello assiduously and in a year was working as a musician.

His humor had a delicious salacious urbanity, and he was incredibly quick. Once I was having lunch with him, Dave Raksin, and Leonard Marcus, then editor of *High Fidelity*. Someone said something about the early 1940s. Hugo said, "I was learning my craft at that time."

"Studying with Robert?" I said—a very bad pun.

Instantly Hugo said, "Your craft is ebbing."

He used to refer to some contemporary composition as "cluster's last stand." Of a certain film composer, he said, "Very gifted, but chromium plated." Of another composer, famed in the profession for having parlayed a small talent into a large career and a larger ego: "He's a legend in his own mind."

Mocking the tendency of movie studios to have lyrics added to improbable film melodies, Hugo said, "I always thought they should have put lyrics to my love theme for *Broken Arrow*. Something like:

'You led me from the straight and narrow.
But you broke my heart when you broke my arrow.'"

When Hugo was working on *Joan of Arc*, Dave Raksin, at the time scoring another picture, encountered him walking through a studio street, head down, lost in thought. Dave asked him how the music was coming.

"I'm just starting the barbecue," he said.

Paul Glass and Hugo once attended an exhibit of modern art at a gallery in Pasadena. The lady in charge made the mistake of asking Hugo what he thought of it.

"Awful," or some such, he said.

Taken aback but oblivious of danger, the woman pressed on: "Oh, Mr. Friedhofer, you think that only because you don't understand the meaning of the French term avant garde."

"Yes I do," Hugo said. "The translation is 'bullshit.'"

When I learned that Dave Raksin was teaching a course on other than music at the University of Southern California, I said, "How come Dave teaches urban affairs?"

"Why not?" Hugo said. "He's had enough of them."

The objects of his jibes rarely resented them; indeed they were often the first to quote them.

There were a number of nicknames for Hugo. Alfred Newman's wife called him The Red Baron and had a plaque made bearing that motto. It sat on his piano until he died. Paul Glass has a friend who, after a long search, found a recording of Hugo's score for *The Young Lions*. The notes of course were in Japanese, one of the few major languages Paul does not speak. "I don't know what it says," Paul told his friend, "but I know the composer: Toshiro Friedhofer."

Earle Hagen called him Hug to his face and The Hug behind his back, and always after I heard that name—in Musso and Frank's inevitably—I too called him Hug.

Hugo arrived in Hollywood in July 1929 accompanied by his first wife, a pianist who never ceased to love him and died only months after he did. She was the mother of Karyl and Ericka, who died at thirty-two of leukemia and whose loss Hugo never quite got over.

Sound was added to movies a few months before Hugo was hired to orchestrate the music for *Keep Your Sunny Side Up*. Thus he was the only composer whose career in film scoring embraced the entire history of the craft. And he had been writing music for movies even before that. Many silent films had full scores that traveled with them and were performed by pit orchestras which, Hugo said, sometimes numbered as many as sixty musicians.

Hugo went to work as a cellist in the orchestra of the Granada Theater in San Francisco when he was twenty-four. One of his friends was an organist named Breitenfeld—Paul Desmond's father. When scores would arrive at the Granada with parts or even entire segments missing, the conductor would assign Hugo to write substitute passages.

In Hollywood, Hugo went to work only as an orchestrator, not as a composer. "No one in those days," he said, "ever did a complete score by himself. I got a reputation for being good at anything in which machinery was involved—airplanes, motor boats, typewriters, ocean liners."

The studios recognized at least one other aspect of his protean intelligence: he spoke German. When Erich Wolfgang Korngold arrived in Hollywood, he spoke no English and so Hugo was assigned by Warner Bros. to work with him. Hugo orchestrated for Korngold all those romantic Errol Flynn swashbucklers. The Korngold scores with Friedhofer orchestration include *Captain Blood, The Prince and the Pauper, Another Dawn, The Adventures of Robin Hood, Juarez, The Sea Wolf, Kings Row, The Private Lives of Elizabeth and Essex, Escape Me Never, Devotion, Of Human Bondage, The Constant Nymph,* and *Between Two Worlds.* When Max Steiner arrived from Austria, like Korngold unable at first to speak English, Hugo was assigned to him too. For Steiner he orchestrated *Green Light, The Life of Emil Zola, God's Country and the Woman, Gold Is Where You Find It, Jezebel, Four Daughters, Dawn Patrol, Dark Victory, The Old Maid, The Story of Dr. Ehrlich's Magic Bullet, All This and Heaven Too, The Letter, Sergeant York, One Foot in Heaven, In This Our Life, Casablanca, Watch on the Rhine, Arsenic and Old Lace, Mildred Pierce, The Beast with Five Fingers,* and parts of *Gone with the Wind.* Indeed he ghost-wrote some of the GWTW score for Steiner.

He always expressed great respect for Korngold and Steiner, but his attitudes toward the two were different. "In Korngold's case," he said, "it goes beyond respect. Not only did I learn a great deal from him, I loved the man." But when he was notified by an Israeli music society that they had planted a tree in his name, he said, "If they've planted one for Max Steiner, I want mine cut down."

Steiner and Korngold were among the many composers—
Franz Waxman was another—for whom Hugo orchestrated. It
was not until 1937, and then only through the intercession of his
friend Alfred Newman at Goldwyn studios, that he was allowed to
write a score of his own. It was for the Gary Cooper film *The
Adventures of Marco Polo*. "I wrote the score," he said, "not to the
picture itself but to my memory of Donn Byrne's wonderful
novella, *Messer Marco Polo*." It is not the only known example of
his scoring something other than the picture itself. A persistent
legend holds that when he was stuck for an idea for a scene in the
The Best Years of Our Lives, he went to a museum and wrote music
for a painting. Hugo denied this. He said the painting gave him
an idea for the music—which is splitting the hair pretty fine.

He was thirty-six when he worked on *Marco Polo*. All the
Friedhofer characteristics were already in place: the restraint, the
perfect orchestral balance, the beauty of line, the sensitivity, and
something that is indefinably but recognizably him. *Marco Polo*
should have been his breakthrough, but it wasn't. Warner Bros.
kept him firmly in place as an orchestrator, and, excepting one
minor film, he was not allowed to write another score during his
eleven years there.

But in time, and at other studios, he was recognized.
Although he continued to orchestrate for others (and Korngold
would let no other man touch one of his scores), he went on to
write the music for *The Lodger, Lifeboat, They Came to Blow Up
America, Home in Indiana, A Wing and a Prayer, Brewster's Millions,
The Bandit of Sherwood Forest, Getting Gertie's Garter, Gilda* (a col-
laboration with Martin Skiles), *So Dark the Night, Wild Harvest,
Body and Soul, The Adventures of Casanova, Enchantment, Sealed Ver-
dict, Bride of Vengeance, Captain Carey USA, Roseanna McCoy* (a col-
laboration with David Butolph), *Three Came Home, No Man of Her
Own, Guilty of Treason, Broken Arrow, Edge of Doom, The Sound of
Fury, Two Flats West, Ace in the Hole, Queen for a Day, Lydia Bailey,
The Secret Sharer, The Outcasts of Poker Flat, Thunder in the East, The
San Francisco Story, Rancho Notorious, The Marrying Kind, The Bride
Came to Yellow Sky, Face to Face, Island in the Sky, Hondo, Vera Cruz,*

White Feather, Violent Saturday, Soldier of Fortune, Seven Cities of Gold, The Rains of Ranchipur, The Revolt of Mamie Stover, The Harder They Fall, The Sun Also Rises, The Barbarian and the Geisha, The Bravados (with Alfred Newman), *In Love and War, This Earth Is Mine, Woman Obsessed, The Blue Angel, Never So Few, Homicidal, Geronimo, The Secret Invasion, Von Richtofen and Brown,* and *Private Parts,* in approximately that order. He also wrote a considerable quantity of music for television, including (with Earle Hagen) the *I Spy* series.

He was in his way a revolutionary film composer. Because the scores to silent films were almost continuous, the early producers of talking pictures, who had not yet grasped the differences between the two media, expected the new scores to be like them. Hugo was perhaps the first to argue for less music. "The trick in film scoring," as Henry Mancini says, "is knowing when to cool it." Hugo, in *Marco Polo,* already knew.

There is another way in which he was revolutionary; he was the first Hollywood composer to write distinctively American scores. The significance of his *Best Years of Our Lives* score is generally considered to be its recognizably American quality. His friend Aaron Copland's scores for *Of Mice and Men* (1939) and *Our Town* (1940) preceded it, but Copland was not a mainstream "Hollywood" composer. Friedhofer's probably had the greater influence on other film composers. Prior to *Best Years* and in spite of the two Copland scores, Hollywood movie music had a European flavor, no doubt because so many of the composers were born and trained in Europe. The early film moguls imported them wholesale, as they imported directors and actors and costume designers. And I would have to point out that Hugo was imparting his American quality to scores well before *Best Years,* and for that matter *Of Mice and Men.* One need only listen to his music for *Marco Polo* to observe this.

Is it proper for a film about an Italian in China to sound American? Verdi wrote *Aida,* which is set in Egypt, and Puccini wrote *Madama Butterfly,* which is about an American in Japan, in their own Italianate styles. Hugo had every right, as they did, to approach his subject matter in his own idiom. Nonetheless, there is a remarkable bit of writing during a segment in which, by montage, we watch Marco Polo progressing from Italy to China through all the countries in between. It lasts probably less than a minute, but during that minute Hugo goes through all the national styles of the countries traversed—and still sounds like Hugo.

He was amazing at this. In *Boy on a Dolphin* he writes in a Greek style and sounds like himself. In *Vera Cruz*, he writes in a Mexican style (of which he was enamored; he loved Mexico) and sounds like himself. In *The Young Lions*, since it concerns a German officer (Marlon Brando) and two American soldiers (Montgomery Clift and Dean Martin), he wrote in both American and German styles, and sounds like himself. In any of his films it is fascinating to observe how much the music adds to the power of the story, and how unobtrusively (unless you're watching for it) it achieves its effect. And how distinctive the style is! Someone— Somerset Maugham, I think—said, "The greatest style is no style at all." Hugo never strove for style; he simply had it.

"One of the factors," Dave Raksin said once, "is his conception of melody and harmony, which maintains the traditional idea of what is lyrical and conjunct.

"The problem with most melodic writing, outside the obvious banalities of contemporary pop music, which is at the level of finger painting, is that in the effort to avoid what has been done, composers too often avoid what should be done. Hugo manages to be lyrical without being sentimental. His music has dignity to it.

"He is a sophisticated and thoroughly-schooled musician fully conversant with twentieth-century music who also happens to know that the tonal system is far from dead."

Which brings us to one of Hugo's worst puns. The music he wrote for one scene in *The Companion* was in three keys. "This was inspired," Hugo said, "by the parrot in the scene. It's Polly-tonality." He used to make these outrageous jokes even in the music itself. Many years ago he was assigned to score a picture about the French Revolution. There is an old and angry maxim among film composers: everybody in Hollywood has two areas of expertise, his own and music. The producer on this picture was a self-important jackass of the old school. Striding the room during the music conference, he said, "Friedhofer, this is a film about the French Revolution, so I think there should be lots of French horns in the music."

Hugo found this so hilariously stupid that he did in fact use "lots of" French horns in the score. And as he neared the end of the picture, he put a capper on his joke. In the last scene, when the escaping lovers espy the cliffs of Dover, he reprised the melody with solo English horn.

The Hug used to say that listening to a film score without the movie was like trying to ride half a horse. He said that if a film score had the weight and richness of texture of the Brahms Fourth Symphony—he particularly loved Bach and Brahms—it would overwhelm the scene and damage the picture. But his own scores tended to undermine his theory. All of them, and especially *The Best Years of Our Lives,* are beautifully detailed. It is regrettable that everything he wrote exists in short segments, although there is always a continuity and form about his scores. I would like to see Paul Glass structure some of them into suites for public performance, being confident that Paul would have been Hugo's own choice to do so. Hugo is one of the few film composers ever to get an occasional approving nod from the classical establishment. His work is particularly admired in Germany. Donald Bishop, Jr., wrote some years ago, "Friedhofer's classicism is one of the finest esthetic achievements in contemporary music, in and out of films."

I turned up one day at the little apartment on Bronson Avenue, to go with him to lunch. In it were an upright black Steinway, a small black Wurlitzer electric piano, four swivel chairs, a big round coffee table on which reposed his typewriter and stacks of the correspondence he was always in the process of answering, a tape recorder, and shelves of records and books. Everything was functional, and there was no chair you could honestly call comfortable. He owned not one copy of the albums of his film scores.

On the wall above a work table, on which was piled his score paper, was a display of plaques commemorating those of his scores nominated for Academy Awards—*The Young Lions, An Affair to Remember, Between Heaven and Hell, Above and Beyond, Boy on a Dolphin, The Woman in the Window, Joan of Arc, The Bishop's Wife.* One year he lost out because several of his scores were competitive to each other. Where, I asked, was the statue for *The Best Years of Our Lives*? "In storage somewhere," he grumped. "Let's go to lunch." He always maintained that an Academy nomination was more honor than the award, since only the music division voted on it, while the award itself derived from the votes of actors, producers, directors, and others who might or might not know what music is all about. And anyway, he had resigned from the Motion Picture Academy, which he despised, many years before.

"I have seen," Hugo said to me once, "two authentic geniuses in this industry, Orson Welles and Marlon Brando. And this town, not knowing what to do with genius, destroys it."

We were discussing his score for *One-Eyed Jacks,* the one film Brando ever directed and for which Brando was raked across beds of broken glass by studio executives and their lackey press agents and—in supine obedience to the moguls—by the newspapers. Brando was made to look the self-indulgent *enfant terrible* for his meticulous shooting of the picture, when in fact he was seeking that evasive goal of perfect craftsmanship. But the picture has now taken on a sort of cult status. Mort Sahl has seen it twenty times or more; I've seen it about ten times, partly for the pas de deux acting of Brando and Karl Malden, partly for the performances Brando elicited from Ben Johnson and Slim Pickens, partly for the cinematography, and partly for Hugo's splendid score. How heartbreaking that main lyrical theme renders the morning scene on the beach, when Brando tells the girl he has been lying to her and has shamed her. Hugo used a distantly lonely solo trumpet in front of strings, one of his favorite devices. He loved jazz and jazz musicians, and that trumpet solo is by Pete Candoli.

"I had ten weeks to work on that score," Hugo told me, "longer than I've had on any other picture.

"Brando had cut the film to about four and a half hours, and then it had been cut further to about two hours and fifteen minutes, at which point it was turned over to me for scoring.

"When I saw it at that length, it was without doubt the goddamnedest differentest western I have ever seen, and I loved it. They sneak-previewed it somewhere in the hinterlands on a Friday night with the kids and the popcorn and all that, and it bombed. They tried this and that and the other and cut it again, and it went out in a very much bowdlerized form. In fact they even butchered the music. Whole sequences I had designed for one scene were shoved in somewhere else. So the score is best heard in the UA record album, which I had the opportunity to edit. That is the real score of *One-Eyed Jacks,* minus about 45 minutes of music.

"By the way, in Brando's cut, the girl dies in the end. The studio didn't like that."

One-Eyed Jacks, in which Hugo's genius is fused to Brando's, is a broken masterpiece. And as for the UA album of that score, if you can find a copy of it, it sells for $150 or more.

The cavalier treatment of film scores—the actual paper scores— by movie studios is notorious. The studios claim that they own the scores, as one owns a suit ordered from a tailor—which in fact is precisely the analogy their lawyers used during a lawsuit filed against them by the film composers, a suit the composers for all substantial purposes lost. And when studios have become pressed for storage space, they have often consigned these national treasures to the incinerator or the dumpster.

The score for *The Best Years of Our Lives,* so highly acclaimed even in academic music circles, was lost for thirty-two years. Attempts by Elmer Bernstein and Dave Raksin, among others, to get Hugo to reconstruct it, failed. "My mind is not where it was when I wrote that," he said. But then it was learned that someone who had worked on the picture had kept a set of acetate recordings of the score, and working from them, Australian composer

Anthony Bremner reconstructed and orchestrated the music. A Chicago producer named John Steven Lasher recorded it with the London Philharmonic Orchestra. And he commissioned a fairly elaborate booklet to accompany the record, which was issued in 1979 to commemorate Hugo's fiftieth year in Hollywood.

Composer Louis Applebaum wrote an excellent technical analysis of the score. And a lot of us wrote tributes for it: Royal S. Brown, one of the few classical music critics to recognize the worth of motion picture scores, George Duning, John Green, Bronislau Kaper, Lyn Murray, Dave Raksin, Lalo Schifrin, and David Shire. I thought Henry Mancini said it best, in two lines: "Hugo is the silent conscience of the film composer. An affirmative nod from the man is worth more than all of the trinkets bestowed by the film industry." And when it was done and packaged, we sent the whole thing to Hugo. And he never said one word to me about it. Not a word.

A few months after that, when Jack Elliott and Allyn Ferguson had assembled what they called The Orchestra, later renamed the New American Orchestra—a virtuosic organization of more than eighty-five of the finest studio, symphony, and jazz musicians in Los Angeles—I suggested that they perform *Best Years* in concert. Hugo at first refused to attend, as he had previously refused to attend a retrospective of his movies. But Jeri Southern prevailed, and we went.

The orchestra gave a shimmering performance, all its members knowing he was there. Most of them had worked for him at one time or another and revered him. Part way through the first section, Hugo said to me in that sepulchral voice of his, "The tempo's a little fast."

"Oh shut up," I said.

And when it was over, the audience cheered as at a football game, and Hugo had to stand up and take a bow. It was, as far as I know, only the second time in his life he had heard his music played in public and received the applause he deserved. And I think it was the last time he heard his music played anywhere.

Claus met him at last. I took Hugo to lunch with him and Allyn Ferguson and actor Michael Parks. Parks can be rather reticent, but I induced him that day to do his eerie reproductions of various famous voices. "It's amazing," Hugo said. "He doesn't sound like an imitation but like a Xerox copy." Claus and Hugo felt an immediate rapport, although I haven't the slightest idea what they talked about: their conversation was in German. "How good is his German?" I asked Claus later. "You would never know he is an American," Claus said.

I had come into a habit, whenever Hugo and I went anywhere, of hovering over him, in a surreptitious way. His step had become faltering and slow, and I was always afraid he would fall. He used a beautiful cane of dark wood that Jeri had given him, which he treasured. Once he left it in my car and he was frantic until he reached me and found that it was safe. As we left Musso and Frank's that day and were crossing a street, I reflexively and involuntarily took his arm. He gave me a withering stare, and I never made that mistake again. But my hands were always ready to catch him if he stumbled. The tragedy was that his body was failing and his mind was not.

He had a spot on his lung which turned out to be malignant, and he underwent chemotherapy. He smoked far too much all his life. He used to say that he needed the cigarette in his left hand to balance the pencil in his right. And then, as I had feared he would, he fell, and broke his hip. He was taken to the hospital for surgery. Ginda came up from Mexico and began making arrangements to put him in a home. Karyl and I both believe that Hugo decided to die. Pneumonia set in, and he lost the power of speech, this most articulate of men.

Jeri sat by his bedside all one afternoon. He looked at her and silently formed the words, "I love you."

After Jeri had gone home, exhausted, a nurse entered the room to make him comfortable. He opened his eyes. Miraculously, the power of speech came back to him and he got off a last line that, days later, set off gales of consoling laughter, because it was so typical of him. He said, "You know, this really sucks." And he died.

When a great tree falls, it makes quite a crash. Without the help of the *New York Times* or the *Hollywood Reporter* (which printed about four lines on his death), the news traveled by mysterious means all over the world. Paul Glass called Roger Kellaway from Switzerland, desperate to know whether Hugo's scores were safe and where they were, saying they would be invaluable to music students for generations to come.

I became agitated about the scores when Dave Raksin told Ginda he was planning a memorial service for Hugo, and she said, "But who'd come?" Whether his full scores still existed in dusty studio archives I did not know, but I knew the whereabouts of his meticulous six-stave "sketches," so complete that Gene DiNovi once said, "When you orchestrate for Hugo—" and Gene proudly did at one time "—you are a glorified copyist." These were still in the apartment on Bronson Avenue. Everyone kept saying that something would have to be done about them. And at last it dawned on me that I would have to do it.

I felt a kind of shock, when I entered that familiar silent apartment, knowing he would never be there again. Then I went to work. I knew where all his scores—each of them bound in hardcover, the film titles imprinted with gold leaf—were stored, and I hauled them out in great armfuls and heaped them on a flat-bed cart I had brought. In six minutes and three trips, I stripped that place of his scores, rushing along the U of the balcony and dumping them in a huge pile in the middle of Jeri Southern's living-room carpet. I left Jeri's key to his apartment on her coffee table, went home, called Roger Kellaway and told him to tell Paul Glass the "sketches" were safe. A few days later Karyl, who is a map librarian at Stanford University, took them home with her; later she donated them to the University of Utah, where they are now available for study. Lawyers say they are worthless. Musicians say they are priceless.

We held the memorial service in a small sunny chapel in West-wood. Dave Raksin conducted a chamber orchestra, made up of musicians who loved Hugo, in a recital of Bach and Brahms.

Elmer Bernstein and Leonard Rosenman and Dave and I made little speeches, and the service was not remotely sad. Indeed the conversation before and after it was full of laughter. Jeri didn't come, which I thought appropriate: somebody had to uphold Hugo's tradition of not attending affairs in his honor.

No life of course is long enough, but Hugo's was, as lives go, fairly long, and it was brilliant, and he left us with a thousand funny stories and a mountain of music whose worth has yet to be fully evaluated.

"Lucky as we were to have had him among us," Dave said that day, "we must not risk offending Hugo by overdoing our praise—which he is even now trying to wriggle out of, somewhere in time.

"Peace be yours at last, dear friend. Sleep well."

GI Jo

Early in Walter Murphy's novel *The Vicar of Christ*, one of the main characters, a Marine Corps sergeant major, is pictured listening on a radio to Jo Stafford's *On Top of Old Smokey* just before a battle of the Korean War.

Stafford's recording of *Blues in the Night* figures in a scene in James Michener's *The Drifters*, and a character in one of the James Hilton novels, talking about what he would select to take to a desert island, includes a Jo Stafford collection in his list.

That scene in *The Vicar of Christ* somehow sets Stafford's place in the American culture. You're getting pretty famous when your name turns up in crossword puzzles; you are woven into a nation's history when you turn up in its fiction. And Stafford's voice was part of two American wars. What Kay Armen and Vera Lynn were to the British in World War II, Stafford was to the Americans, and the effect lingered on into the 1950s and Korea. Why she became such a favorite of Americans scattered around the planet in those wars has gone unexplained, and perhaps the question of her popularity has never been examined, as was that of Frank Sinatra, Elvis Presley, and the Beatles.

Possibly it was her way of *letting* a song happen rather than shoving it at you soaked in personal style. There was nothing sexually aggressive about Stafford, she did not seem to challenge anyone to conquer her. She was a very pretty girl, as seen in pictures that were hung up in the barracks of soldiers and over the swaying bunks of sailors, but she seemed more like, well, the girl next door than like the sweatered catch-me-if-you-can girls such as Rita Hayworth, kneeling on a bed, bosom bulging in a satin nightgown in that famous *Life* magazine photo. To me, listening to Jo Stafford from a vast distance in my high-school years, she seemed like the wise older sister, singing a piece of advice, "A heart that's true— there are such things." And now that I know her, she still does. There is also a deeply maternal quality about her; sometimes when I telephone to speak to her husband, Paul Weston, I halfway feel I should be saying, "Can Paul come out to play?"

She came across, in those war years, as someone who did not give a fig for stardom, did not want to stand above the crowd, did not consider herself better than anyone else. "Not caring what you own, but just what you are . . . " And that impression, as it happens, was exactly correct. That is what she's like, this decent, enormously intelligent, and staunchly egalitarian lady.

She was often voted "GI Jo" by companies or squadrons. The term by now perhaps requires explanation. Uniforms, rations, and other things issued to American soldiers in World War II were marked GI for "government issue," and soldiers themselves became known as GIs, or GI Joes.

At a military hospital in Europe, one of Stafford's recordings was, by vote of the patients, played every night at lights out. Once in New York, two young fliers, just back from Europe, told her that they'd almost been court-martialed because of her. Returning from a mission over Germany, they had, against regulations, been listening to Armed Forces Radio. They'd disrupted the flight pattern over their home field rather than change bands (to get their landing orders) during one of her songs.

The favorite of all her records among servicemen, she believes, was *I'll Be Seeing You.*

Jo Stafford slipped almost unnoticed into the American consciousness as the lead singer with a Tommy Dorsey vocal group called The Piped Pipers. That's what she liked doing, group singing, and she became a star half by accident because of a song called *Little Man with a Candy Cigar*. She went to Dorsey and said, "Tommy, this is the first time I've ever done this, and it'll probably be the last, but I want a favor of you. I want to do the record of *Little Man with the Candy Cigar* solo." He said, "You got it." From then on he assigned her a lot of solos. For the rest of the 1940s and well into the 1950s she was part of the fabric of American life, as she is now part of its memories. A retired Army general, well advanced in years, wrote her that he was so disgusted with the state of the world that he wanted to retreat to a farm with his Jo Stafford records and just forget it.

Like all of us, Jo has aged, but she hasn't really changed that much, and time after time people recognize her in supermarkets or gas stations and tell her how much this record of hers or that one meant to them during the war years. She still receives mail from old soldiers and fliers and sailors who were consoled by her voice during that ordeal now more than forty years in the past, and remains touched by them, and answers them.

"Yes, it means something to me, those letters," she said. "I'm a very patriotic lady, and in those years I felt very deeply about those kids. I used to see a lot of them at the Paramount Theater, because New York City was their embarkation point, and they'd be on their way, and my dressing room used to be full of them all the time. I couldn't turn them away."

"Your patriotism, however," I said, "is anything but the uncritical kind—the love-it-or-leave-it stuff."

"Oh absolutely not, that's like saying if you love somebody very deeply, you never criticize them." She looked at Paul, with a strange mixture of affectionate smile and gritted teeth and said, "That isn't true, is it?" And Paul laughed, probably at something that had happened that day.

She never did want stardom and eventually gave it up, not with a conspicuous public announcement of retirement but gradually and quietly, first by withdrawing from public performing and later by ceasing to record. She concentrated on raising her two children.

Stafford's marriage to Paul Weston has been settled, steady, and warm. Product of a profession whose practitioners are noted for psychological instability, she is sane, steadfast, and as far as I can see, very calm. One day in 1947, when she was at the height of her stardom, Jo passed Country Washburn, chit-chatting with some of his cronies, in a corridor at Capitol Records. "There's the girl who can do it," she heard him say. That's a line to catch your attention, and she asked what it was that she could do. Washburn explained that he was planning a satiric recording of *Temptation,* as it might be done by a hillbilly singer—the term in use in those days. The girl he had scheduled for the session had, for one reason or another, fallen out, and he thought Jo could do it. So Jo made the record under the pseudonym Cinderella Stump. The song in its hilarious new incarnation was called *Timtayshun.* It was an immediate and enormous hit. The entire record industry, and its press, was speculating over who Cinderella really was. Not even Jo's manager knew. When at last he found out, he was furious. He asked her what kind of deal she had made for herself. She told him there was no deal; she had made the record for fun, and for scale, and was receiving no royalty at all.

What made the record only the funnier, and this is true of her second and later alter ego, the astonishingly incompetent society singer Darlene Edwards, was the sheer accuracy of it, the authenticity of the style. You cannot satirize what you do not know, and Jo knew whereof she was singing.

Her mother was Anna York Stafford, a distant cousin of Sergeant Alvin York, the farm-boy sharpshooter decorated in World War I. Anna York was born in Gainesboro, Tennessee, where she was noted as a virtuosic player of the five-string banjo. She married Grover Cleveland Stafford, who moved west in the hope of making a fortune in the California oil fields. He never did, but he always worked, first as a roughneck, then as a driller, finally as a foreman. Life for the Staffords was sometimes hard during the years of the Great Depression, and they lived from paycheck to paycheck. Jo was born the third of four girls on a tract of land known as Lease 35 at Coalinga, California, a small town that lies between highway 101 and Interstate 5 in a limbo about halfway between Los Angeles and San Francisco. The land thereabouts is dry, and Coalinga's chief claims to fame are Jo Stafford and a bad 1983 earthquake.

Hard at times or not, the Staffords' life was full of music. "When I was in high school," she said, "I had five years of classical voice training—all the breathing exercises, lying on my back, bouncing books on my diaphragm, doing scales. I had eyes to be an opera singer. I was always in the glee club in high school, and I thought to be an opera singer would be a good thing. But it takes more than five years to become an opera singer, and when I got out of high school, I had to go to work." The training helped make her a sight-reading shark and contributed to her accurate intonation. Her ear is so precise that she makes her fictional Darlene Edwards sing sharp or flat to ear-grating effect. It is hard to sing out of tune on purpose, only too easy to do it unintentionally, but Jo can do it effortlessly at will.

Years ago she told me that the trick to that kind of accurate vocal intonation is to think the tone just before you make it.

"I can't tell you physically how you do it," she says. "It's a mental thing. You know the song, you know the note you're going for. And a split second before you sing it, you hear it in your mind. And it gives you a real edge on hitting that note right."

Yes, but that doesn't fully explain it. The phenomenon of pitch in the voice is a mysterious one anyway, since the vocal cords contain no sensory nerves, which is why laryngitis is painless.

"Do you think that discipline grew out of your group-singing experience?" I asked her. "When you have to sing lead, you're responsible for the pitch of everybody."

"Yeah," she said, "you're responsible for the shape of the whole chord, as a matter of fact. You change everything . . . How can I explain this? I did a multiple recording of Christmas songs. I had done multiple recording years back on *The Hawaiian War Chant*. I did the lead first and then filled in the three parts underneath. When I heard the results, I said, 'I will never do that again.' So when I made this Christmas album, I put all the parts, starting with the bottom one, in first, and sometimes there were as many as eight tracks. I put the lead on last. Then I could control the way that sound was.

"In different chords, Paul made me realize, although I'd always done it, you do not sing A-flat the same as G-sharp. When you're sitting on top of the chords, you sing the lead differently on each one. I think it has a lot to do with overtones.

"I have a theory that when you sing absolutely straight tone, without vibrato, you lose overtones. So if you aren't dead center of the pitch when you take the vibrato out, it's going to sound awful."

But it takes great security and control to do what she did, since it involves, at least in legato passages, thinking one tone while you are still producing the one that precedes it. Paul said to her only recently, "I still don't know how you do that." She does it, though, which is why she is admired by such superb vocal technicians as Bonnie Herman, the lead voice of The Singers Unlimited. Since Jo had long been one of her idols, in part because of her lead work with the Pied Pipers, Bonnie was surprised some years ago to get a fan letter from her. They have been friends ever since. Jo says she doesn't have absolute pitch. "But I have pretty good relative pitch," she said. Pretty good?

Jo joined her older sisters, Pauline and Christine, who were already in the music business, to form a vocal trio. It was an age of sister groups, producing the Boswell Sisters, the Andrews Sisters, DeMarco, Clark, Dinning, and Clooney Sisters, and more; Jo considers the best of them were the King Sisters. Girl vocal groups, she said, normally have a high light texture because of the range of the female voice, but Alyce King was able to sing quite low, which gave body to their sound. "Alice had a B-flat down on the bottom," Paul said.

The Stafford Sisters had their own radio show on Los Angeles radio station KHJ. They performed as well on *David Broeckman's California Melodies* and, for five nights a week, on *The Crockett Family of Kentucky* shows. "The Crocketts," she said, "were a real, authentic, country group—not Nashville country, but country

country. Folk. They were awfully good, good musicians. We had a couple of arrangements, my sisters and I did, that were satires on country folk singing." All three Stafford girls did studio work as well, and Hugo Friedhofer affectionately remembered them running from one movie studio to another on their appointed rounds.

Jo remembers that when she was singing back-up for Alice Faye in films, the latter would, at the end of a day, deliberately fluff a take, to force the job into overtime so that the girls could earn a little extra money. Alice Faye and Jo are still friends.

The Stafford Sisters replaced Jo with another girl when Jo joined an eight-voice group called The Pied Pipers. And it was at this point that she met Axel Stordahl and Paul Weston.

He was born Paul Wetstein in Springfield, Massachusetts, of a German Catholic father and an Irish Catholic mother. "He is Irish in everything except music," Jo remarked once. "When it comes to music, he is German." Meaning, one presumes, precise, thorough, and disciplined. His writing is characterized by spare, clean voice-leading, and it is highly individual.

Paul grew up in Pittsfield, Massachusetts. His father was a teacher in a girls' private school. The school had a phonograph, which he was allowed to take home at the Christmas break. Though it was a big and bulky machine, he brought it to the house on skis. And he brought records, the kind that were blank on one side. One of them was *Whispering Hope*, sung by Alma Gluck and Louise Homer.

After high school, Paul went on to study economics at Dartmouth. He claims he learned just enough economics to pass the exams, but this seems unlikely in view of the fact that he was graduated cum laude and Phi Beta Kappa. That was in 1933. Like so many young intellectuals of the time, he was in love with the young music called jazz. He had led a band at Dartmouth and, in 1934, while he was doing graduate studies at Columbia University in New York, he sold some arrangements to the Joe Haymes orchestra, which the late Rudy Vallee, then the nation's heartthrob, heard on a radio broadcast. Vallee commissioned him to write some charts for him. Paul's father was dismayed at the thought that his son might desert economics for music. But in those Depression years, Paul points out, nobody much was looking for young economists, and circumstance colluded with desire to make him a professional musician. His father relented when Paul sent home for deposit a check bearing Vallee's signature, which caused a considerable dither at the local bank. Paul continued to write for Vallee and Haymes and for drummer Phil Harris and his orchestra. (Harris would later marry Jo's friend Alice Faye.)

In summer of 1935, the battling Dorsey brothers, who could never agree on anything, including tempos and the way a rhythm section was supposed to sound, broke up their band. Tommy took over the Haymes band and offered Paul a job as staff arranger. He took it and wrote for Dorsey for five years. It was a brilliant arranging staff, including as it did Sy Oliver and Axel Stordahl. The charts on *Stardust, Night and Day,* and *Who?,* among others, are Paul's.

One of his closest friends was Stordahl, whose real name was Odd Stordahl. It doesn't sound odd to a Swede, but it does to an American ear, and he changed it to something almost as odd, namely Axel. The signature on the record-date contracts for Frank Sinatra's first Bluebird sides, including *Night and Day,* reads Odd Stordahl. Paul calls him Ax, and there is always affection in his voice when he says it, so long after Stordahl died of a heart attack.

In 1938, Paul, Stordahl, Dorsey's featured singer Jack Leonard, and Herb Sanford, the BBDO advertising executive who produced the Raleigh Kool network radio show on which the Tommy Dorsey band was playing, rented a house in Los Angeles. It was at this time that they first encountered the Pied Pipers. "Paul was going with Alyce King of the King Sisters, Ax was going with Yvonne King," Jo said. "The Kings knew about the Pipers. They'd heard us. They told Paul and Ax, 'You really ought to hear this group.' So one afternoon we went over to Paul and Ax's house and had a sort of singers' jam session."

"Half the group singers in town were invited," Paul said. "Like the Music Maids from the Bing Crosby show, and the Kings.

The Pied Pipers came in the front door, and they went right to the refrigerator and ate up everything in the house.''

"We were very poor," Jo said almost plaintively.

"Even the ketchup. Ax and I never got over that. The ketchup was all gone, everything that was in the refrigerator."

"I don't remember that ketchup," Jo said, laughing.

"Then they started singing. They had Jo and three guys and four other guys, and they worked in sections. Like, they'd have a sax section versus the brass section, then the two sections would be together, and four of them would sing unison here against four parts. We'd never heard anything like it.

"At this point Herb Sanford came home and heard them and went crazy. He went to Tommy and said, 'We've got to have them on the Raleigh Kool program.' And Tommy saw a chance to get the Pipers on the program without his having to pay anything, since Herb was pushing them. The band went back to New York, and the Pipers got in their cars and drove to New York. On the basis of doing one radio show!"

"You have to be awfully young to do that," Jo said.

"The sponsor," Paul said, "was in England. Each week the agency mailed a recording of the program to the sponsor. One of those great big glass discs. But as they took it to the post office, they broke it, so that it got to England in pieces, so this old Sir Hubert or whatever his name was didn't know what the hell was going on. He knew he had Tommy Dorsey and he knew he had big ratings. Unfortunately for the Pipers, he came to America. He was sitting up in the booth, at NBC. Now their arrangements were pretty crazy anyway, but they were singing 'Hold Tight, Hold Tight, foodly racky-sacky, want some sea food, Mama.' And this Englishman jumped and clawed at the glass and said, 'Get them off my show, get them off!' So they were fired. They stayed in New York for a few months."

"We stayed until we had just enough money left for our train tickets home to Los Angeles," Jo said. "I had gone down and picked up my last unemployment check. It was pretty panic city. And I got home and there was a message to call an operator in

Chicago. I didn't know anybody in Chicago, but it was a collect call, and I had nothing to lose. I returned the call and it was Tommy. He said, 'I can't afford a group of eight, but if you have a quartet, I'd sure like to have you join the band.' Dick Whittinghill had left the group by then, and we actually were down to four. So that was it. We went with Tommy."

Tommy Dorsey was noted for being a martinet, a volatile Irish miner's son who couldn't even get along with his own brother, the affable and widely liked Jimmy. Benny Goodman had a similar reputation for tyranny, but Dorsey, unlike Goodman, is often remembered by those who worked for him with a strange grudging affection. There is another difference. Goodman demoralized musicians. Dorsey somehow inspired them, and the Dorsey band in the years Jo was with it had an *esprit de corps* unlike any other, a collective vanity that made them think they could carve any other band. By and large they were right. It was a superb band whose recorded output doesn't seem to date. It executed excellent hot charts by Sy Oliver with burning zeal, particularly when Buddy Rich was booting it, and played ballads probably better than any other band of the period, as often as not built around its leader's mellifluous solo trombone. It was a band with an extremely broad emotional range.

And Dorsey was able to hold together some deeply disparate and brilliant temperaments, including—not long after Jo joined the band—Frank Sinatra and Buddy Rich, who were perpetually at each other's throats. How they remained friends is a mystery. What is more, they even roomed together. Sinatra has said that he himself is amazed that they both came through the experience alive. Legend has it that Sinatra once threw a cutglass pitcher of water at Buddy backstage at the Paramount in New York. I once asked Jo if it was true. "Sure," she said. "I was writing a letter to my mother at the time, and the water splashed all over it."

Lee Castaldo, who later changed his name to Lee Castle, was close to the Dorsey brothers, and at one point studied trumpet with their father. Lee said Tommy was the kind of man who knew the diagram of every water pipe and electric line in his house, and who always knew—or wanted to know—everything that went on in his band. In another famous incident, Buddy Rich blew up in the middle of a performance at the Paramount, quit the band and walked off the stage. Buddy headed for Florida, where his mother and father were living. A day or so later, Lee got a phone call from Buddy, asking Lee to send him his drums.

Dorsey, as Lee discovered, had anticipated the call and had paid the hotel's telephone operators to tip him off when it came. A few minutes later Lee got a call from Dorsey, inviting him to come to his room for breakfast. Lee thought this distinctly strange, but he accepted the invitation, and wondered all through the pleasant matinal chit-chat what it was all about. As they finished their coffee, Dorsey suddenly snarled, "That son-of-a-bitch Buddy Rich called you to send him his drums, didn't he? Well, you're not going to do it!"

But Buddy got his drums, and in due course he and Dorsey were reconciled.

Paul and Jo both got along with Dorsey. Paul said, "I only ever had one argument with him. It was someplace like Louisville, Kentucky. He was rehearsing one of my arrangements, and he did something that he hardly ever did. He started to make some changes. Axel and I weren't used to that. And Tommy was very good about this. I haven't thought about this for 30 years. He was making the changes, and I was throwing a pencil up in the air and catching it. And the brass, the evil ones, started to laugh. So Tommy knew something was going on behind him. All of a sudden he turned around and caught me and he fired me. So I was out of the band for about three hours. A lot of people got fired from that band for a few hours."

Jo said, "One night in Texas, half of the band got fired. Tommy was in one of his drinking phases. And he was pretty well smashed. And he had almost a concert arrangement on *Sleepy Lagoon*. There's a part where he has to go up to a real high note. And this note just splashed all over the stage. So he stopped the band."

"This was in front of an audience?" I asked.

"Sure. We were playing a dance. It was such a horrendous mistake. He said, 'Stop. Take it from letter C.' So he tried. And again, splash! all over the stage. He stopped the band about three times. On the fourth time it started getting to the players. And they start giggling. The whole saxophone section started. And then it's like the measles, it spreads. Tommy turned and he said, 'You're fired, and you're fired, and you're fired.' He fired about half the band. And they all got up and picked up their horns and left. I can still see it. Freddy Stulce walked by the Pipers and said to us, 'See you later.' We played the rest of the night with about half a band."

She laughed, and Paul joined her. They reminisce about the business without regret, finding the laughter in life.

Paul said, "Did you ever hear the story about Jimmy Dorsey starting over again on a tune? It was up in Milwaukee. And there was an early morning show, and Jimmy'd had a few the night before. One of his big numbers was *Flight of the Bumble Bee,* which is not too good at 10:30 in the morning with a hangover. So he starts. And it fell apart. So he said angrily, 'Take it from the top.' And he counts it off—probably a little faster, just to show them.

"And some guy in the audience yells, 'Why don't you play it right?'

"And Jimmy yells, 'Why don't you go and fuck yourself.'

"The theater manager came out and took Jimmy by the elbow and led him off."

He chuckled some more at memories of the Dorseys, then said, "When Jo came with Tommy, I was just leaving the band. Dinah Shore had asked me to be her arranger and musical director, and I also had a chance to do an album with Lee Wiley. I wanted to branch out. Tommy said, 'Okay,' but then he got thinking about it, and he thought, 'I'll bet he's goin' with Glenn Miller.' And he made a speech one night at rehearsal about it. But I wasn't going with Miller. I guess," he said, turning to Jo, "I wrote one arrangement that you guys sang."

"Yeah," Jo said. "It was a Mercer song. *I Thought About You.*"

Paul settled in Los Angeles in the summer of 1940 to write for Shore, the Bob Crosby band, and for movies. He worked at Paramount Pictures with Bing Crosby, Bob Hope, and Betty Hutton. It was at Paramount that he met Johnny Mercer, who made him Capitol's musical director.

He carried on this executive position, producing such things as the early King Cole Trio albums, while turning out an incredible amount of writing for Mercer, Stafford, Betty Hutton, Maggie Whiting, and, later, Gordon MacRae and Dean Martin. In 1943 he went to work on *The Johnny Mercer Music Shop* network radio show. He also began to record a series of instrumental albums, the first of which was *Music for Dreaming*.

In the late 1950s, when stereophonic records were first released to the public, those albums were re-recorded. They are remarkably good stereo, even today, and Weston's writing remains as fresh as it was at the time. The format was that of the dance band augmented with strings, with one exception, a charming album called *Carefree* in which he used four fluegelhorns, four trombones, and four French horns, no strings and no saxes. A dance band can drown a full string section. In recording, one has two options with such an instrumentation: you can crank up the strings electronically or you can tone down the brass and saxes to achieve a natural acoustical balance. Paul did the latter, and the writing had a soft classical purity, almost a Mozart quality. Sometimes he would use four clarinets in harmony, as the Dorsey band often did in its ballads, and the Isham Jones band before it. It is a sound that is often heard in concert bands, and it is a particularly warm one, now almost vanished from popular music.

The albums had a gentle and tender quality about them, the strings forming cushions for such fine jazz soloists as Babe Russin, Eddie Miller, Barney Kessel, and the late Don Fagerquist. And they perfectly embody Paul's temperament, which is sunny, sensible, warm, generous, fair, and very humorous.

Johnny Mercer had told Jo back in her Dorsey days, "Some day I'm going to have my own record company, and you're going to record for me." He was as good as his word. He signed her to the label within a year of its founding, and she began to record a string of hits, one of which came from a suggestion of Paul's:

"When Jo and Gordon MacRae were going to do some duets, I remembered that record of *Whispering Hope* that my father brought home. And they recorded it. We never found a disc jockey that played it, we never found anybody that bought it. And in the Bible belt it sold well over a million copies. And it's still selling."

When in 1950 Paul went from Capitol to Columbia, Jo went with him. Paul wrote the charts on an incredible five hundred or more of her recordings, not to mention sessions for Rosemary Clooney, Doris Day, and Frankie Laine. At Columbia, her hits included *You Belong to Me, Make Love to Me, Jambalaya,* and *Shrimp Boats,* which Paul wrote. Whatever the cause of their affinity, in 1952 Jo became a Catholic convert and they were married. They had known each other twelve years, ever since she and the Pipers pillaged his refrigerator, so they hardly married in haste.

At this point we have to consider two more biographies, those of that inextinguishable duo Jonathan and Darlene Edwards.

Musical jokes are probably as old as the art itself, and fictional musicians with which to make them have been around for a long time. Peter Schickele's P.D.Q. Bach is a particular favorite of musicians. So are Jonathan Edwards, the incomparably incompetent cocktail pianist who insists that what he plays is jazz, and his off-pitch but earnest wife Darlene.

The Edwardses came into being at a Columbia Records sales convention at Key West, Florida. Paul and Jo, along with George Avakian and the late Irving Townsend of Columbia's a&r staff, were having a late dinner in a restaurant where they had to endure one of those wrong-chord pianists who somehow find work for tin-eared restaurateurs and bar owners all over the planet. The pianist left for the night, and Paul, who gets more than usually funny after about two drinks, went to the piano and began to play *Stardust* in excruciating imitation of him. Avakian and Townsend fell out, as the old expression had it, and, laughing helplessly, insisted that an album should be made in that style. Avakian came up with the name Jonathan Edwards, after the famous preacher of the Colonial period, because, he said, it had a "properly ossified ring" to it.

On the way back to California, Paul had some second thoughts. He wasn't sure he could sustain the gag for an entire album. He pressed Jo into service as Darlene, Jonathan's wife. They went into the studio to make *The Original Piano Artistry of Jonathan Edwards*. The drummer on that first date was Jack Sperling. Paul had to fire him because he couldn't stop laughing. Every time they would try a take, Sperling would drop his drumsticks, collapse with face in his folded arms across his snare drum, and laugh until he cried.

The album was a best-seller shortly after its release in 1957, and the dreadful duo sustained their curious brand of artistry— bars with beats missing or added, wrong chords to befog the mind, incompleted and meandering runs and what Jo calls "crumbling thirds," and Darlene's eerily inaccurate intonation—through *Jonathan and Darlene Edwards in Paris, Songs for Sheiks and Flappers, Sing Along with Jonathan and Darlene Edwards,* and the comparatively recent *Darlene Remembers Duke, Jonathan Plays Fats.* (Ellington's *Don't Get Around Much Any More* starts on the third; Darlene starts it on the tonic and lets it fall from there.) Leaping into the contemporary market, they did a single on *Stayin' Alive* and *Copacabana.*

It is a dubious distinction to have a song in one of their albums, for Darlene has a bizarre taste in lyrics. You do not realize how dreadful the words to *You're Blasé* really are until you hear Darlene do them. ("You're deep, just like a chasm, you've no enthusiasm . . . ") The same is true of *Cocktails for Two* and, alas, Ellington's gorgeous *Sophisticated Lady,* which deserved better than "smoking, drinking, never thinking of tomorrow, nonchalant . . . " and "when nobody is nigh . . . "

The recordings have had some curious effects. Paul was playing golf with the head of a large corporation, who mentioned that on a trip to New York he had picked up an album called *Jonathan and Darlene Edwards in Paris.* He asked Paul if he'd heard it, and Paul, thinking this was a joke, allowed that he had. The man said, "He's pretty good, but I don't think she's all that hot." And Paul realized the man was not joking.

In 1961—after several years of doing television in America— the Westons moved for a summer to London, where they did a series of television shows for the ATV British network. The shows were seen throughout the British commonwealth, and their faces became as familiar in England as they were in America. One night they went to a small restaurant near their home in Hampstead. The cocktail pianist smiled as they entered and immediately went into an imitation of Jonathan Edwards, which Paul and Jo thought was a charming and amusing tribute. They smiled and nodded appreciatively to the pianist. The pianist went into his next tune, in the same style. When he used a chord that possibly not even Jonathan could have come up with, Paul realized the man actually played that way. Paul had a mouthful of red wine at the time. It got sprayed all over Jo's white dress.

The fans of Jonathan and Darlene, particularly within the music business, are legion. Leonard Feather said that Darlene was the only singer to get off the A train between A and B-Flat. When the first album came out, he gave it 48 stars in *Down Beat*.

One of the devotées of Jonathan and Darlene is George Shearing. If he knows Jo and Paul are in an audience, he will immediately play *Autumn in New York* in Jonathan's style, to the undoubted bemusement of members of the audience who are not in on the joke. Still another fan is actor Art Carney, who wrote Jonathan and Darlene a fan letter—in the personna of Ed Norton.

Once you get into the lunacy of Jonathan and Darlene with the Westons, they become curiously real. Paul and Jo talk about them as if they were, and you can see that Jo has a certain strange affection for Darlene. "She's a nice lady from Trenton, New Jersey, and she does her best," Jo said. *Los Angeles* magazine sent a writer to their home to interview Jonathan and Darlene, who supposedly live with the Westons, permanent sponges in their household. Paul and Jo slipped into the roles, and, as Jonathan and Darlene, complained about food and the fact that the Westons made them go into the bedroom when famous people came to the house.

Jo said, "It was crazy time. Because when he asked a question, the interviewer wasn't asking me, he was asking Darlene."

"Once we got into it," Paul said, "it was easy. Jonathan was saying that he played a much better stride piano than Fats, and Darlene came up with things off the top of her head. She said, 'Well, actually, a five-four bar gives you an extra stride.'"

Jonathan told the interviewer, "We do things that other people have thought of and foolishly abandoned."

"The thing about Jo," Paul said, "is her versatility. She accomplished more in more different directions than any singer I know. When you think that *Whispering Hope* was a religious seller in '46 or '47—one of the first religious songs that a pop singer had ever done.

"And then there's *Jo + Jazz*. She's not a jazz singer, but she did a good jazz album. She was the first pop singer to do American folk songs with an orchestra. And that was in 1946. She could do show songs, she could handle a rhythm song and a ballad and whatever. I sound like an agent or something. But I think people sometimes don't realize how wide her scope was, in all kinds of American music."

The one negative in her career was that some critics said her singing was cold.

"That used to be the party line," she said. "I never made it with the critics. I think what the critics didn't like was that it was simply singing. There wasn't much . . . "

"There was a disgusting normality about it," Paul said.

"Maybe. I don't know. I think maybe a lot of 'em resented that too. I'm basically a pretty dull person. I was never on smokin' anything or drinkin' anything."

"When you're struggling, they love you," Paul said.

"When *Little Man with a Candy Cigar* first came out," Jo said, "the critics couldn't say enough wonderful things, they were absolutely thrilled, it was marvelous. And so because of that, I thought that's the way it was going to be. But from then on, kids, forget it."

"Well, particularly when she got radio shows and hit records," Paul said. "Then it was: She's cold." Paul is always protective of her.

"They're suspicious of commercial success," I said. "It's an American conviction: if it's popular it can't be good; if it's good, it can't be popular. Which is odd, in view of the country's galloping commercialism. But then perhaps it's a reaction of critics against commercialism. We've all seen trash sells, but it does not follow that what sells is necessarily trash. The former is the premise of the record industry, the latter is the premise of critics."

Commerical success Jo surely had. Columbia gave her a diamond award when her sales reached 25,000,000 records—and that was *after* her period at Capitol. She was the favorite woman singer of Americans in the peak years of her career, according to the *Billboard* magazine charts. In 1972 a writer and researcher named Joel Whitburn published a book analyzing the success of various recording performers between 1940 and 1955. Whitburn assigned a point for each week a performer was listed in the *Billboard* chart. The results were: Bing Crosby 693, Perry Como 606, Eddie Fisher 386, Sammy Kaye 323, Jo Stafford 310, Patti Page 306, Vaughan Monroe 290, the Andrews Sisters 279, Nat Cole 274, and Glenn Miller 272. Jo's one-time band mate, Frank Sinatra, is conspicuous by his absence. He had only one Number 1 record during that period, according to *Billboard*—although I must say that I have always found the *Billboard* charts suspect.

Nonetheless, whether those charts are indeed an accurate reflection of popularity, there is no doubting that Jo's was enormous. In itself, it seems to have meant nothing to her. "And anyway," she said, "if I'd gone funny in any way, I had a family that would have brought me right back down to earth." (To this day she remains in close contact with her sisters.) Public performing simply was not attractive to her. She found far more satisfaction in the recording studio. Of all the compliments she ever received, she still remembers most vividly, and treasures, one from the late Conrad Gozzo, the great lead trumpet player whom Paul often booked for her dates. "Musicians don't usually go into the booth to listen to a take," she said. "But that day Gozzo came in, stood there listening, and at the end of the song, he pointed a finger at me, then turned and walked out. Without a word." She was always a heavy favorite of musicians. Lester Young said he wanted to have his own big band with Jo Stafford and Frank Sinatra as his singers.

Her two children were reaching the age of danger. Jo thought more and more about her responsibilities at home. In 1959, with a lucrative Las Vegas contract awaiting only her signature, she decided to give up public performing—Darlene, interestingly enough, did not—but she continued to record until the mid-1960s.

The California show business landscape is strewn with the wrecks of what have been called the Beverly Hills Brats, the sons and daughters of famous parents who have themselves attempted show business careers to embarrassing results. There are exceptions, but many of them have been burned out by drugs, drinking, or other indulgences, some of them obnoxious figures, others quite tragic.

When Amy Weston was in her adolescence, she and Jo had a confrontation in which Amy defended herself on the grounds that she wasn't a doper. Later, I remember, Jo said in astonishment at the new age dawning, "I'm supposed to be *grateful* that they're not drug addicts!" Yes. Our world had come a long way from "A peaceful sky, there are such things . . . "

But her judgment that her family mattered more than a career was obviously a right one in that Tim and Amy got through the adolescent years undamaged by the come-ons to destruction that were all around them. Now in their thirties, they are disciplined and intelligent and professional. Tim Weston is a respected guitarist and composer, Amy is an excellent singer divorced from saxophonist Bryan Cumming. And Jo, whenever she can arrange it, is the adoring babysitter of two grandchildren, one of them presented to her by Amy and the other by Tim.

Her passion is history, which she reads voraciously, particularly that of World War II. Her knowledge of it is almost awesome. This grew at least in part out of her symbolic association with the war and her awareness of how the young servicement felt about her. Once I was discussing the loss in heavy seas of Allied amphibious craft during the Normandy landings at Omaha and Utah beaches. She knew exactly how many were used at each beach, how they foundered, how many were lost, and how many got ashore. During a dinner-party discussion of an action off Mindanao some years ago, a retired navy officer contradicted her on a detail. Politely but firmly, Jo held to her point. The officer said, "Madame, I was *there!*" A few days later he dropped her a note to say he had consulted his logs. She had been right and he wrong.

Jo has given a lot of her time to charity. She is a past president of SHARE, an organization devoted to work with mentally handicapped children. Well after Jo had given up performing and, finally, even recording, Darlene continued to work. Her last public performance was given May 19, 1978, on the occasion of SHARE's 25th anniversary. She shared the spotlight with Jo's old band-mate, Frank Sinatra.

If I like to talk history with Jo, I always seem to end up talking politics with Paul. He may claim to have forgotten whatever he ever knew about economics, but if a new tax bill is proposed or there is a change in the prime interest rate, Paul's analyses of the implications are always instructive.

Paul is involved with the Crippled Children's Society of Los Angeles of which he was president for three years. His mornings are devoted to golf, which he plays at the Bel Air Country Club, sometimes with Les Brown.

The Westons are liberal Catholics, and in an age when presidential rhetoric brought out of the woodwork all the bumpersticker patriots, the gun people and assorted other crazies, they remained unintimidated liberal Democrats.

A few years ago, Paul set up Corinthian Records to get back the masters of Jo's albums and reissue them—along with those of Jonathan and Darlene. Time-Life Records has issued an album of twenty of Jo's best sides, including one of Darlene's. Jo, typically, said, "I don't understand that. How can anybody listen to twenty songs by *any* singer?" Twenty of Paul's orchestral tracks have been reissued on compact disc.

Fortune smiled on the Westons. But she has smiled on many other people in show business who have alchemically converted her bounty into failure or disaster or tragedy, and been demolished by the hubris, indeed the madness, that intense public acclaim so often induces. The Westons have handled it rationally and with grace.

Jo will never sing again. She is firm about that. She did it, she loved it, and it's over. Could she do it if she wanted to? Time takes a toll on voices, particularly those of women. The vocal cords calcify as people grow older which, in extreme age, produces a high cracked sound. But that doesn't happen to everybody, and Bing Crosby sang well in his seventies. Assuredly Jo could do it. One day in July 1986, when I was talking to her about some theoretical musical matter or another, she demonstrated a point. That clear voice went up and down a scale in perfect intonation, like a flute. It was a fragment, a brief bit of music flung into time, but it was so good that it startled me.

American accents derived originally from those of England—that of Brooklyn, for example, from that of East End London dock workers who were brought over to do the same jobs here—and then were modified by those of people from other places. In Frank Sinatra's highly characteristic enunciation, one hears the slightly dentalized t and d that one so often encounters in the speech of Italian Americans from New York City and the communities around it—though not, interestingly, in those from Boston or Providence, Rhode Island.

Scholars of dialect tell us that American accents flowed westward in swaths, those of the American Northwest being derived from those of the Northeast, those of the Southwest from the Southeast.

The roads around Gainesboro, Tennessee, slant south-south-west between the ridges of the Cumberland Plateau. Gainesboro is due east of Gallatin. It is surrounded by towns with flat-footed no-nonsense names likes Nameless, Commerce, Gentry, Prosper-ity, Rough Point, Difficult, and Defeated. ("How can anybody lis-ten to twenty songs by *any* singer?") Not too far to the east is Oak Ridge, home of the macabre American Museum of Atomic Energy, where man's bleak future was engineered. Gainesboro is at 36 degrees 20 minutes north latitude. Coalinga, California, where the roads run straight and square to each other on the flat land of the central valley, is at 36 degrees 8 minutes.

The *g* is disappearing from the gerund in the English lan-guage. Indeed, it *has* disappeared in many parts of England and the United States, even though we continue to write it in a word such as *going*, as we do the vanished *l* in *palm* and *salmon*, the lost gutteral in *drought* and *thought*. Jo drops the *g* in gerunds in her speech, though not, interestingly, in her singing. Nonetheless, she has a California-modified Tennessee accent. She almost sings "ah" for the personal pronoun I, and she pronounces "on" almost as "own." That is how strongly Tennessee persists in her speech, not to mention her character.

One of the two main streams of American music, the one that led to what we now call country-and-western, has roots that go back to Scottish, Irish, and English balladry. One of the elements in its singing style is a way of skidding up to a note from a major or minor third below.

There are two primary forms of vibrato. The first is a pitch vibrato. A finger on a violinist's left hand slides up and down on the fingerboard, a trombonist rapidly vibrates the slide, to pro-duce an oscillating. If the intonation is good, the "note" produced is the exact center of what is actually a rising and falling sound, and the ear accepts it as that tone. The second kind of vibrato is a volume vibrato. A note becomes louder and softer. Flute players use this kind of vibrato. It is produced by increasing and decreasing the force of the air pressure from the diaphragm.

In opera and most forms of American and European popular music, singers use a pitch vibrato. But many folk and some country-and-western singers have a volume vibrato. It is a variation of intensity.

Jo's Tennessee background shows not only in her accent but in her vibrato. Paul's right. She's not a jazz singer. She is what one can only describe as a highly educated folk singer working mostly in other idioms of American music. You hear her affinity for folk music when she sings *Tennessee Waltz*. She may make fun of the style in *Timtayshun*, but she sings it with ease and respect in *Tennessee Waltz*, sliding up thirds to her notes. But you really hear it when she does a folk song such as *He's Gone Away (Over Yandro)*, her reading of which is chillingly beautiful.

Her vibrato is puzzling. It seems to be compounded of both kinds—she says that it's quite unconscious on her part, something that just happens. You wouldn't think that such an acoustic phenomenon would be evasive of analysis, but it is. The engineer with whom she worked at Capitol used to remark on it because it never pushed the needle on the VU meter into the red. This is what probably caused some critics to call her cold, her perfect cool control, her failure to chew the scenery and make you aware of the effort.

And it is probably what caused the kids from Tennessee and Kentucky and Kansas and Missouri and Montana and Wyoming, and incidentally from Ontario and Saskatchewan and Alberta, to love her, this small-town girl singing those big-city songs. And the calm of her style, that was probably just what they needed—the sound of rationality in the madness and horror of Wake Island and Guadalcanal and Iwo Jima and the Casserine Pass and Anzio and Monte Cassino and then Remagen, where the Germans forgot to blow the bridge.

No wonder they made her their GI Jo.

Jo Stafford was the voice of home.

A Journey to Cologne

Part I

When I was a twenty-one-year-old neophyte newspaper reporter still in shock from sudden immersion in a world of homicides, suicides, highway deaths, fires, and politicians, I was sent to interview a singer. She was only four years older than I, but she had become famous when I was in high school. She was an original and powerful talent. She was also, which I did not realize then, extremely shy. In the solipsism of the young, I thought I alone suffered from this painful affliction. I had the further disadvantage of being in awe of her. And so we sat there in her room at the Brant Inn in a shared discomfort, paralyzed by reticence, groping our way through one of the classic stupid interviews.

The Brant Inn stood on the shore of the western end of Lake Ontario, just at the start of the Niagara Peninsula. Its interior was decorated to look like an ocean liner, to suggest, I suppose, journeys to far-away places and romantic encounters under other skies. I first went there to hear the Lionel Hampton band, probably in 1944, when British and American and Canadian bombers were finishing off Cologne, among other cities. But particularly Cologne, because it was a great rail center.

During the early years of World War II, the roads in the Niagara Peninsula were lined with hitch-hiking young airmen in the blue uniform common to Britain and Canada and all the Commonwealth countries, as well as men who had slipped out of the occupied lands to fight in the RAF. That uniform was a unifier: so many men from so many countries wearing it, together in the common cause. Under what was called the Commonwealth Air Training Plan, they were all sent to Canada for instruction, out of the range of the German bombers. My mother and father were always giving them rides and bringing them home for dinner. Our house in St. Catharines became a sort of hostel for them. I gave them what I could: I let them play my records.

A number of the young men who came to our home were from Lancashire, where my father was born, and although he had lost his accent, he could tell by theirs where they came from, sometimes within five or ten miles, and they received an especial welcome. So did the Americans. A flier's nation was identified by his shoulder patch—United Kingdom, Australia, New Zealand, France, Poland, Norway, Netherlands, Belgium. For the first two years of the war the United States remained legally neutral. Therefore the American volunteers in the Royal Canadian Air Force could not wear U.S. on their patches and so, in an odd little legal nicety, they were identified by home state. The patches read New York, California, New Mexico, Alabama, Montana. An inordinate number read Texas, and, needless to say, their wearers said they were in the Royal Texas Air Force. We loved them, because they had come to join us when we felt so alone and it seemed Britain might fall. Long after the war, when I was a foreign correspondent on military assignment in Europe, I met the RCAF base commander at Gros Tonquin in France. He had a thick Brooklyn accent. He was one of those boys.

One of the Englishmen who came to our home was named Tommy. He was a little older than the others, in his mid-thirties, as I recall. Because he was mature and stable, he had been assigned for training as a bomber pilot. After the war, when the burgeoning airlines were hiring former military fliers, they passed over fighter pilots, knowing they had been selected for recklessness. They wanted the bomber pilots, who had been chosen for

steady nerves and sound judgment. Before the war, Tommy had
been a golf pro in Hamburg. His wife had been killed in November 1940 in the bombing of Coventry. I never knew a man with
more conflicting desires. All he wanted to do was to kill Germans
to avenge her, and then, after the war, to go home to Hamburg
and his friends there and play golf. I visited Hamburg after the
war. It seemed you could stand on a pile of rubble and see the
whole city. I wonder if Tommy was one of those who flattened it.
And Cologne.

By 1944, of course, all those young fliers were gone: gone to
England, gone to strafe fleeing Germans in France, gone to
destroy those rail yards at Cologne.

Now the Brant Inn too is gone. Some faceless high-rise stands
in its place. I do not remember what I wrote about the singer.

In Geneva, Switzerland, in January of 1984, in the small and Spar-
tan apartment of the composer Francy Boland, I was telling him
how much I admired his writing. He too is, if not shy, at least very
reserved. I had recently been exposed to an enormous amount of
his work in the thirty-six albums of the Clarke-Boland Big Band,
only two of which were ever released in America. One of his compositions, *Sabbath Message,* a brooding and ominous work, truly
threatening, is a remarkable jazz composition, not just a melody
stated by the orchestra followed by some solos backed by section
figures and culminating in an out-chorus reprise of the tune. It is
writing in the tradition of Duke Ellington and Gil Evans. It is
architecture in sound, not orchestrated song, making dazzling use
of Roger Guerin, Benny Bailey, and Jimmy Deuchar in solos, and
a sax section that speaks as one voice, made up of individualists
Derek Humble, Carl Drevo, Ronnie Scott, Billy Mitchell, and
Sahib Shihab, the whole magnificent machine driven by Kenny
Clarke with that impossible alchemical combination of sensitivity
and demonic fire that was Klook's alone. There was never a drummer like him, and Francy Boland is one of the great composers in
jazz history. The band they led was one of the best of them all.
Some of its alumni insist it was *the* best, and Johnny Griffin, who

took Billy Mitchell's chair in 1965, has been known to get tears in his eyes remembering it. I had been listening to it for nearly a month in Italy, eleven years after its demise, feeling as if I had discovered the lost treasures of the Incas.

I didn't say all that of course. Or maybe I did. Apparently I said enough to make Francy Boland uncomfortable. The thought going on inside his forehead was in French but the slight scowl on its outside said in any language, "Who is this clown and what does he know about it?"

Francy is small by American averages. He has the firm neat build of the steady tennis player. If Disney were to make a film about jazz, I would want to see Francy played by a chipmunk: motionlessly alert, then moving suddenly, then stopping again to watch and listen, frozen in mid-step. He is like that, with a keen, mustached, bespectacled face. He moved. He drew a record from a shelf and played it. "This is some writing," he said in French. "Do you know what it is?"

Strings running in several rapid streams, straining but not breaking tonality, harshly pretty. "Prokofiev," I said. It was a reasoned guess. He took the record off. Prokofiev's *Romeo and Juliet.* He sat down and the conversation resumed. Compliment accepted. I have wondered since how things would have gone had I been wrong. Certainly in that moment I had no idea what friends and comfortable collaborators we would be in the months ahead, and how attuned my sense of the absurd and his would become. When, later, we were rehearsing in Germany, we became frustrated with a rattle-trap, gap-toothed hotel piano we were sentenced to use for sins committed in a previous life. At some point Gigi Campi, the producer, asked if the piano was all right. "That piano?" Francy said venomously in his Belgian accent, dismissing the instrument with a contemptuous Gallic flick of the wrist. *"Burn it!"*

"Why?" I said. "That won't help it."

One day a few weeks before that, while we were working on the charts for the album and having lunch at La Cave Valaisanne in Geneva, which is the world's most uninteresting famous city, and one of the prettiest, we were talking of that curious deadfish morality of the Swiss, who sold weapons to both sides during the war and would not hestitate to do so again, and also of the notable dearth of good-looking women among them—Francy says that if you see an attractive whore in Geneva, she's almost certainly French.

Francy Boland loves American music, American mystery novels, and American movies, especially horror movies. He is odd man out in liking military music, and he adores that of John Philip Sousa. He even arranged *High School Cadets* for the Clarke-Boland Big Band, usually referred to as the CBBB. He hates the kind of music that has grown up in the long shadow of Arnold Schoenberg and the cabal that imposes it on Europe and America, and above all Germany. He loves the work of Arthur Honneger, which he says is little performed now because of that influence. He played me a taped performance by a Belgian orchestra of a concerto he had written for clarinet, one of the several instruments he plays. "It's pure serial technique," he said.

"And pure bullshit," I said in English.

"And pure bullshit," he said, also in English, then in French: "I wrote it because they said I didn't know how."

He was born November 6, 1929, and received the Prix de Solfège et d'Harmonie from the Royal Conservatory of Music at Liege in 1950. He heard his first jazz concert in 1942, noting that there were German officers in the audience, although jazz was officially proscribed by Hitler as decadent Negro-Jewish music. He began to play semi-professionally in 1945. After the war he went to Paris. In 1951, he began writing arrangements for singers at Barclay Records. His very first chart, for some singer he has forgotten, was for a song with these lyrics:

La lune est grise, mon coeur aussi, which is, *The moon is gray, my heart as well.*

"Do you know what that is?" he said. "*How High the Moon* in French."

"But that's horrible," I said. "It's even worse than the lyric in English."

For a while Francy was the hot young arranger in Paris. (One of his friends was Nat Peck, the trombonist from Brooklyn who had joined the Glenn Miller Army Air Corps band in 1944 and stayed in Europe when the war was over.) Then Francy took sick. The disease was diagnosed as tuberculosis. He went home to Belgium to recover. When he returned to Paris, Michel Legrand's career was cresting, and Francy was relegated to a second tier.

Belgium has tended to produce better jazz musicians than France. Francy thinks the reason is its long association with the English language. Gigi Campi, who is an astute historical and social observer, says, "In my opinion, it's also because Belgium is a political compromise and hasn't any corny folk music tradition to overcome." Whatever the reason, the Belgian jazz players include Sadi (whose full name is Sadi Lallemand, which he refuses to use because Lallemand means "The German"), Toots Thielemans, and the late Bobby Jaspar and Jack Sels. As a pianist, Francy doesn't have that nervous, flaky, rushy French time. His playing is dark, pensive, and unfettered, and rhythmically it goes right down into the ground. Aside from his stature as a composer—in the older and larger sense in which it meant a man who made the orchestra his instrument, rather than a songwriter—Boland is one of the finest jazz players Europe has produced.

In 1958 he moved with his wife to New York, where his daughter Miriam was born. He worked in a Chet Baker quartet, found himself on a band bus traveling with a Birdland All-Stars group, seated behind Lester Young and Sarah Vaughan, an experience he recalls with a kind of awe. He did some writing for Count Basie. Mary Lou Williams took up his cause and recommended him to Benny Goodman, who also wanted Francy to write for him. But the American experience was not pleasant. Francy had fallen in with one of the jailhouse labels, as they are quaintly known in the trade, one of the companies owned by gangsters, the old-fashioned kind with guns, rather than their successors with Phi Beta Kappa keys and computers and p.r. men, and he was robbed a lot. And his marriage was under strain. He took his wife home to Europe. There is a picture of her on the wall in Francy's hall, taken in some happy moment of youth. Her name was Marie-Therese. She too was Belgian. She was very pretty. She's dead.

"You're writing *what?*"

That's the question I heard most often in the early days of the project. Artie Shaw, for one, asked it. And later on I heard, "Did you meet The Man?" Lyricist Hal Shaper wrote me from England, "Some of us can claim to have written songs with Harry Warren. But writing songs with the Pope? That's a real conversation stopper."

"Where did this thing start?" That was another of the questions.

Any given event is the consequence of countless previous events. You might say that this album began when a Wehrmacht truck nearly killed a young aspirant actor in Poland during the German occupation. Or you could say it traces back to October 20, 1914, when the congress of the Italian Socialist Party in Milan expelled from membership a former schoolteacher and anti-clerical tin-pot novelist named Benito (after Juarez) Mussolini. When he was rising to power in the early 1920s, financed by rich industrialists and landowners, his *squadre d'azione,* action squads, were striding the land in their black shirts. They took a particular interest in a certain Paolo Campi, a man of honor who had been one of those who expelled *Il duce,* the leader. He had been twice a member of the Italian parliament and was now the vice-mayor of Milan as well as mayor of the little town of Gallarate. Gallarate is a gem-like village, sleeping on a hill in the Italian lake country, from which on a clear day you can see the Alps shining with snow. The blackshirts invaded Mayor Campi's office. He told them to get out, saying he had been elected to his position and they had not. They smashed a typewriter into his face, then began to flog him. They poured castor oil down his throat, a favorite device. Then they dragged him naked into the pretty cobbled street, tied him to a cart, and wheeled him through the village for everyone to see, his body wracked by spasms and fouled with diarrhea. A member of the Carabinieri who had both guts and a gun put a stop to it.

He wrapped the mayor in his cape and took him home. The mayor's wife, Gennarina, a woman of great strength—you can see it in her photos—took him across the border into Switzerland and nursed him back to life. Physicians repaired nineteen separate wounds in his face. Then she took him to the Weimar Republic of Germany, first Berlin and then Cologne, where she founded a chain of ice-cream parlors that was to be very successful. In Cologne, on December 15, 1928, eleven months before the birth of Francy Boland, she had her third child, a boy she named Pierluigi, the common contraction of which is Gigi. Pierluigi Campi means Peter Louis Fields.

Gennarina Campi left Cologne in 1943 in the midst of one of the two hundred and sixty-two Allied bombing raids that left twenty thousand casualties, sent most of the rest of the population fleeing into the surrounding countryside, smashed the railway yards, and demolished 90 percent of the city, including ninety-one of its hundred and fifty churches. When the raids were over, the great cathedral, the largest example of High Gothic architecture in northern Europe, stood alone in the rubble, its twin spires black against the sky.

Gigi Campi still remembers that train trip to Italy. In a small satchel on her lap his mother carried sterling, diamonds, and jewelry, and a little bag of dictionaries. It had a double bottom filled with gold coins. On top of the satchel's contents she had put pads of cloth smeared with ketchup and limburger cheese. A Gestapo officer approached her while Gigi, only a boy, sat rigid with fear. The man demanded to know what was in the bag and made to put in his hand. With an affectation of outrage, she slapped it away, demanding that he show a little respect and letting him see and smell just enough to turn his stomach. The man shrugged and left them, and they crossed the border into Italy.

Warsaw was in ruins—the Stukas took care of that in 1939, as we can see in the motion pictures the Germans made with such pride. Without ammunition, food, water, or electricity, the city capitulated on September 7 of that year. The German occupiers harried the inhabitants for five years; they considered the Poles one of the inferior peoples. In Warsaw they imprisoned and tortured or shot in summary street executions some one hundred thousand of them. They carried nearly half a million Warsaw Jews off to extermination camps. In their campaign to wipe out the Polish culture, they destroyed monuments and closed theaters, libraries, and scientific institutions. And then one of their trucks partially crushed a young actor and playwright, nearly killing him, and unleashing events whose consequences we do not yet know. Recovering from his injuries, the young man began thinking in a new way about his life, and he turned from his dreams as a playwright and actor to become a priest. He continued, however, to write his poems: musings on the human spirit, observations on the condition of man. These poems were published in the postwar years in various Catholic journals under a pseudonym, presumably because they spoke for humanity and against war. By now Poland, which in its long history has enjoyed one short happy time—the years between the two world wars—had a new tormentor, or rather an old tormentor returned, the Russians. Outside a small circle there was little interest in the poems until their author, Karol Wojtyla, took a new name, John Paul II.

Signora Campi returned to Cologne, or what was left of it, after the war. Her husband died in Italy in 1948.

Growing up among the Germans, surrounded by their conformity, their ineradicable conviction of their superiority, their unquestioning dedication to *Ordnung*—order—and their proclivity for spying on each other, her son Gigi was hurt, which at times he will even admit. Afraid of being called a dirty little Italian, he became addictively fastidious, the kind of person who cannot bear it if your spoon is not aligned on your saucer just so, and will not hesitate to tell you. He draws plans on paper, makes endless notes in a neat architect's hand, sets up diagrams, tries to impose *Ordnung* on the arts, uneasy with the artist's ability to make order in the mind at a cost of circumferential chaos. He walks with a very straight back and issues metaphysical pronouncements such as "Jazz is dead!" That is all very German. The other side of the man is Italian. Or maybe it is another man entirely inside him—warm, funny, generous, loyal, solicitous, perceptive, appreciative, sensitive, and lonely. And in the wink of an eye he can turn back into the German: cold, superior, critical, and unceasingly seeking to get something on everyone, in order to establish control. It is the most puzzling phenomenon you have ever encountered. He says *I hate* more than any man I ever met. A partial list of his hatreds includes perfume of all kinds, underscores in movies, psychology both Freudian and otherwise, underfried potatoes, cats, and French critics. He is an impresario whose word is as good as a contract, a music publisher with a reputation for not stealing, and an insomniac with limitless energy and an inflexible will to carry through what he begins. He is somewhat taller than Francy Boland, with a well-cut refined face and gray hair to which he pays considerable attention and wears in a kind of bouffant cut. Gigi Campi conceived, founded, financed, managed, and recorded the Clarke-Boland Big Band. It happened this way:

For thirty-two years, from 1948 to 1980, he operated the Cafe Campi in the rebuilt downtown Cologne, only a few hundred yards from the cathedral. It became one of Germany's cultural centers, a gathering place for artists, designers, novelists, and musicians, including Karlheinz Stockhausen and Kurt Edelhagen. One evening in the cafe, Edelhagen talked of the difficulty of organizing and rehearsing a jazz band in Europe. He said it took a lot of time. Gigi, the Italian side of whose character includes a love of argument, said he could put together one of the finest bands in the world in Europe, and do it within a month. On a bet he set out to do so, planning the band around Francy Boland, who at the time was writing for Edelhagen, and Kenny Clarke.

Two weeks later the CBBB, a remarkable orchestra composed half of European musicians and half of American expatriates, was in the studio, recording its first album.

Artists born west of the Atlantic have been going "home" to Europe ever since the two American continents were colonized, a rite of passage Gershwin celebrated in *An American in Paris*. In the

1920s, there was a mass transplantation of American writers to Paris. For nearly three generations, it was virtually *de rigueur* for American composers to conclude their training in studies with Nadia Boulanger at Fontainebleau. Whether painters, writers, instrumentalists, composers, or even fashion designers, they have gone to find the headwaters of their work, with one exception: jazz. The jazz musician brought to Europe something new, a form that was not invented there.

The Europeans have always been especially susceptible to it, and partly for this reason, Sidney Bechet lived much of his adult life in France. Before World War II, Coleman Hawkins spent long periods of time there, becoming the father, according to Francy Boland, of a school of very good European tenor players. From June 4 to September 5, 1937, Benny Carter led an eleven-piece orchestra at the Kurhaus Hotel in Scheveningen, Holland, made up of white musicians from Britain and Holland and black musicians from the United States and the West Indies. "Benny never gets credit for that," Leonard Feather said. Leonard recorded the band, with Coleman Hawkins as guest soloist on some sides, at The Hague in August of that year. "It was the first racially mixed orchestra," he says.

Bill Coleman lived in Paris, where Bud Powell spent the last years of his life. Don Byas and Ben Webster ended their days in Holland. Johnny Griffin has lived in Europe, at first in Holland and later France, since the 1960s. In Denmark there is a tight little colony of American jazz musicians, including Edmund Thigpen, Richard Boone, Ernie Wilkins, Kenny Drew, and Sahib Shihab. Benny Bailey lives in Munich, bassist Jimmy Woode in Zurich, Art Farmer in Vienna. The late Kenny Clarke lived at Montreuil-sur-Bois, near Paris. Obviously a lack of racial pressure is one of the reasons many musicians have chosen to live in Europe. "But there are as many reasons for living over here as there are musicians doing it," Ed Thigpen said. "Race is only one of them." And to those Europeans who announce their liberalism to black American artists by decrying American bigotry, Thigpen has been known to say, "We wouldn't have any bigots if you hadn't sent them to us."

Not all the American musicians living there are black. Al Porcino lives in Munich, Red Mitchell in Stockholm, Sal Nistico in Bonn.

The dispersion effect of jazz has been enormous, around the planet, and there are innumerable splendid jazz players of all nationalities, many of whom say their introduction to the music came through Willis Conover's *Voice of America* broadcasts. Jazz has become a world music. One of the best of these overseas players was the Swede Ake Persson, whom Duke Ellington would, whenever possible, take along on his European tours. In the years after the war, only the Swedes, such as Bengt Hallberg and Lars Gullin, seemed at ease in the harmonic and rhythmic vocabulary of bebop. There was a reason. All of continental Europe, including Norway and Denmark, had been under German occupation and unable to get the new American records. Josef Skvorecky's haunting novels and short stories document the persecution of jazz in Czechoslovakia. But it was nowhere more bitter than in Germany itself. Those Germans who loved jazz—and there were a lot of them, as there was an extensive anti-Nazi German underground—had to keep their prewar records hidden, and they could obtain no new ones. But the Swedish musicians, including Persson, who was born at Hassleholm, February 25, 1932, were cognizant of musical developments in America. The English had an edge, too: they had Robert Farnon (moonlighting charts for the Ted Heath band) and Glenn Miller in their midst even as the war raged. One of the finest English musicians to come up during this time was the alto saxophonist Derek Humble.

Clarke, Boland, and Campi drew on this large pool of players, both the best of the Europeans and the best of the Americans living there, to build their band. They made Benny Bailey the lead trumpet player. "I didn't know I could play lead," Benny told me in Düsseldorf, when we recorded. "They thought I could. That band brought things out of me that I didn't know I had. Out of all of us. It was greater than the sum of its parts, and all of us played above our level." He shook his head ruefully. Too little known to Americans because of his long sojourn in Europe, Benny

Bailey is one of the most magnificent of jazz trumpet soloists, and he proved to be one of the great lead players as well. He still is.

Humble and Persson played lead alto and lead trombone respectively. These three gave peculiar and highly personal edges to their sections, which is part of the explanation of the band's personality and power. Humble and Persson are both dead, Humble by an ironic mischance, Persson a particularly macabre suicide.

"What happened?" I asked Shihab, who loved him.

Shihab took on a cold and brusque manner that he assumes to hide hurt and anger, flicking icy glances at me through his glasses. He is almost tall, a light-brown-skinned man with a splash of freckles on his long face and a small beard. There is something noble about him.

"Cat tried it three times. Third time he made it."

For eight or ten weeks each year for ten years after that evening in the Cafe Campi, the band would come together, as in the gathering of some clan, to record and travel, playing festivals all over Europe, tearing up London audiences that jammed Ronnie Scott's Club, while Scott played tenor in the sax section. It wrote a chapter in jazz history that went largely unnoticed in the United States. Of its thirty-six albums—including one with Stan Getz as guest soloist, another with Carmen McRae—only two came out in the American market, one on Atlantic and one on Columbia. John S. Wilson accurately took the measure of the band, giving it a rave in *High Fidelity*. The recording engineer was always Wolfgang Hirschmann, and two decades after the first albums were made, the sound is outstanding. There is no barrier, you can hear every detail in the voicings, as if peering through clear water to a pebbled bottom. The albums were released in Europe mostly on Hans-Georg Brunner-Schwer's MPS label, which was never able to get good distribution in the United States. And so most American jazz fans, including the most ardent devotees of big bands, know almost nothing of the CBBB.

Ever since the big-band era ended, musicians have been gathering voluntarily into this orchestral form for the sheer joy of making an exuberant roar. But the great mature players cannot afford to work for road-band money. The traditional compromise has been the "rehearsal band" made up of players who feed their families through more commercial work. And those who work in the studios—and, even more so, those who have turned their backs on it—complain that it takes the edge off their playing. The Clarke-Boland band was made up for the most part of men who played jazz full time for a living. The band had two drummers, Kenny Clarke and Kenny Clare, the English drummer with the look-alike name. They functioned in such rapport that you didn't seem to be hearing two drummers but one very large and very propulsive drummer. Kenny Clare died within two weeks of Kenny Clarke, as if their destinies were locked together.

Klook was the wonder. You listen to what he did with cymbals and slip into amazement when the colors change as in a light show, before your very ears. He plays yellow and then the sound turns to red or blue or some other color and you cannot tell exactly when it happens. And the center is always *there.*

The band had the fire of youth and the emotional depth of maturity, both in its solo and ensemble work. Above all it had *esprit.* And those who were part of it cannot forget the experience. It haunts them, as war haunts men afterwards. They talk about it, laughing at memories. They remember a jazz festival in Sicily when they had to follow the Ellington band late at night, when the audience was already sated. They claim they blew the Ellington band away, while the audience cheered and Duke's men, most of them friends of theirs, listened in amazement.

They remember a tour of England with other groups. The bus was inadequately heated. Blankets were issued. When they got on the bus after one concert, they found Philly Joe Jones, traveling with another group, already settled in a seat near the front, sunk low, wrapped in his blanket, his hat down over his face. Idrees Sulieman, a sensitive soul, was one of the last to come aboard. He couldn't find his blanket. He thought—wrongly, as it turned out;

it was down somewhere in the darkness—that it had been stolen. He grabbed the ignition keys to the bus and said that it would not leave until his blanket was returned. He continued like this for a time, hurt as much as angry, saying finally, "We are supposed to be like brothers in this band! Cats! There is a coward on this bus!"

And from under the hat of Philly Joe Jones, a voice rumbled: "But a warm one."

But a warm one. They will smile and shake their heads after telling the story again.

What happened to that band?

Some of those who were involved say that Gigi withdrew his support after some of the French and German critics said the band was old hat. This is credible, in view of his constant statement that "Jazz is dead!" But he denies it. If it is so, it is a tragedy. Some of the world's most misguided jazz criticism comes from France. I remember once being in Paris with Bill Evans. In the intermission of his concert, a fledgling French jazz critic introduced himself to me and then said of Bill, "You know, *we*"—sometimes the English too will speak to you that way, and certainly the Germans; it is all in the way they say *we* "—we consider him passé."

"It may come as a great shock to you," I said, "but *we* don't care what you think."

Gigi Campi denies that the critics had anything to do with the disbandment. He says the burden of the band became too great. And that is also credible. He had sunk huge sums of money into it which he had never fully recovered, he says. The tapes of the albums sit on shelves in the basement of his large home on the side of a lake no more than a ten-minute drive from the village where the blackshirts almost killed his father. The charts are there, too, along with photos of the musicians, clowning, laughing, working.

"What finally finished the band is this," Gigi said. "In 1970 Willard Alexander wrote to me that a very well-known club in Las Vegas was excited to have the CBBB play there. Willard wanted to discuss a possibility of building around the Vegas engagement a college tour plus one appearance at Carnegie Hall.

"According to American law, engagement contracts have to be signed by the leader of a band, which had not happened to Francy and Klook in Europe, because I was signing the contracts for them.

"Francy and Klook and I had a meeting in Paris. They were afraid of the risks of a U.S. tour with their signatures on contracts holding them responsible for the whole financial operation, even though they knew they would have the backing of Hans-Georg Brunner-Schwer and myself, guaranteeing to cover all hotel and transportation costs.

"I was so discouraged by their uncertainty that I gave up. That was the end of the Clarke-Boland Big Band."

Whatever the story, the band could not be reconstituted now. Klook is gone. Even in the last months before he died, he seemed tired when I talked to him. He was seventy-one and had never fully recovered his energy after an earlier heart attack. He is buried in France.

Derek Humble was a heroin addict. Gigi once asked Klook, "How much does he use?" Klook said, "He uses in one day what I used to use in a week." Humble was also epileptic. According to Gigi, he had a seizure in an English pub and collapsed. The medication that could have saved his life was in his pocket, but no one there knew what was wrong with him, and he died.

No one seems to know with certainty why Ake Persson did what he did, and Shihab doesn't even want to talk about it. The Clarke-Boland Big Band was dismantled in 1973. A few months later, on May 24, 1974, Duke Ellington died. Persson considered his experience with these two bands the peaks of his whole career, and now it would never be again. The suicide rate in Sweden is high. A certain amount of American propaganda has intimated that this is an insidious consequence of socialism, but the fact is that the Swedes have had a high suicide rate for centuries. Many Swedes believe it is due to the long cruel winter in the deepest part of which there is almost no daylight.

On February 3, 1975, Persson telephoned Gigi in Italy from Stockholm. He said, "Get me out of this country!" Gigi told him to get on a plane and come to Italy. On February 4, three weeks short of his forty-third birthday, Persson got out of his car in downtown Stockholm, set his trombone in its case against an iron rail fence, hung his briefcase on one of the spikes, got back into the car, put it into gear, gathered speed, and drove out onto the ice of the harbor. That is a salt-water harbor, and even in winter the ice cannot be all that strong. It gave way and the car started to sink. Ake Persson apparently realized at the last moment what he had done and changed his mind. A policeman who saw it all said he could hear him screaming as the car went beneath the dark winter waters.

Campi produced three more albums with the band, but without Clarke, who was ill at the time. Boland's writing is wonderful, as always, but the spirit is not the same. Persson's replacement in the band, ironically, was Frank Rololino, who would also commit suicide.

When Karol Wojtyla became the first non-Italian pope in four centuries, his writings, including a play and his poems, were given in perpetuity to the Libreria Editrice Vaticana, the Vatican publishing office. Now that their authorship was known, they were translated into ninety languages.

Mario DiNardo, a Roman film producer who has friends in the Libreria Editrice Vaticana, became aware of the poems and asked his friend Gigi Campi if he thought any of them could be set to music. After examining them in their Italian translations, Campi perceived the difficulty of doing so. But he promised to try to find a composer who might solve some of the inherent problems, the biggest being that the poems are in free verse.

The line between prose and poetry has grown faint in the twentieth century, with meter replaced by vague rhythms, if any at all. What modern poetry really is is an allusive euphonious prose cut into short lines according to impulses best known to the author. Any meandering jottings can now be referred to as "poetry," and some university teachers of "creative writing" actually forbid students from using regular meter or rhyme, destroying the discipline of the craft at the root. In the past poets wrote sonnets the way musicians practice scales—as a strict exercise through which to attain mastery.

Because it has recurring structural patterns, traditional metrical poetry is easier to set to music than "modern" poetry, which is free-form and lacking firm meters. Indeed the problems attendant to setting the latter to music become moutainous. Six composers to whom Campi showed the poems of Karol Wojtyla finally concluded they were insuperable.

Tito Fontana is an Italian composer, pianist, and businessman to whom Campi mentioned the matter. Fontana is a tall man whose once-fair hair is turning white, a man of bearing. He is married to Lea Pericoli, a strikingly beautiful woman who once represented Italy at Wimbledon and is now a television sportscaster and fashion commentator. Fontana has a love of poetry, having tried his hand at it himself. He asked Campi if he might try to solve the problem. Campi said he was welcome to.

Fontana collaborated in the task with another composer, Sante Palumbo. Tito wrote some of the melodies, Sante wrote others, and they worked jointly on still others. And they succeeded where everyone else had failed, making a quite elaborate demo with rhythm section and synthesizers and the Milan studio singer Paola Orlandi. The demo finally was released in Italy as an album under the title *Concierto per la Pace,* concert or concerto for peace. It is quite lovely, and moving.

The impossible having been accomplished once, Campi decided to try for twice: he wanted to have the songs translated into English in an effort to reach a world market. He and I were introduced through Sahib Shihab, and on a visit to Los Angeles, Campi asked if I thought the Fontana-Palumbo-Wojtyla songs could be adapted into English. After he returned to Milan, I studied them and concluded the problems were insoluble. I found the music lovely—strange, wandering like a stream through a meadow as it followed the course of the words, difficult to sing, with tempo changes and constant modulation, drawing on all sorts of musical styles and sources, from bebop to European circus waltzes. It was hard to memorize and impossible to forget. But how could one possibly fit the English language to melodies determined by the Italian translations of poems written in Polish, without doing violence to the meanings of the originals? And I could not take liberties with them, as I would with a Jobim or Aznavour song, in view of their authorship and the political, not to mention religious, sensitivity of the material. I told Gigi Campi it couldn't be done.

I did not foresee his persistence. In the weeks that followed, he would telephone from Italy, charming, humorous, and gracious. I studied the texts in Spanish, Portuguese, and English, as well as Italian, which I found I was learning by osmosis, to see if other translators had introduced enough variant factors to suggest that I might take at least some liberties. And I did find some discrepancies. I told Gigi I would like to look at the Polish originals. He telephoned the Libreria Editrice Vaticana, and the next day I had them.

But I couldn't read them. I called Lalo Schifrin, who shares my interest in languages. He too said, "You're writing *what?*" I explained the problem and said, "Who do we know who speaks Polish?"

"Bronislau Kaper," he said.

But of course. Kaper was Polish. I called him, and he said, "You're writing *what?*" And I explained the problem again. Bronnie said he would be glad to help. We set a time and I went to his elegant home in Beverly Hills. I was unaware that he had cancer; Lalo said later that he didn't want his friends to know.

Bronislau Kaper was one of the finest of film composers. His scores include *San Francisco, Gaslight, The Swan, Butterfield 8, Mutiny on the Bounty,* and *Lord Jim.* One of the songs from one of his films that achieved an identity of its own is *All God's Chillun Got Rhythm. On Green Dolphin Street* and *Invitation,* from the scores of two of his films, became standards with jazz musicians, and one of them, *Hi Lili Hi Lo* was a favorite of Bill Evans. Kaper was born

February 5, 1902, in Warsaw, and educated at the University of Warsaw and the Warsaw Conservatory. He came to the United States in the 1930s, when the storm troopers were beginning their work. He already had a reputation in Europe as a film composer.

He was a karate practitioner who at eighty-one looked sixty-five or less. Bronnie Kaper was a wonderfully dear man, slight, wiry, and good-looking, with an urbane wit unexcelled by anyone in the film industry except maybe Hugo Friedhofer. He always made you laugh. He made you feel glad you were alive. And he made you feel you were his equal.

And so I arrived at his house with the Polish texts. We sat down and he began to explain them to me. He would grope for a phrase, then express an idea the best way he could. I would reshape it into more idiomatic English. He said, "You do a very good job of translating my English into English."

That afternoon we made new verbatim translations of the poems that Tito Fontana and Sante Palumbo had set to music. I thanked him as I left. As he shook my hand he said, "You know, this has given me such a spiritual feeling that I may run for pope myself."

"Now now, Bronnie," I said laughing, "you know a Jew can't be pope."

"Don't count on it," he said. "I'm not dead yet."

Six weeks later he was.

Despite having unadorned verbatim translations, I still saw the difficulties as insurmountable, and wrote Gigi that I could not hope to complete the project unless two requirements were met: I must have Vatican permission to take subtle liberties with the texts; and I must have the permission of Tito Fontana and Sante Palumbo to take similar small but important liberties with their music. Finally, I suggested, it would be best if I wrote the lyrics in Italy, where I could consult with Fontana and Palumbo.

I anticipated that if the composers did not balk, the Vatican would. A few weeks later I was on a plane to Milan.

Part II

I hadn't been in Europe in fifteen years when I walked into the terminal building at Linate Airport outside Milan that January afternoon. The first things I noticed were the machine guns and the dogs. Neat little machine guns. Combat analyses from World War II showed that most killing is done in distances of less than twenty-five feet. Short-barrel weapons are less accurate than long but given the intimacy of modern killing, accuracy doesn't count for much. And so the new small machine guns, or SMGs, as opposed to LMGs, the large machine guns such as the M-16 that was used in Viet Nam, are neat, small, and imprecisely efficient when they squirt bullets with incredible rapidity around airports and other public places in these days after Lod and the Munich Olympics and the murder of Aldo Morro. They were Uzis, weapon of choice of the U.S. Secret Service. You don't aim them, you just vaguely point and swing them, and if you take out a few women and infants along with the bad guy, well, those are the breaks. And so I was struck by the machine guns and the German shepherds on leashes whose assignment is to sniff out dope. I was very glad to see Gigi Campi waving and smiling in a crowd beyond the customs and immigration desks.

They train the dogs, he told me in the car as we swung out of the airport parking lot, by turning them on. The dogs get to dig it and so go about their sniffing altogether eagerly. Sometimes, he said, you'll see a dog and its handler wandering among the valises, glassy-eyed and both of them stoned. He made me laugh.

With what for Gigi Campi amounts to admirable restraint, he waited at least twenty minutes before asking me if I had written any of the lyrics yet. The answer was no. And within me, I still was wondering if the task could be accomplished at all. And I felt strange here, going north on this freeway, then leaving it to pass through Lombardy villages. And I thought of the long Austrian occupation of this part of Italy as we passed road signs in a language whose rules of pronunciation I did not even know. I am at ease and at home in France, but I felt strange here, and dependent on Gigi. Maybe I shouldn't have come.

Gigi's home is just outside Cazzago-Brabbia, an exquisite village whose people by common assent have kept the accoutrements of the twentieth century out of its streets.

Gigi is an architect by training, though he gave up the practice long ago, repelled by the rush to a sterile and humorless T-square-and-triangle aesthetic that makes hospitals and hotels, offices and apartment buildings all look alike, and Sao Paulo like Manhattan like Milan—the legacy of le Corbusier, Mies van der Rohe and the Bauhaus.

The last building Gigi designed was this house on a country lane, at which we now arrived. It is guarded by a high wall of river stones, beautifully set in place by hand, and by a black wooden gate which rolled quietly aside when he pushed a button in a hand control in the car, admitting us to a lakeside estate that covers ten or fifteen acres. The house is striking, wide and low, an interesting amalgam of Japanese and Italian styles, engirdled by a wide railed porch paved with gray granite. There is a swimming pool in the basement, which is next to an office on whose shelves rest the tapes of all those unobtainable albums by the Clarke-Boland Big Band, and photos of the band and the dead Ake Persson and Derek Humble. I did not yet understand how deeply those who participated in it mourned the passing of that band.

I wrote the first of the lyrics that weekend at that house. Gigi, so impatient on the one hand for me to write them, would on the other hand interrupt the painful solitary reflection that is the only way I know to get lyrics written, to regale me with his hospitality, take me out to restaurants—and the cuisine of that area is in a class with that of France—or play CBBB records at blistering volume. It was a strange weekend, and I was coming down with the flu. But I managed to escape from time to time, to walk down over a frozen meadow to the ice that rimmed the lake, and look across to the mountains called the pre-Alps, occasionally faintly visible through the spectral winter mists. Or I would hide in the room he had assigned to me, lie on the bed, stare at the ceiling, affecting a forbidding aloofness not because I felt it but because I needed solitude to try to solve the problem of the first song. I no longer needed the tape—I could hear Tito Fontana's music in my head—but I listened to it again and again.

The floor plan of that house is completely open. It is designed for entertaining but not for living. It is not made to be alone in. It is beautiful, all done in stone, but it lacks privacy and it contains not one decent light by which to read. And since Gigi designed it, made it what he wanted it to be, it tells us a great deal about him, about his restlessness, his incapacity for repose, and his abject terror of solitude. The only thing you can do in that house is talk, and if you had no one to talk to, it would be desolate. "It is full of ghosts," he said before the weekend was out. "Derek and Ake and my wife." She had died suddenly, in Florence, in a hotel room, while she was on business there, of a heart attack, only two years before. And a year from now, Kenny Clarke would join the ghosts in Gigi's house, and less than two weeks after Klook, Kenny Clare. "A few more deaths and jazz will be finished for me," Gigi said that weekend. But he doesn't listen to the new people, has never even heard of the brilliant young players who have come up in America. In his loyalty to his friends, which is fanatic, he tries to hold onto faces and events in a past that is unceasingly being formed from the impalpable present as one by one those we know fall away behind us, like people waving farewell from a railway station while we look back from a train that is gathering speed. I don't like it either, but it is the way of the world.

And I was there to write. From the penciled notes I had made with Bronislau Kaper, I began to construct the first lyric from the poem called in Italian *Maddelena*. In French that is *La Madeleine*, and I thought of the great Roman-style church in Paris named for her—Mary of Magdala, who adored Jesus. Pope John Paul's poem seemed to me to have a melancholy sensuality. And I thought of another army of occupation, long ago in Palestine, the Roman, one of whose favorite methods of execution was crucifixion, particularly cruel because it takes the subject days to die, which explains why when the "honorable counselor" Joseph of Arimathaea "went in boldly unto Pilate, and craved the body of Jesus. And Pilate," who never wanted him executed in the first place and who knew perfectly well how long it took to die on a cross, "marveled if he were already dead," and sent for the centurion, who said the man was indeed dead.

Tradition sees Mary of Magdala as a courtesan who was lifted from a tawdry life by Jesus. There is a heretical legend that the wedding in Cana was her marriage to the man who had saved her (the gospel fails to tell who got married). That would freeze the blood of any Protestant fundamentalist, not to mention undoubting Catholics, but would not seem unreasonable to Hugh Schoenbaum, who wrote *The Passover Plot,* or D. H. Lawrence, who wrote *The Man Who Died,* both of which hypothesize that the body was removed from the cross alive. There is another theory, elaborately explored in *The Sacred Mushroom and the Cross,* that Jesus never even existed but was a symbol in a drug cult. The anger of St. Stephen, which blazes across the centuries, refutes it. No fiction writer could have or did invent that man.

Joseph of Arimathaea took the body to a tomb and rolled a great stone to its access. "And when the Sabbath was past, Mary Magdelene, and Mary the mother of James, and Salome, had brought sweet spices, that they might come and anoint him. And very early in the morning the first day of the week, they came unto the sepulchre at the rising of the sun." John says that "Mary stood without at the sepulchre weeping" after finding the body gone. It was from this that I took the cue. And gradually the poem of Karol Wojtyla took form in English, and I wrote it out on music paper, notating the slight rhythmic changes I was making in Tito's melody so that I wouldn't forget them. The lyric seems to portray an emotionally devastated woman who has just begun to glimpse the full historical significance of the man she has lost, as she stands before the empty tomb. And the line "and my lips without makeup" I took to mean: because of him, I'm no longer a whore. As I listened to Tito's music in my mind and put the words on paper, I found myself constantly on the verge of tears.

The spirit was here,
then all at once it vanished,
and I am alone in this old place.

And so I am filled with a sadness
that will endure
while I live in this body.

And in the spirit
it will find its nurture,
where there was nothing but hunger.

The sorrow of love
will continue,
through the weeks, months,
and years

and like the roots
of a dry tree in summer
are my tongue and my palate,
and my lips without makeup.

The truth
takes such a very long time
to erase all the error.

And always,
the drought of the world
is felt not by me,
but by him.

    The liberties I took were delicate. In Polish, the line reads "like the roots of a dry tree." In Italian, dry tree is "albero secco," which contains five syllables as did, therefore, Tito's music. The music at that point is lovely and had to be preserved. So I added a little, writing "dry tree in summer," which contains five syllables and matches "albero secco" and thus the melodic line but does not violate the meaning.

    Gigi seemed ecstatic when I showed him the lyric, and I took a breather, and again we listened to the Clarke-Boland Big Band, with Gigi constantly grabbing my shoulder or my arm to be sure I didn't miss this passage or that. He moved. He stomped. He

laughed to the music. He conducted the orchestra. He sang coun-
termelodies. Obviously he knew every line of every chart that band
ever recorded. He sang top parts, he sang inner parts, and he sang
them in tune and in time. Amazing.

"I haven't listened to these records in a long time," he said.
And I realized how much he wanted me to love what he and
Boland and Klook had created. He was succeeding.

One of the most impressive players in that band was Sahib
Shihab, whose work on baritone I knew and liked. I had heard him
too on alto with Thelonious Monk. I remembered him from his
days with the Quincy Jones big band as a decent and sensitive man.
He had been living in Copenhagen for many years now, and we
had corresponded quite a bit. But now I was really hearing him.
What a superb baritone player! On alto, his playing—at least in
the early days—had a filial resemblance to that of Charlie Parker
and a fraternal relationship to that of Phil Woods. But on baritone, he had a sound somehow like an alloy of that of Gerry Mulligan and Pepper Adams or Cecil Payne, which suggested to me
therefore a lineage from both Lester Young and Coleman Hawkins. Comparisons in jazz can be and too often are extended into
absurdity, and Shihab was, I could hear, very much his own man.
The baritone, as Mulligan says, "is a hard horn to fill," and Shihab
fills it full, playing with immense power and imagination. It is not
enough to say that Shihab is one of the finest of baritone soloists,
because (as he would say to me later in Switzerland) there have
been few of them. Sahib Shihab is one of the finest of all saxo-
phonists, not to mention flutists, a wonderful player whose controlled inner anger occasionally is released in great hilarious honks
and unexpected roars. There have been few jazz musicians as
under-recognized as Sahib Shihab.

The touch of the flu with which I had left California grew worse
that weekend, and by Monday, when we drove to Milan, I felt, as
others who had suffered it that year had described it, as if I were
going to die. Normally I would have been fascinated by Milan,
lying there in the blue winter mists, but that morning I was too

sick to care about anything, and Gigi—the stranger on whose mercy I was at this moment so dependent—became seriously worried, as he told me later, and he decided to find a hospital. We searched the suburbs of the city and at last saw a sign saying *Ospidale*. I felt as helpless as a child as Gigi spoke in Italian to a nurse at a desk. Surprisingly quickly I was shown to an examining room where a handsome avuncular doctor with white hair asked me questions through Gigi, sent me for a chest X-ray, examined it, said that I did not have pneumonia but only that devastating flu, told me to stay in bed, and wrote a prescription. I noted in the doctor, X-ray technicians, and nurses alike the implicit assumption that anyone who does not speak your language is mentally defective. They would speak slowly and loudly to me, as if thereby to penetrate the wall of my stupidity, and, as sick as I was, I found it funny, and understood something fresh about the nature of prejudice.

Gigi checked me into a small hotel with an English name near his office, the Lord Hotel, spoke in rapid Italian to the desk clerk and two or three other men about my condition, gave them some money and the doctor's prescription, installed me in my room, told me that he would go to his office and come back, and left. After a time an elderly man I had taken to be a clerk of some description returned with the prescription, a package of things, including—syringes! He tried to explain something to me in Italian, and finally I asked him in desperation whether he spoke French.

"Ah," he said brightly, "mais je suis français!" Thank God. In the middle of Milan I had found a Frenchman. He told me his name was Freddy, and he was a licensed paramedic. I had forgotten: the paramedic system was developed in Europe, first in Ireland and then in Russia; and in Italy there are paramedics attached to the hotels. Freddy had for years worked on ocean liners between Le Havre and Quebec City. He said the doctor had prescribed a course of shots for me over the next three days, and I had to take all of them.

The first day passed in a fog of fever and pain. But by the next morning, I was feeling better, and I went over to Gigi's office, which is on the Piazza del Duomo. It is in a peculiar old building with a creaking elevator I never learned to trust which rose in a sort of central courtyard through a series of balconies with low railings not intended for the reassurance of acrophobes. Gigi occupies two offices on the fifth floor, one at the rear of the building in which he lives, the other at the far side of the courtyard. The latter commands the most striking view in Milan. I walked to its "French" windows and looked out across the central piazza of the city at what to me is the most magnificent cathedral in the world, that fabulous foolish gingerbread statue-covered edifice with its countless spires like the fingers of upthrust hands. It had taken centuries to build and was completed on the orders of Napoleon. I am not a cathedral fan, but that of Milan is the most wildly imaginative building in the world, and one of the most beautiful.

Gigi introduced me to Tito Fontana, who owns a recording studio in the Corso Venezia, a few blocks to the rear of the cathedral. He placed his office, which is on the second floor of the building, at my disposal. It contained the essentials: a piano and a tape recorder. And each day I would walk there, enjoying the solitude of a strange city. The Italians disparage Milan. It is a working city, busy and efficient. But I found it very beautiful as, searching for just the right words to render those poems into English without doing them violence, I wandered to La Scala or to the castle of the Sforzas, which is now a great museum of art and furniture and the armor of ancient wars.

"Who were the Sforzas?" I asked Gigi one day.

"A family of Italian bandits," he replied contemptuously. Gigi is a member of the Italian Socialist Party, and at one time had written for *Avanti*, the party's daily newspaper.

I went to work on *The Armaments Worker*. It is a powerful piece, partly because of understatement, expressing the moral dilemma of everyone willy-nilly caught up in the rush to destruction, watching helplessly as those strange creatures with a compulsion to power seize the controls of the system to wallow in the dementia of their own celebrity. Our contemporary Sforzas.

> I have no say
> in the way of the world.
> I'm not the one
> who commences the wars.
>
> I go along,
> I do my job,
> I do no wrong,
> but I don't know.
>
> And that's the question
> that always haunts me.
> I have no say and yet
> I do no wrong.
>
> I turn little screws
> with my fingers,
> making parts of the weapons
> that threaten us all.
>
> And I still have no say
> in the destiny lying before us.
>
> I could create
> another fate,
> making the world
> safe for the people
> longing to live their lives.
>
> And I would know then
> the sacred reason,
> the glowing meaning
> of this existence.
>
> No one then could destroy us
> by their actions
> or deceive us
> by their words.
>
> The world that I help make
> is not a good one.

> But I'm not evil,
> and I didn't invent it.
>
> But is that enough?

As the various lyrics began to take shape, Gigi's enthusiasm rose, and Tito shared it. They kept telling me how beautiful the lyrics sounded in English, which amazed me, since the conventional wisdom holds that Italian is the most beautiful language in which to sing. I began to think that Gigi's improbable project just might come to pass.

The next song I worked on was *The Actor.*

A strange irony of our time had passed unnoticed by the press. In Rome there was a former actor pleading for peace who had experienced first-hand the horrors of the most terrible war in history. In Washington there was a former actor pleading for war and ordering or threatening or preparing invasions, who had never seen a shot fired in anger; during that same war he had made movies about patriotism and bravery while other men died. Both of them had been felled by bullets in assassination attempts.

Acting is a strange profession, involving a talent for deception. Elizabeth Ashley has said that the probable value of affecting to be a rock or a tree in Actor's Studio classes was that you would never be called upon on the stage to do anything comparably embarrassing. She is doubtless right. You must achieve an utter lack of shame about doing and saying even preposterous things.

I have heard it said by actors that the greatest actor in the English language is Michael Parks. Temperamentally incapable of playing the Hollywood game, he goes chronically under-recognized—a sort of Sahib Shihab of actors. He observes people constantly, their mannerisms and speech habits. He told me once about "this guy I met in a bar last week, an ex-Marine who had been in Viet Nam. He was the kind who of guy who . . . No, wait, I'll do him for you." And he turned away from me for a moment, like a vaudeville comic putting on a hat and spectacles. When he turned back, his face had taken on that purplish hue of the advanced alcoholic. Even the texture of his skin seemed to have changed. "Did you ever spin a gook with an M-16?" he snarled. It was awesome—brilliant and terrifying. Michael had *become* that man. And then the man disappeared and Michael became Michael again. He dismissed my astonishment saying, "It's only a matter of credibility."

> So many people inside me,
> living their lives,
> seeing all that I see,
> speaking only through me.
>
> I'm like the channel of a river
> and there's always running through me
> all the passions and illusions of men.
>
> But I also have my own life
> that I feel that those others within me
> may in some way be changing.
>
> Sometimes I feel
> I will melt into all men
> with their yearnings
> and their follies always like my own.
>
> So many voices I hear,
> so demanding—
> they're all around me.

By studying the poems of Karol Wojtyla in Italian, I had acquired their vocabulary. Absorbing the sounds of the language through endless repetition of the songs in the album and the enunciation of the singer Paola Orlandi—whose Italian is exquisite—I was passively acquiring an understanding of its rules of pronunciation and beginning to hear it in the streets. I bought a grammar and at nights, at the hotel, began to study the language formally. I thought of Jobim. Soldier Latin, he calls the Romance languages. Enshrouded in the solitude of my assignment, I was falling in love with Italy in general and Milan in particular.

Milan has a particular and grim image in the common memory, as Dallas has one as the place where John F. Kennedy was killed. Milan is the city where Mussolini and his mistress, Clara Pettaci, were executed and hung by their ankles in a filling station. The photos of the two of them, arms dangling, Mussolini in jodhpurs and boots, Pettaci with her skirts dangling up from her waist to reveal her underwear, are indelible in the memory of anyone who lived through that period. The next weekend, when Gigi and I went back out to the house at Cazzago, I asked him what had happened.

"Everyone forgets," Gigi said, "that fascism didn't begin in Germany, it began in Italy. We showed them how."

When Mussolini and his mistress, attempting to escape to Germany, were captured by anti-fascist Italian partisans, mostly socialists and communists, a debate began over how to dispose of him. It lasted well into the next day. And the socialist Sandro Pertini (the current president of Italy, a man revered and considered a likely candidate for the Nobel Peace Prize) walked in on the meeting. He said that the British and Americans would undoubtedly establish war crimes tribunals, and Mussolini would be brought to trial. He said the trial might last up to two years, during which thirty years of Italian shame would be displayed before the world, and in the end the Allies would probably execute him, along with the German war criminals. He told the partisans they must make up their minds what they were going to do and then do it quickly.

So they took Mussolini out and shot him, along with Pettaci. But was it necessary, I asked Gigi, to hang them up in public, like deer awaiting dressing?

"That was in retaliation for things that had been done to the partisans," Gigi said. "Pertini was very upset about it."

There is a famous story about Chet Baker and Romano Mussolini, the dictator's son, who was—and is—a jazz pianist. Supposedly they were to record together in Rome. Supposedly they were introduced at the date. Supposedly Chet Baker said to Romano Mussolini, "Hey, baby, sorry to hear about your old man."

I asked Gigi if he had heard the story. He had. Did he know whether it was true? No, but he believed that it well might be—and so do many other people.

By now Gigi, in a great and frantic flurry of activity, was organizing the concert and recording sessions. I couldn't believe it. The material wasn't even written, and he was already casting and planning the session. There were all sorts of plans. Plans came, and they went. One was to record it in concert in Rome, another to do it in Milan. He wanted a big orchestra, and there would be at least five trumpets, all great players—Benny Bailey, Rick Kiefer, Idress Sulieman, Art Farmer and Rolf Ericson, as it turned out.

I argued with him. "Why five trumpets?" I said. "This is essentially a vocal recording, and we certainly don't need a split lead or all that power."

"Shh," he said, putting a finger to his lips. "It's almost the Clarke-Boland Big Band. Let me have my dream."

To my great joy, the growing probability was that Sarah Vaughan would be the singer. But Gigi wanted two singers. He wanted Benard Ighner, and had already spoken to him. Gigi's late wife had loved Benard's song *Everything Must Change*. A line from the song is on the wall of her crypt. I wasn't convinced we should use two singers, and if we did have two, I felt, the other singer should be white.

If we were to do a project that would be a plea for international brotherhood and understanding, then our performers should represent two races. And one of the songs would create a casting problem, if the singer were not white. One of Karol Wojtyla's poems, called *The Black,* represented a vision of Africa in the mind of a European. I was already translating this piece, which ultimately became:

> In you, O my brother beloved,
> is a continent vast and unending,
> where you see great rivers
> run dry in their beds
> and the sun consumes

all that it touches,
just like a crucible
melting down iron.

In you, I sense
my own thoughts,
like echoes.
They may be different
but in essence
they use the same scale
in weighing and dividing
verity from falsity.

And suddenly, the ecstasy
of measuring those thoughts
in the same scale of values
comes shining through,
a light that burns
in your eyes and my eyes;
but in spite of the differences,
the essence
has always been the same.

If the song should be sung by a black American, its effect as a statement of brotherhood between the European and African cultures would be compromised, if not completely destroyed. Indeed it could then be construed to suggest a tacit understanding between black America and black Africa of hostility to the white world.

And so I said that if we used a second singer, that singer should be white.

"We," Gigi said, head a little back, his lower lip out, "We," in that way it seems not only the French and British address us barbarians from the New World but sometimes the Italians too (although I must always remember that Gigi is also German), "We don't have those problems here." Meaning: unlike you racist Americans. I couldn't even be bothered replying.

This was another of many disagreements Gigi and I were to have, some of them bitter and loud. I simply went on writing. And

I would wander through the castle of the Sforzas, studying paint-
ings of Christian martyrdom, men getting their heads cut off, men
shot full of arrows, men on crosses, and I thought of all the battles
fought and people slaughtered in the name of Jesus, and looked
at the armor, magnificently crafted, and pikes and swords and
shields.

By my second week in Milan, the worst of the flu had left me,
and I picked up the phone and dialed a number. A woman's voice
answered in Italian, and I said, "Franca, is Gerry there?" and told
her who was calling. I heard her announce it in the room, and an
astonished voice say to her, "Where is he *calling* from?" He took
the phone.

"Lees," he said.

"Mulligan," I said.

"Where are you?"

"Here. In Milan." Gerry and his Italian wife Franca live part
of each year there now. And so they invited me to lunch. I dined
with them in their beautiful apartment and Gerry played me some
new pieces at the piano, pieces with a strong Italian flavor to them.
I love his writing.

The next night I had dinner with Tito Fontana and his wife,
Lea Pericoli, wonderful gracious people. They couldn't believe
what I told them of the extent of religious intrusion on the political process of the United States. A European politician who
invoked the name of God for votes would be finished. Nor could
they believe it when I told them American money is inscribed *In
God We Trust,* until I showed them a one-dollar bill.

Rushing onward with his plans for the recording, Gigi
decided we should go to Switzerland to see Francy Boland. We
flew to Geneva and discussed with Francy the size and composition
of the orchestra. Our flight back the next morning was canceled
because of a snow storm. We took the train to Milan, emerging in
the great pompous fantasy of a railway station erected on the
orders of Mussolini as a statement of Italian grandeur. Gigi
despises that building, although I thought it had a strange sort of
pretentious appeal. Because Gigi had pointed out so many build-

ings erected during that period, I was beginning to be able to detect for myself the curious grandiose architecture of the fascist period. With his acute sensitivity to history, Gigi was giving me invaluable gifts of insight. When I wasn't fighting with him, I found him the most estimable and delightful of companions.

My time was running out. I had to return to America because I had signed a contract to do a singing engagement at the Chateau Laurier in Ottawa with Roger Kellaway. Roger wanted to rehearse for a few days in New York. I had booked my ticket for a forty-eight hour stopover in Paris to see my son. I told Gigi I would finish the songs in America.

Gigi asked me to make a demo of those already written before leaving. My throat felt like sandpaper after the flu but we went to Tito Fontana's studio anyway. All I could do was my best. I used the tracks from the album Paola Orlandi had recorded—which were of course in her keys, about a fourth too high for me. Somehow I got through the songs. I thought the tapes were terrible, but Gigi and Tito were enthusiastic about them.

After the last take, I began to gather up my lead sheets in the studio. Through the double window to the control room I could see Gigi and Tito gesticulating wildly and apparently angrily. When I opened the door to the room the noise of their dispute exploded. Tito was pounding a table with the flat of his hand, saying, "No, no, no!", which is pretty much the same in all western languages. Until now Tito had struck me as being a contained sort of man, but I was confronted now with his intensity. Since I could not understand the argument, I withdrew from the room as graciously as I could.

Not until Gigi and I were at dinner did I ask what it was about. "Well," Gigi said, "I told Tito that I thought we needed two new songs, not by the Pope. They should have new lyrics by you. He got very angry and started screaming and said it would violate the form, and we should only use poems by the Pope."

"But I agree with Tito," I said. "The problem in this project is unity. We do not need two singers, and we do not need two voices in the lyrics. There should be no lyrics by me."

We argued. Finally I let the matter drop, deciding that I simply would not write the two songs and that would settle that. Again I underestimated Gigi's intransigence. Somehow or other he would get me to write those new songs, and I would realize in the end that on this point, he was right.

The next day Gigi took me to the airport. I boarded the plane from the rear, walked toward its middle, saw a beautiful woman coming toward me—and walked into Lea Pericoli, Tito's wife! I knew perhaps seven people in all of Italy, including Gerry and Franca Mulligan, Gigi and his secretary, Tito and Lea, and Freddy the paramedic. What were the odds that one of them would be on the same outbound flight with me—and in a seat behind me at that? Another passenger agreeably exchanged seats with me and I flew to Paris with Lea, on her way there to cover a fashion show for Italian television. The flight was rough. She said, laughing, "I hope your fellow lyricist is watching out for us."

My son Philip, now twenty-seven and six-foot-two, met me at Charles DeGaulle Airport. His full name is Alain Philippe. He was named for two of my closest friends, one a Dutch Jew whose mother died in the bombing of Rotterdam, the other a French Polish Jew whose mother died at Auschwitz. *"Bon jour, mon fils,"* I said.

"Bon jour, mon père. Ça vas bien?" He kissed me on the cheek, as the French are wont to do.

"Pas mal. How's your mother?"

"Fine. My grandparents want to see you."

"Oh no. That would be very uncomfortable."

"They said to tell you they have no bad feelings about you. They still love you."

"Well, I dunno. . . ."

He was very insistent. "It'll be cool," he said, and finally I said, still doubtfully, "Okay." As we got into the bus that would take us to the Métro, I asked him the eternal music business question: "Are you working?"

"I'm playing some cocktail piano, some jazz dates, some other things. Practicing my brains out."

I stayed with him in his apartment that night. In the morning I went for a walk in the rain. It had been so long since I had seen Paris, and I walked down the Champs-Elysés in tears for sheer love of the place.

I took the Métro to Porte Dorée, as I had countless times before. The neighborhood was completely unchanged, the same little bakery called Flamarion, the same cafes, the same magazine store, the same charcutiers. I was unprepared for the intensity of feeling I would have walking up that busy boulevard, the unanticipated inundation of vivid memories, such as watching Phil take his first steps across the street there in the Bois de Vincennes.

I knocked on the door of the apartment of my former in-laws, and was admitted, and took my ex-mother-in-law in my arms. She cried and I cried. She seemed so small and walked now with a cane after a hip operation. But her cooking was as always; I went shopping with my son for my favorite goodies, and then we had a glorious lunch. I looked at my nephew Franck, whom I adored when he was a little boy, and at my ex-father-in-law, who had white hair now. His people were well-to-do before the war, impoverished at the end of it. When I first knew this family, in 1954, some foods were still scarce in France and I brought them coffee from an RCAF PX at Gros Tonquin.

This man, my ex-father-in-law, one André Ducreux, patriotic soldier, was in the French tank corps at the start of the war. Due to corruption in the French military, his tank simply ran out of gas. He was captured, treated well, and released. But the experience left him embittered. I knew the story of the Occupation of Paris almost as a personal memory, almost as if I had lived through it myself, from my years as a member of this family.

I remembered too taking Phil and Franck on an outing to the Château de Vincennes. I thought it would be fun for two little boys to explore a fine old castle. We came all unexpectedly on a plaque in its lower level commemorating the hundreds and hundreds of French people who had been stood up against this wall and executed by the Germans. I tried to keep the two boys from seeing it, but it was too late. Franck could already read, and Phil was learning, and so I had to discuss with them how many people had died on this spot and what war is. All that now seemed so long ago.

The telephone rang. Phil answered it. Then he said to me, "It's my mother. Would you like to speak to her?"

The conversation was not as awkward as I might have imagined. "You've almost lost your accent in English," I told her. When I met her she spoke hardly any English and I hardly any French.

During the last winter of the war, the walls of this apartment were sheeted with ice. She suffered through meningitis without medication. On the day of the Liberation, she went to the Place de la Bastille with a young boyfriend. They stood in the cheering crowds. There were still snipers on the rooftops. He fell dead at her feet. She was seventeen.

I had not realized how much I regretted estrangement from this family. Because my son exists I have ties of blood to France. He healed something that day, by making me come here for lunch.

It came time to leave. My ex-father-in-law shook my hand, then got tears in his eyes. "Go on, scram," he said in French. *Vas y.*

Phil took me to the airport the next day. Roger Kellaway and I rehearsed for two or three days in New York, then flew to Ottawa a day before our engagement because it was closing night for Zoot Sims. I'm glad we did. He played beautifully, thrillingly. He always did. But he was having some pain and he played sitting down.

After the set he said, "So you guys are opening here tomorrow?" Then he said to me, with a kind of astonishment, "All the years I've known you, and I didn't know you could sing."

"Well, Jack," I said, "all the years I've known you, and I didn't know you could sing either." And he laughed. I had no idea that this was the last evening I would ever laugh with Zoot Sims, and that little more than a year later Roger would play at his memorial service.

As we settled down to hear Zoot's last set, I glanced at a card on the table that listed coming attractions. The pianist to follow Roger and me was Romano Mussolini.

Part III

The week in Ottawa passed pleasantly, Roger played brilliantly, and I sang reasonably well, then we flew back to New York on one of the small feeder airlines. Roger showed me a copy of the company's magazine, open at an advertisement. "Have you seen this?" he said. It was a fashion ad, smiling male and female models wearing sports and other clothing—all of it bulletproof. For a moment it seemed like something in *National Lampoon* and then I realized it was quite serious. The text described the dashing cut of these clothes that might save you from an assassin's bullet. At first I laughed. Then I thought of John Paul II and Ronald Reagan and Anwar Sadat and George Wallace and John Lennon and Malcolm X and Martin Luther King and Bobby Kennedy and Jack Kennedy and all the lesser political figures similarly cut down whose names we don't even remember. I thought, "What kind of world has it become?" Machine guns in Milan airport, bulletproof windbreakers advertised on a tiny airline over Canada.

From New York I flew home to California and a meeting with Sarah Vaughan. The most important matter now was to find out if she would do the project. I called her, and my wife and I drove, one Sunday afternoon, over to her house.

Sass lives in a San Fernando Valley community called Hidden Hills. There are two accesses to Hidden Hills, each of them gated. You have to announce your name to a guard, who then telephones the house of your destination to get permission for you to enter. The guard called Sass, then waved us on.

She lives with her mother and her daughter Debby, an exquisite beauty with light brown skin and delicate features. There is a fairy-like fragility about Debby. She looks light enough to fly. Men, and women too for that matter, are startled when they meet her. Sass recorded Bill Evans' and my song *Waltz for Debby* for her when she was a wee little thing. And now Debby had just graduated— "Thank God!" Sass said—from the University of California at Santa Barbara with a degree in communications. Sass tries to conceal it but you can see how proud of Debby she is. That afternoon, a few minutes after the guard called from the gate, Sass was sitting at her kitchen table with Debby, June Eckstine (Billy's ex-wife), and an actor friend who read the Tarot cards. He told her, "You know a man who is going to approach you about a project that somehow has something to do with religion. You'll do it and you will be remembered for it long after we're all gone."

"That man," Sass told him, pointing to the front entrance, "is about to walk through that door." And a minute or two later I rang her doorbell.

It is one of those homes that center on the kitchen, a big country kitchen. My wife and I joined them at the broad wooden table. I put a tape of the Italian album into a small cassette player, spreading typewritten copies of the English lyrics on the table, and started the tape.

"Sing them for me," Sass said.

"They're not in my range," I said. I had no eyes to sing for Sarah Vaughan.

"Sing them anyway," she insisted.

So I put the tape back to the start. At that point, someone said, "Look!" and pointed at the window and a vine-covered fence just outside it. A great flock of doves was gathering on the fence, in the leaves, and on the sill, like an audience arriving. You see doves occasionally in Southern California, but not commonly, and not in flocks. The symbolism gave us all shivers.

And so for an audience of Sarah Vaughan, her friends, and a flock of doves, I sang the songs, and when I finished, the doves flew away. I swear it. "Oh boy!" Sass said, watching them go.

"Well?" I said.

"They're beautiful," Sass said. "It's a whole new way of writing songs." She had caught it all. She had heard the beauty of Tito's writing. The openness of the forms, the lack of melodic repeats, the absence of rhyme, did not throw her.

We had our singer. I hurried home and telephoned Gigi.

What we did not have was a conductor. Gigi phoned me a few days later. He said that a reporter from the German magazine *Stern* had told him that we could get Leonard Bernstein for our conductor, we'd get the cover of the magazine.

"Who cares about *Stern*?" I said.

"All over the world, journalists read *Stern*," Gigi said.

"Not the journalists I know," I said. "Besides, we need a conductor who is sensitive to jazz, and I don't think Leonard Bernstein is." As it turned out, the issue was academic: Bernstein was booked up for three years in advance.

During this time, all possibilities of an early Italian premiere for the work—when and if I ever got it written—collapsed. Undaunted as always, Gigi made arrangements for a concert in Cologne to be underwritten in part by the German television network. This, he assured me, was to our advantage. He said we would be far better off working with German television crews. Now what about a conductor? Could I get André Previn?

André Previn is a different case. André is an accomplished jazz player himself. The critics may have damned his jazz playing in the past, but it is indisputable that of all the major symphony conductors in the world, none could even approach him in sympathy for and comprehension of jazz. André was an old friend and I could comfortably approach him. I tracked him down and phoned him in England. He was then still conductor of the London Symphony Orchestra and the Royal Philharmonic—the directorship of the Los Angeles Philharmonic was pending. The project fascinated him, but by now Gigi was locked into a June concert date and André was committed to conducting at Tanglewood in June.

Various other names had been suggested to Gigi by one person or another, and then Lalo Schifrin's name was mentioned. Lalo and I have written songs together, including two complete Broadway shows, both of which, to our deep chagrin, went unproduced and lie in filing cabinets, though I consider his music for them brilliant. He is a highly accomplished musician, and he had the further advantage of having worked with Sarah Vaughan in the past. I got him on the phone.

"Remember when I called you," I said, "about the poems of the Pope, and asked you who we knew who spoke Polish, and you suggested I call Bronislau Kaper?"

"Yes," he said, sounding cautiously curious.

"Well, you're not going to believe this," I said, and outlined the project as it had thus far progressed and asked if he might be interested in going to Germany with me and conducting.

"Man," he said, laughing, "you and I have been involved in some weird jobs together, but this is the weirdest." He said he wanted to hear the music before making a decision. I mailed him a copy of the Italian album. A few days later he called back, said he liked it, and would indeed be interested in working with us.

We had Sarah Vaughan and Lalo Schifrin committed, at least in principle, to the project! And I began to realize how many nationalities were involved in it.

After a conference with the German television people, Gigi set the date for the concert and recording sessions: June 30, 1984. The location had been changed from Cologne to Dusseldorf, which is immediately nearby; indeed the two cities are contiguous. I assumed that the recording sessions would be held *after* the television show and concert, when everyone would be rehearsed to perfection. If only it had been so—the fear and tension that would have been avoided. In the meantime, Gigi said, it was essential that I go to Geneva to write the rest of the lyrics and to consult with Francy Boland about the arrangements. He said he was renting an apartment there for me and Sahib Shihab, who would do all the copy work. I told him I could not come before early April, since I was committed to do a concert and a couple of college lectures.

Sahib Shihab wrote to ask me to buy and bring the paper he would need, because American score paper is much superior to that available in Europe. I sent his shopping list to a composers' supply house in Hollywood. After all, what was a little paper to add to my luggage? When I packed it, it filled two suitcases and weighed a hundred and twenty-two pounds.

I went first to Milan since Gigi said he wanted to consult with me about certain matters of the program and press coverage of the concert. I was sitting in his office waiting for him to get off the telephone when a man with a familiar face entered. But I hadn't seen that face in twenty-two years.

"Sahib?" I said, a little tentatively.

"Yeah," Shihab said, and we shook hands.

The next day, Shihab and I set off by train for Geneva, toting the suitcases full of score paper. I was not as yet comfortable with him, and certainly did not foresee that the weeks he and Francy Boland and I were about to spend together would, in retrospect, prove to be among the happiest of my life. His Muslim religion didn't bother me. Ahmad Jamal and Dakota Staton had, early in the 1960s, taken actions preliminary to suing Ralph Gleason for identifying them, in his syndicated newspaper column, with the Black Muslim movement, which was notable chiefly for its open hatred of white people. Ahmad, a likable and immensely decent man, told me at that time that for him and for Dakota, conversion was a matter of religious conviction. They had, he said, no such hatred of white people. I think that my slight unease with Sahib Shihab came from a suspicion that he might be puritanical. He shattered it just after we crossed the Swiss border.

We had a compartment to ourselves. And suddenly, he sang an outrageous obscene parody of *Bye Bye Blackbird*.

There is a particularly excellent red wine called Dole that is made in French Switzerland, near the rise of the Rhone, but doesn't travel well. They carried it, I learned, on this train. I ordered a bottle and got Shihab to teach me that parody. We laughed our way through the Swiss mountain passes, all the way to Geneva, where Francy met us, and installed us in an apartment that he had sublet from his daughter, Miriam, born in New York City while Francy was traveling with the Birdland All-Stars, and her husband, nicknamed Reoc, pronounced Ray-ock, a French Swiss art teacher.

Sahib Shihab was born Edmund Gregory on June 23, 1925, in Savannah, Georgia. "That's Johnny Mercer's home town," I said one night in the kitchen while we were cooking our dinner.

"That's right," he said, turning the veal sausage as I sipped some Dole. "It was in Savannah, Georgia, that I first came to this planet." There is a dry and surrealistic quality about his humor, as if this existence were merely an illusion, which of course it is. "My parents moved to New York City when I was three, so I know very little about Savannah. My father was a cook on a merchant vessel. When I was twelve I lost my mother. He was on the sea at the time, so I was in the city alone. I did have some family there, and they looked out for me until my grandmother came to collect me and my mother's body. We took her to her birthplace to bury her. Charleston, South Carolina.

"I was already playing saxophone. I was musical from the beginning. I liked the sound of the saxophone, and my mother bought me an alto, because that was all she could afford. Elmer Snowden, who had played banjo at one time with Duke Ellington, was a friend of the family, and he knew the saxophone. He was very helpful. He picked out the best one available, and it was a Buscher. My first instrument. And he gave me my first lessons. I played in my first band in New York when I was twelve, just before my mother died. It was led by Luther Henderson.

"After my mother died, I lived in Savannah for a year with my grandmother. I played in the only good band in the town. It was led by a bass player named Larry Noble, and we traveled on weekends. My father came to get me after a year, and we moved to Schenectedy, in upstate New York, where I finished high school. I played in the jazz club there, and had my first child. I was seventeen. I wanted to marry the girl, but my father thought that it would interfere with my education, so that was the end of that idea. My father and mother were very religious, and sang in the church choir. She had a contralto voice, and I could pick her sound out easily.

"After high school I went to New York, and for the next three years I played with many of the great artists of that time. Somehow I got to Boston, and I played with the Perry brothers. Ray Perry played alto and was the leader. He also played a most fantastic electric violin. It was the first time that I saw a violin like that. Joe Perry played tenor and Bay Perry was on drums. It was a nine-piece band, and we had a good band. I remember one matinee, Ray asked this piano player to sit in, and I noticed that he never looked at the keyboard. He fascinated me—and everyone else—with what he was playing. And the tempo was swift. His name was Bud Powell.

"On trumpet was a cat named Leonard Graham, who later changed his name and faith. He is now known as Idrees Sulieman. That's how long I've known him. In the band opposite us was a cat named Gerry Mulligan. I was nineteen.

"The world was at war, but being a conscientious objector, I didn't serve.

"Boston was a very clean town then, and I fell in love, my first love, with a very beautiful, brilliant, twenty-one-year-old virgin. This girl I really wanted to marry. And I had the approval of my father.

"I got an offer to go on the road with Buddy Johnson, and I took it. This was the real beginning of my road experience. Buddy had a record that was warm at the time. The song that made the noise was sung by a man whose name I can't remember. It was called *Baby Don't You Cry*. The singer was drafted while we were on the road and the only one who could duplicate his sound was me.

"I left Buddy in Chicago and joined Fletcher Henderson's band. I played second alto until the first alto was drafted. This was my first experience with the hot seat, as I call it. It was also the first time I saw so many sharps. Fletcher had written a chart on *Swanee River* in the key of E, which puts the E-flat horn in C-sharp. This was an experience.

"I also got experience directing the orchestra and the show on the off night. This was Monday. At that time, bands would work for weeks at a time. It was wonderful. We worked a club on the South Side, the old Club Delisa, and then we had a month at another club called Rumboogie. It was here that I got the news that my first love was pregnant. It was a blow for me.

"Roy Eldridge was working at a club called El Grotto, and he needed an alto player. He was going to New York after they finished the gig, so I took the job. This was my first time of meeting Eddie Lockjaw Davis. This was the time of Charlie Parker, Dizzy Gillespie, Thelonious Monk, Bud Powell, Miles Davis, Max Roach, Sonny Rollins, and many others. Fifty-second Street was jumping. It was like an oasis of jazz. One could go from one club to another in seconds, they were so close together.

"I was very confused and disappointed with the way people of color were being treated when I met Talib Daoud, a very good first trumpet player. I used to think him strange, because he was always in a hurry, and he always had the *New York Times* under his arm. I wasn't thinking at the time, and I was only interested in the sports page. Therefore I thought him to be a very intelligent man, and out of reach from the cats, so to speak. One night he approached me while I was standing in front of the Spotlite, a jazz club on 52nd Street. He said that he wanted to talk to me. I couldn't imagine why, but I thought, 'Maybe he has a gig for me,' and I went with him to his pad. We sat down and he started to talk. Everything he was saying made a lot of sense. He lived with his mother, I remember, and in one of the rooms he must have had a thousand books. I remember asking him if he had read all those books, and he said he had. He took me through history, and my eyes were opened.

"We talked of many things, and then he showed me the Quran. There were many Islamic books that he lent me, and once I began to read them I couldn't put them down. I found them most interesting, and full of truth. This was the beginning of my Islamic studies. I was pretty loose in my teens, trying to follow the cats, and doing all the wrong things. I had had very little guidance.

After the death of my mother, I got most of my experience in the streets. Talib Daoud presented a whole new world to me, and I accepted it. It was easy for me to understand things of a religious nature because I came from a religious background. I have always believed that there must have been a supreme mind in the making of this vast and wonderful universe, and I found the answers to most of my questions in studying Islam. Would you like to pour me a glass of that wine?'' he said, almost ready to serve dinner.

"I thought you Muslims didn't drink," I said.

"I do not always live up to my faith," he replied with a suppressed smile, and I poured him some wine and we had dinner.

The next day he and Francy and I went to lunch in a Chinese restaurant in downtown Geneva. The menu was in French, which Francy and I had to translate for Sahib. Francy had eyes for a certain meatball dish. I said to him in French, "We can't have that, it contains pork, and it's against Sahib's religion." "Ah," Francy said in his growly Belgian accent, "you don't have to tell him, do you?" I immediately translated this for Sahib, and we laughed.

A few days later I got Sahib to take up the story again, as we were walking through a glorious botanical garden near the shore of Lac Leman, looking at the spring flowers in the sunlight. "Talib Daoud was instrumental in bringing the first missionary to New York," Sahib said. "We were so enthusiastic with these truths that we wanted to tell everybody. There were a lot of people willing to listen, but many could not bring themselves to accept the teachings. A lot of people thought that this was another fad, and that it would soon go away. They were wrong about that. I began to realize that it's very difficult for people to face the truth.

"During that time, Art Blakey and a few other musicians decided to get a band together. This was the beginning of the Messengers. It started with eight pieces and grew to eighteen. I remember that the members of the first Messengers were Art on drums, Gary Mapp, bass, Thelonious Monk, piano, Cecil Payne, baritone sax, a tenor man from Brooklyn whose name I can't remember, Ray Copeland, trumpet, Haleem Rashid, trombone, and myself on alto.

"We used to generate jobs by renting a ballroom in the Bronx on Sunday afternoons and having featured guests. On one of these occasions, Charlie Parker was to be the featured guest. We were all looking forward to it. Bird came late to the gig, and then when he showed up he said to me that he wouldn't read the notes, and I said, 'No sweat.' I would play the charts and when a solo came, I would give him a cue, and he would blow. Well. The first solo for alto came, and Bird got up and took his solo. When he sat down I thought it was all over, but the people wouldn't let it finish there. I thought to myself, 'Just what is there left for me to say when Bird said it all?' Bird said to me, 'Man, all one can do is play what one knows,' so I got up and played, and the people loved it. Bird gave me courage, and I'll never forget it."

"You know," I said, "I've never known an artist of real worth who didn't have doubts, and they can only be overcome through courage. Paul Tillich, the theologian, said that an act of courage allows you to experience God. How old were you when you became a convert to Islam?"

"Twenty-one," Sahib said, "Many musicians who were in the Messengers accepted the faith also. But very few continued to follow the teachings. I'm still trying to follow the teachings but I'm not doing a very good job of it, I must admit. However, I find it difficult to turn my back on the truth.

"Art was living on 117th Street at the time. We used to have our meetings there. I experienced my first real Muslim at one of those meetings. This man was a dignitary at the United Nations. He came up to Art's house in a Cadillac limousine driven by a man of color. Everyone in the block was on the lookout for this event, because we had talked it up but people didn't want to believe us. When they saw this long black Cadillac stop in front of Art's house, it was a different story. This very distinguished guest got out with a beautiful red fez on his head, and he was very tall. Everyone started to whisper. This man came into Art's house to

meet his brothers in Islam, and made prayers with us on a bare
wooden floor. His humbleness was overwhelming.

"This man was Sir Muhammad Zafrulla Khan, who was, at
that time, a judge on the World Court of the League of Nations,
right here in Geneva. This was very impressive to us all. We, the
brothers in Islam, used to go all over the city of New York, preach-
ing the message. But many people turned a deaf ear to what we
had to say.

"Harlem was jumping at that time. There was Small's Para-
dise, and Minton's Playhouse, and later came Basie's. The Apollo
Theater was the proving ground for many artists. I played in the
band behind many artists who are superstars now. I also played in
a number of small combos during those rich, beautiful days. Art
Blakey, Thelonious Monk, Oscar Pettiford, plus I was on many
recordings in the New York area. When Birdland opened, things
began to move downtown. This was the time that Dizzy needed a
baritone player, because his baritone player was leaving. I didn't
have a job, so I bought the baritone player's horn. It was a Dolnet,
and the player's name was Bill Graham. That's when I started playing baritone. I worked with Diz for a couple of years, and we
played Birdland often. I remember making a big-band record date
with Art Blakey, and there was this tenor player sitting next to me.
When he took his solo, it was something else. His name was John
Coltrane. On that date were people like Melba Liston, Jimmy
Cleveland, Donald Byrd, Cecil Payne, Kenny Dorham, Ray Copeland. Those were the days, fantastically rich and musical days.

"I came in touch with Talib Daoud again. He had started to
manage Dakota Staton, and they married. I became her musical
director for a while. Then I joined Illinois Jacquet's band. He had
a seven-piece group, and we went on the road. He took the group
to Europe, and this was my first time out of the States. He had
musicians like Mathew Gee on trombone, his brother Russell on
trumpet, I was on baritone, Ossie Johnson was on drums, Johnny
Acey on piano, Al Lucas on bass. Sarah Vaughan and Coleman
Hawkins were the heavies with us. We toured Europe and finished
in Scandinavia. The Swedish people impressed me very much,

because I was beginning to lose my faith in mankind at the time. These people had to be putting me on! They were so nice, so understanding. We were only going to be in Sweden for a short time, so I thought it was just an act. I wanted to return and live among these people for a time. My chance came when Quincy Jones called me for a job with a show that was going to play Europe. This was in 1958, and the show was called *Free and Easy*.''

I remembered vividly. It was an all-black company doing a remake of the Johnny Mercer-Harold Arlen *St. Louis Woman.* I met Sahib and Melba Liston and Jerome Richardson and Phil Woods and Benny Bailey, all of whom were in that band, just after the show folded. It went broke in Europe, and Quincy had to pawn his soul to Mercury Records to get his musicians home.

Sahib stayed in Scandinavia, settling in Copenhagen, where he married an extraordinarily pretty Danish girl and started a new family. "Do you ever feel a desire to go back to America to live?" I asked one morning when we were having croissants and coffee, in a little cafe that had become one of our haunts, and following the fortunes of Jesse Jackson in the *International Herald-Tribune*. It was in the *Herald-Tribune* that we read Basie had just died, and then that Red Garland was gone.

"Yes," he said. "I'm an American. And that's my home. But I can't go back and just be some nigger."

Gigi arrived from Milan, Nat Peck from London. With Sahib they sat in Francy's small apartment and listened to Clarke-Boland Big Band records, on some of which Nat played trombone. There was something sad about it, like the reminiscences of old soldiers.

Gigi said he needed another tune for our project, he wanted a hit, a big hit. He had asked Lalo Schifrin to submit a tune or two. We went out to lunch and then sat on the quay by the lakeside, watching the great jet of water that shoots two or three hundred feet in the air to no particular purpose. Then Gigi and Nat went away again and Francy and Sahib and I went back to work.

The first problem we faced was that nobody had set keys with Sarah Vaughan. Gigi had been negotiating the terms of her contract with Harry Adesso, her manager, and Sass, quite rightly, would not start work until it was settled. I shouldn't have come here so soon. Had I stayed in California until her contract was signed, I could have gone to her house and set those keys. Now I was trying to accomplish this from halfway around the world by long distance telephone. Sass and I discussed the tunes, and she gave me keys. I could only pray they were correct, because with the size of the orchestra Gigi was planning—about eighty—and the scope of the project, I estimated that at least a quarter of a million dollars would go down the drain in Düsseldorf if Francy's charts should turn out to be in the wrong keys.

The apartment had two bedrooms. In his room, Sahib had set up a trestle table on which to do the copying. I needed a keyboard of some kind. Francy took me to a music shop where we rented a small but adequate electronic instrument, which I set up in my room.

A sense of the frantic was beginning to infuse the project. Every morning, early, Gigi would phone from Milan, first to Sahib and me, then to Francy. These calls began to affect the three of us like Chinese water torture. Their purpose seemed clear: to exert pressure and accelerate the work. In fact they slowed it by breaking the continuity of concentration. It would take two hours or so to find the rhythm again.

I finished another of the lyrics, called *The Children*. It presented a structural problem, which I resolved by using some of Tito's musical material to create a double release, giving the melody an odd but arresting ABBA form.

> All at once it seems they grow up.
> They find out what love is,
> and then they're adults.
> Hand in hand they wander,
> unaware of crowds that

flow around them,
silhouetted profiles in the sunset.
Their hearts are like
captive birds inside them,
and in the throb of every heartbeat
is the pulse of all mankind.

Silently they sit together
on the riverbank
in the moonlight
by a lonely tree.
The mist hasn't lifted,
the earth is a whisper.

Like April kites
their hearts are soaring
somewhere overhead.
Although it has always been like this,
will it change when at last
they go their way?

Here's another way to see it:
a cupful of light
is poured on a flower,
suddenly uncovering in each of us
an unforeseen dimension.
What has been started within you,
will you some day spoil it,
or will you keep it safe inside you,
always knowing right from wrong?

Lalo sent me two lead sheets by courier. One melody struck me as perfect for a finale—a rousing gospel tune, which brought to the concert a black American Protestant feeling, thereby implying that the issue of man's survival is the common dilemma of all men and all religions. I thought of our planet as viewed from space, and its obvious fragility, on which Eugene Cernan and the other astronauts have commented. Slowly and painstakingly I turned Lalo's melody into a song called *Let It Live,* plagued by uncertainty, reading the lyric line by line to Sahib, in need of his reassurance. Finally, at lunch, I read the first half of it to Francy.

Gigi's calls would come about 8:45. He would say, brightly, "Any progress?" And I would say, "No." He found out that Francy had heard part of the lyric. Sounding hurt, he asked why he was excluded.

Why indeed? Lionel Tiger wrote a book called *Men in Groups* about the almost mystical loyalty and sense of union that occur among men in military units, athletic teams, hunting parties, and other co-operating groups. We had established a routine. I would go for long walks in the morning, working on the lyrics in my head. Francy and I and Sahib would meet for lunch, then go back to Francy's apartment, where he would ask for my thoughts on the charts and have me set tempi for the songs, which he would note with a metronome and then mark on the charts. He accepted most of my suggestions, particularly as they pertained to the meaning of the lyrics, but he turned one of them down flat: I wanted to use an accordion on *The Actor*, to set up a circus-like ambience. "Absolutely not," Francy said. "I'll do it another way," and he did.

After lunch Sahib would go back to our apartment and copy the parts from Francy's charts in a beautiful hand. And I would go for another walk or, on warm days, sit in the sun in a cafe I found on a stone island right where the Rhône flows out of Lac Leman, and search for ideas I liked enough to write down. You don't write lyrics, you find them. And then at night we would have dinner at one restaurant or another, or Sahib and I would cook, and we'd laugh or talk about sad things. While we were not aware of it at the time, Francy and Sahib and I had become a group. Alec Wilder used to refer to "getting into your bubble" to create. We were in one, together, groping our way toward solutions. Tony Bennett said to me once, "In the immortal words of Erroll Garner, 'Stumble—straight ahead.'"

Before the adventure was over, we were teasing Gigi about his passion for *Ordnung*, saying, in the terrifying and chaotic days and then hours before the concert, in fake German accents, "Ve must haff *Ordnung!*" Finally I exasperated him to the point where he said to me, "Without *Ordnung*, there would have been no Clarke-Boland Big Band." Quite so. But that is the compact between the artist and the entrepeneur.

In telling Gigi that it took a long time to create a good jazz band in Europe, Kurt Edelhagen was being German. It is not an accident that the Germans have shown the least ability to play jazz of all the peoples of Europe. Edelhagen saw it as a step-by-step (one of Gigi's favorite phrases) plodding process of assemblage and *Ordnung*. When Gigi said he could put together one of the greatest bands in history in Europe within a month, it was the impulsive genius of the Italians that spoke. Yes, it took *Ordnung* to get the band booked and working and paid, but it took *inspiration* to create it, and Gigi in his argument with Edelhagen had an Italian inspiration that is one of the most fortuitous moments in jazz. The right brain had a vision; the left brain made it come into being. And when that band was burning, Clarke and Boland and Shihab and Persson and the rest weren't *thinking*. They were grooving.

In Geneva, Sahib and Francy and I attained that lovely balance between loneliness and companionship, between tension and relaxation. And, I see now, we didn't want anyone breaking the bubble. Not even Gigi, who had made the adventure possible. And Gigi is a prodigiously creative man who—in common with a lot of artists—doesn't understand the creative process, and whose enthusiasm I misread: he simply wanted to be involved in the work. Now it seems to me that we were unfair to him. But I didn't have time to think it all through then. I was busy. I didn't want him dragging me out of the cave, out into the eye-hurting light of the rational. Yet he would do it every morning, and it would take me hours to get back to the cave. And so I said to him, irritably, "Look, why don't you stay off the telephone and let us get some work done?"

And we didn't hear from him for several days. Francy, with a grin, started talking about "*la trêve*"—the truce. Then one day, at lunch, he said, "*La trêve est finie. Gigi m'a telephone ce matin.*" The truce is over. Gigi called this morning.

Francy had played me a tune he had just written. Gigi came up to Geneva for a day, and I said, somewhat to Francy's surprise, "Francy's got a tune I think would make a good opener. Play it for him." Francy played the tune, which was in C-minor, a haunting thing. Gigi liked it immediately.

He went back to Milan and I sat in my cafe, or I walked, and looked for a lyric. Sometimes Francy and Sahib went with me, and Sahib says he saw the lyric take shape in my head as we strolled along the lake front, past the old League of Nations whose purpose was shattered by the bullies and the jingoists and the soldiers wanting more toys, looking at statues to dead heroes and dead dreams, past a house in which Napoleon had once lodged his Josephine, thinking about Heisenberg, about the Leakeys and their unearthed apes who appear to have been our ancestors in Africa, about man's nobility and cruelty, that cruelty that dragged people from their homes in that self-same Africa to a hideous slavery in America, that bloody history that had given me these two new friends. Sahib says I gathered the materials for the song out of the air as we walked.

There is a beautiful stone railway bridge that crosses the Rhône gorge in a series of tall arches. And there is a pedestrian walk along one side of it. Alone on that bridge one day, leaning on the guard rail, peering down into the clear green waters of the river far below, I saw how the concert should open. And by the time I got back to the apartment, the lyric for Francy's tune was complete in my head.

> We come from a distant past
> that we've forgotten
> And now we look up and aspire
> to the stars.
> We are the mystery
> not even we can decipher—
> the mystery of man.
>
> A story is told in stone
> and broken arrows,

in traces of cities unknown
lost in sand,
in columns and castle walls,
silent and unseeing statues—
the history of man.

A wind stirs in the trees,
like voices in dreams,
and then, just when it seems
we know what it means,
suddenly it's gone.

The miracle is the mind
asking the questions,
seeking to find itself
if it can,
only to see itself
endlessly echoed in mirrors—
the mystery of man.

I phoned Gigi and told him he was now welcome to hear everything: the material was complete. I no longer needed the bubble. He listened to the latest lyrics over the phone, writing them down at the other end. Since English is not his language, it took a day or two for him to understand them. And then his calls became constantly more enthusiastic. How much more time did we need? Not much, I told him. Sahib was anxious to get home to Copenhagen—he had gigs to play—and would finish the copy work there. Francy and I took him to the railway station, and then I was alone in the big old apartment. Francy needed me for consultation, but that was all, and I had nothing to do all day but read, mostly French translations of the American espionage and detective stories Francy adores.

Francy had said almost nothing to me about his wife, who had died two years before this in her early fifties. Indeed, I knew more about her from Gigi than I did from Francy. Not long after Sahib left, we were having lunch in a pleasant cafe all of whose waitresses had become like friends to Sahib and me, a place unknown to me six weeks before and now comfortable and familiar. I watched one of the girls serve a dish of sherbet and found I could not remember the word for it in French. I asked Francy what it was called.

"Sorbet."

Then, after a silence, he said, "At the end, that was all my wife could eat. A little spoonful of sorbet. I watched her wither away." And he talked about her to me for the first time.

Finally the last of the charts were written. It was five weeks until the concert. It hardly seemed worth my going back to California, and Gigi and I decided I should come to Milan and help him plan the concert and talk to the English-speaking press. My one reservation was that I had been away so long from my wife. And Gigi, in one of those acts of spontaneous generosity that I learned are part of his character, said, "Bring her here. I'll send her a ticket."

I told Francy about it. "Ah," he said. "Now you know both sides. It is impossible to stay angry at him. It's maddening."

In those last days in Geneva, there was little for either Francy or me to do. We drove out to little country cafes, sat on terraces and looked at the fields of yellow rape flowers in the foreground of the mountains. Always in his car we listened to tapes, almost all of it pre-bebop jazz. I had forgotten how fluent some of those rhythm sections were. The trips with Francy were a re-education in the jazz of the 1930s and 40s. There was a lot of Lester Young, and Basie, and Ellington.

On the last day I took some pictures of him, sometimes with his tongue stuck out in whatever the Belgians call the gesture we know as the Bronx cheer. There is a tramway station in central Geneva in which there are three life-size bronze statues not of great heroes but of contemporary middle-aged members of the Swiss *bourgeoisie*. One is a man who stands there besides a suitcase. Another, immediately beside the tracks, is a woman who searches in her handbag for money or a streetcar ticket. The third is a man in a cap. He is seated on one of the waiting benches, smoking a short cheroot and reading a newspaper.

Francy thinks these statues are stupid, three realistic monuments to Swiss mediocrity. And so I took a bunch of photos of him with them, staring at the lady with the purse, sitting beside the man with the newspaper, leaning nonchalantly on the man with the suitcase.

And then the last day was gone. We took the little electronic keyboard back to the music shop and paid the rental. Then he drove me to the station. "Sahib's gone, and now you'll be gone," he said, and I knew how much he missed his wife. I tried to make him laugh. "At least you'll be alone. I'll be with Gigi!" I would not have dared make that remark to him or Shihab six weeks earlier, when I was still an outsider.

I can still see him, in a knit red sports shirt, standing on the platform of the Geneva station, growing small as the train pulled out for Milan.

Part IV

Those last weeks in Milan, leading toward a concert I did not in my heart believe would ever actually occur—the whole thing was too wildly improbable, even to me—passed in a blur. Gigi has a taste for working with women; even his lawyer is a woman. And for the Pope Project, as we had all come to call it, he had assembled a singular group of them, all attractive, briskly competent, and very intelligent. One of them was Verena Baldeo, a tall slim Austrian of Hungarian ancestry, a motion-picture unit production manager based in Rome, just back from a job in Tunisia and set to leave right after the concert date for a big film in the Soviet Union. Another was Ilia Ferrari, a trim, small, pretty woman with a thorough knowledge of music publishing—she had worked for years for Ricordi, the Italian publisher known chiefly for its opera scores. Still another was Marina Quaresimin, Gigi's almost emaciated and very pretty chain-smoking young secretary from Turin who spoke a variant of English all her own. Verena is athletic, and cavalier in her attitude to clothes; Ilia and Marina very stylish in the Italian manner. After Geneva, Milan was a feast for the eyes. So many of its people, men and women alike, of whatever age, are arrestingly good-looking, and well-dressed.

Gigi is half-owner of a restaurant called Ai Ballos, a name I was told is untranslatable Milanese slang. The other owner is a prosperous printer, a communist to whom Gigi says the most corrosive things you can imagine. Why they are partners mystifies me, in view of Gigi's socialist hostility to communism. In spite of this, however, when Enrique Belinguer, the head of the Italian Communist Party, died, Gigi got a hint of tears in his eyes. They had been friends in youth. "But he was a puritan," Gigi said. "He could never appreciate a beautiful woman." Gigi explained to me that Belinguer and the Italian communists had supported the emplacement of NATO missiles in Sicily because of their distrust of the Soviet Union.

The floor above Ai Ballos is a pension of eight rooms, small and undecorated but comfortable and clean. Gigi installed Verena and me there, the only tenants at the time. My room looked out on a great courtyard surrounded by apartment buildings. I came to recognize some of the women of these buildings as they opened their windows in the mornings, and even some of the neighborhood cats as they proceeded on their rounds. I loved the textures of the light falling on balconies and on bedding hung out to air. I learned to use the streetcar system, instead of taking taxis; or I would walk to Gigi's office each day, to feel myself a part of the city's life.

Ai Ballos is one of the finest restaurants I have ever encountered, anywhere, and Verena and I had free run of the place. We would sit there of evenings amid its bright linens and shining glassware and she would ask me about American politics, and I would ask her about those of Europe. All Gigi's friends are of a color, compassionate and concerned for humanity.

We worked frantically in preparation for the concert. Gigi planned an elaborate twenty-page trilingual printed program, which it fell to my lot more or less to write, biographies of the people involved which were then translated into Italian and German. And Gigi asked me to deal with the press, working with Ilia

Ferrari. A storm of publicity began to turn around us as articles appeared in Italian and German newspapers and we got phone calls from as far away as Tokyo. Even one of the communist papers, intensely anticlerical, praised the project as a positive statement for peace. Explaining to reporters my own role in this undertaking, I gradually became irritated by a recurring question: "Have you met the Pope?"

At lunchtime everything halted. Gigi would send Verena out for gourmet food that we would consume in the kitchen at one end of his suite of offices, looking out on the rooftops of Milan. Or we would repair to a restaurant called the Mercante in a nearby square, one of whose buildings dated from the fourteenth century. I thought the Mercante was as good as Ai Ballos. Its professionally solicitous owner looked like a round and shorter version of Henry Mancini—no doubt one of Hank's distant tribal relatives. The Mercante for lunch and Ai Ballos for dinner, an Italian ritual of pleasure for which I found I had a ready affinity.

And then we got some ominous news. Sarah Vaughan had not received the music. And she was about to leave for a series of concerts before meeting us in Germany. No one could learn those songs quickly; they were as difficult as operatic arias, and more so than most. Sass needed lead time. Gigi called Sahib Shihab in Copenhagen. Sahib assured him that lead sheets had been sent. Then we learned that Lalo Schifrin hadn't received the scores, even though we had received some of them in Milan. And all the while I nursed a secret worry. I had taken down the keys to the songs over the telephone from Sass, writing them on a scrap of paper in the poor light of an unwindowed hallway in Francy's daughter's apartment. What if I had gotten them wrong? If I had, we faced a disaster. Gigi would lose two or three hundred thousand dollars in one night, and it would be my fault. I did not let him in on my secret fear; he had enough to worry about.

One of his writer friends translated the program notes into Italian. For the German translations, Gigi flew in a writer and broadcaster from Cologne named Manfred Miller, a delightfully humorous and sensitive man. Plans solidified for presentation of the concert at the Tonhalle, a concert hall in Düsseldorf noted for its acoustics. Gigi had hired a complete string orchestra from Cologne. In the meantime, one by one, the jazz players had confirmed the dates, including some friends I had not seen in years, such as Ed Thigpen and Art Farmer. I had recommended Mike Renzi for piano, but Mike told us at the last minute that he couldn't get out of a previous contract. We called Bobby Scott in New York, and he agreed to play piano on the session. And what if I'd taken the keys down wrong? I tried to put the thought out of my mind, proof-reading the type for the program. At last my wife arrived at Linate Airport. She was as startled as I had been, she told me later, by the machine guns and dogs.

Janet had never been to Italy. She was as enthralled by it as I was. We began to be aware of a warm pro-Americanism among the people. Nor was this the affectation of shop-keepers anxious for the tourist dollar. Ai Ballos is in a working neighborhood, not a tourist area. At the end of the day, Janet and I would go to a little outdoor cafe to sip Campari or white wine. The place had its regulars, whom we came to recognize and who came to recognize us. Gradually they tried to include us in their conversations, and soon we were part of that little company. One day we went window-shopping, near those canals that Hemingway mentions in one of the early stories. A stooped and very old woman paused and smiled at us and said to Janet, *"La dona e molta bella."* By now I could understand that: the lady is very beautiful. It was a strangely touching moment.

We asked Verena about attitudes, since her work took her all over Europe. She told us that in her business, movies, and in most businesses, Americans are respected for craftsmanship, intelligence, and professionalism. It was her dream to work in Hollywood for a year. All our experience during those weeks in Europe confirmed the high regard in which Americans are held, even though emigration to the United States has slowed to a trickle, now that the standard of living of Europe surpasses that of America.

On weekends we all repaired to the house at Cazzago for what was in essence a party. June began to slip away, and Sass still hadn't received the music. Nor had Lalo.

At last our work in Milan was done. The program was printed and shipped to Germany, and Gigi prepared to follow it. He said there was no point in my going to Germany immediately. I would not be needed until Sass arrived the following week. He handed me the keys to a car and the house at Cazzago, and left with Verena and Marina. Country roads that a few months ago had been strange to me were by now friendly and familiar, and Janet and I spent a lazy week exploring the city of Varese and the villages of Lombardy, including Gallarate. I looked at its little streets and imagined the blackshirts dragging Gigi's father over its cobbles, these very stones.

Of all his aversions, nothing comes close to Gigi's hatred of fascism. "Everyone forgets," he said to me one day, "that the political right became popular not only in Germany. There was a great support for fascism in Belgium and Holland. We have tried fascism in Europe, and we know it doesn't work. But the United States has not, and that is why you keep flirting with it."

The days at Cazzago passed idyllically, and then it came time for us to join Gigi in Düsseldorf. We took the train through Switzerland and up the Rhine valley, past Remagen, where Luther Hodges' men found that the Germans inexplicably had not blown the bridge. They telephoned Patton at his headquarters and asked him what to do, and he said, "Cross it!" and Allied forces made their first penetration into the heartland of Germany. We passed the great cathedral at Cologne, its twin spires rising high in the evening above the city built on the rubble created by, no doubt, some of those blue-uniformed boys who used to hitch-hike past the Brant Inn. Gigi met the train.

On the evening of his departure from California, Lalo Schifrin at last received the scores. He upgraded his plane ticket to first class so that he would have room to spread them out and study them. He and Donna, his wife, and their son Ryan arrived in Ger-

many on June 21, Lalo's birthday. He immediately made a pilgrim-
age to Beethoven's home in nearby Bonn.

Lalo and Donna were lodged in downtown Düsseldorf at the
Steinbergen Park, an elegant hotel of the old school that somehow
had survived the bombing. Gigi and the rest of us, due to lack of
accomodations near the Tonhalle, were at a sterile commercial
Novotel in Neuss, a small town just outside Düsseldorf founded
by the Romans and celebrating its two thousandth anniversary. It
was far from the concert hall, far from the restaurants, far from
the action. Gigi took one look at it and said, "The cats ain't gonna
like this." And the cats began to arrive: Tony Coe and Chris Lawrence and Rick Kiefer and Jiggs Whigham from England, Gianni
Basso from Italy, Jimmy Woode from Switzerland, Shihab and Ed
Thigpen from Denmark, Sal Nistico from Bonn, Art Farmer from
Austria, the Van Lier brothers from Holland, Sadi from Belgium,
Rolf Ericson from Sweden, Benny Bailey down from Hamburg,
Bobby Scott from New York, tall and thin and very distinguished
now with hair and beard almost white, and of course Francy up
from Geneva. As the Mercedes-Benz taxis pulled up one after
another and discharged these remarkable passengers, some of the
finest musicians on this planet, I began to feel the scope of the
project. What a band! And what if I'd got the keys wrong?

And everywhere there was Paolo, Paolo Campi, Gigi's tall and
handsome son, named for the grandfather beaten by the blackshirts. Paolo did everything. He co-ordinated the fleet of taxis
between the Novotel and the Tonhalle. He translated for us. He
was indispensable. Twenty-seven years old at the time, Paolo runs
a successful bar and restaurant in the huge high-ceilinged basement of what was once the Cologne railway station. It is across a
plaza from the great cathedral—a matter of perhaps two hundred
yards away. Allied airmen were under orders to destroy that station but leave the cathedral standing. They did it. You have to walk
around that plaza to appreciate the precision the boys from the
Royal Texas Air force and their ilk had achieved. They sheared
that station off at street level, as with a scythe. All that remains is
the cavernous basement which, with a new roof, houses Paolo

Campi's thriving business. The cathedral suffered only a little scarring from bomb fragments.

The time for the first rehearsal arrived. We went in our fleet of cars to the Tonhalle. It is high-domed and circular, the shape of an orange juicer, a beautiful modern brick building built on a base of gray stone blocks, the remnant of some Wagnerian edifice erected in Hitler's time and taken out by the bombers. It is on the river front. From the stage entrance at the rear you look out across the Rhine, of whose dirty waters even the Romans complained. Since Sarah Vaughan had not arrived yet, Lalo decided first to rehearse the instrumental sections of the suite. He stood on the podium, baton in hand, and gave a tempo. The first thing I heard was Shihab, soloing on soprano saxophone on the release of *The Mystery of Man.* I had known Lalo since he joined Dizzy Gillespie's quintet, the same week I joined *Down Beat* in 1959. My son Phil arrived from Paris. I introduced him, or rather re-introduced him, to Ed Thigpen. When Phil was two or three, Ed, staying with us in our apartment in Chicago, would, with the strength in those drummer's arms, pick him up with one hand and hold him high in the air, letting him giggle helplessly. Lalo too used to come to that apartment. He showed me Jobim's *Desafinado* on my little Wurlitzer electric piano there. It was my introduction to Jobim's music. So many things were coming together on that stage in Düsseldorf.

At last Sarah Vaughan was to arrive. Gigi and I went to the airport. A number of newspaper reporters and photographers had gathered. They interviewed Gigi and me as they waited for her. "Have you met the Pope?" one of them asked me. I stood by the glass wall that kept us out of the baggage area. At last I saw Sass and Harry Adesso, her manager, both of them looking tired from the long flight. I waved. Her face lit up. At last she and Harry cleared customs and emerged. One of the reporters asked her, "Have you met the Pope?"

"No," she said sweetly in that little girl's voice her friends know so well. "But I'd like to."

"And what do you think of Düsseldorf?" the reporter asked. "I just got here," she said. She answered some more questions of that kind, then said to me, "Gene! Where's the music? I've got to see some music! I'm going crazy, I haven't seen any music!"

"Here," I said, handing her a big envelope.

"Oh!" she said, kissing it. "At last!" She hugged it to her. We got into a limousine, her luggage following in another car, and headed to the hotel. She had three days to learn the songs. And what if the keys were wrong?

After she checked into the hotel, we went by taxi to the Tonhalle, about half a mile away. Lalo grinned broadly as she walked onstage. She waved to old friends in the jazz side of the orchestra as the Europeans on Lalo's left applauded her.

I can't remember where it happened. The moment was so ghastly that it is outside place or atmosphere or time. I don't know whether it was at the Tonhalle or the hotel or where. Music in hand, Sass said, "Gene, these keys are wrong." I did not say, "That can't be." I knew it could. Had we been in the United States, I would have known what to do. In California, I would have gotten on the phone and called Billy Byers and Albert Harris and maybe Jack Hayes and a team of copyists and whomever else they all said we needed and the stuff would be transposed overnight, with any necessary revision of the voicings accomplished in the process. In New York, I'd have called Larry Wilcox and Emile Charlap and cried, "Help!" But in Europe? In Germany? Where they do things just so, in order to have *Ordnung*? You do not improvise, you do things by the book. *Ordnung, Ordnung.* How was I going to tell Gigi?

I remember Shihab was standing by. He, not I, said, "That can't be." He'd worked with her in the past and knew her registers. He looked at the music. "It's too low," she said.

"You do it up an octave," he said.

"Can I get it written out that way?" she said. I had encountered this kind of precision in another singer, years before, one with absolute pitch. If the note on the paper was B-flat, it was B-flat. She could not transpose at sight. "Sure," Shihab said. And I came back from what felt like the brink of the grave.

All that afternoon Lalo rehearsed the orchestra, as Sass sat on the stage and studied the songs. Back in an impromptu control room, a dressing room at the end of a long trail of black electric cables, Wolfgang Hirschmann the engineer, hero of the Clarke-Boland albums, sat with Francy and Nat Peck, recording the proceedings. At the end of the session, Sass and I said we needed a cassette player and a tape of what had been recorded. Stores were already closed. But somewhere Paolo Campi managed to buy a cassette player, and had a tape of the rehearsal prepared for us.

Next morning I arrived at Sass's hotel suite. We played the tape, and I sang the songs for her, enthralled by Francy's charts. I had seen her sight-read before. Roger Kellaway and I wrote a song called *The Days Have No Names* for the score to a bad little NBC movie-of-the-week called *Sharon: Portrait of a Mistress*. It is a difficult song, but Sass had been the singer. She walked into the studio and sight-read it with ease. These songs were much more difficult, and she had six of them to learn.

Fortunately two others were to be performed by Benard Ighner and a choral group from England. Francy was rehearsing them back at the Novotel.

A singer under such pressure is operating at two levels. She, or he, is not merely reading music. She is also reading words and trying to understand their meaning. She is reading two things simultaneously and trying to fit them together, two languages really, facing problems much more complex than those of a trumpet player reading a single line in an arrangement. Until you have memorized a song and can do it without conscious thought, the way one rides a bicycle, you cannot be at ease with it, cannot descend into the interpretation of it. Nor are you a detail in the background scenery; you *are* the show.

We worked all morning on the material, then went over to the Tonhalle to rehearse with Lalo and the orchestra. It was then that I discovered that there would not be a separate recording session following the concert. In theory, we were supposed to be recording now. I was horrified. I said to Gigi, "We've got to track this stuff without voice. If it's a mess, she can overdub later!"

Gigi said that it was not necessary, and that she needed the rehearsal time with the orchestra. "How much separation are we going to have?" I wanted to know. She was rehearsing with microphone. Surely the sound of her voice on the loudspeakers was entering the string and piano mikes. "There will be plenty of separation," Gigi said. I was doubtful. Bobby Scott had told me about a device that will remove the vocal from even a phonograph record; perhaps Wolfgang Hirschmann had some arcane way to cancel given frequencies and eliminate leakage. In any case, Sass and I were too busy to worry about it. We proceeded on into what Francy, a year later, in a funny letter to me, called *"l'enfer de Düsseldorf"*—the hell of Düsseldorf. We sat side by side on two chairs on the stage, to Lalo's right. We went through *The Madeleine*. Francy had written, at my suggestion, a completely rubato chart. Lalo had to conduct to her; there could be no winging one's way through the changes on this one.

Sass was pouring every ounce of her talent and concentration into the songs. I was the only person in the world who knew them, knew the little nuts and bolts and wheels inside them. And for that reason, Sass would not let me stray far. I sat at her left throughout that long afternoon. We were frightened, and in the fire of that fear some sort of bonding occurred while my admiration for her kept on growing.

The camera crews aggravated our problems. They were not flexible, like our crews, and nowhere near as good. The myth of German efficiency and technical excellence was dying before my eyes. I have done quite a bit of television, both as writer and singer, and I know how Canadian and American crews work, their creativity and improvisational flair. There was none of that here. One camera was mounted on the floor just below the stage, to stare up at Sarah. We got a complaint that the music covered her face. Donna Schifrin, Lalo's wife, who is tall, beautiful, dark, and with high cheek bones bequeathed by her Cherokee forefathers, has a dry Oklahoma way of expression. She said to Janet, "That camera's got wheels on it. Why don't they move it?" But no, this was the shot that had been plotted in advance, and this was the way it would be.

"Can't you do something about those lights?" Sass protested.

No, she was told, the camera crews too had to rehearse, and they needed the lights. *Ordnung.* Sweat seeped into her eyes. If she's unable to master those songs, I thought, there isn't going to be anything worth shooting.

When the orchestra dispersed that afternoon, Sass said she needed a piano in her room. Paolo found her a Fender-Rhodes somewhere, a rattle-keyed but serviceable nightclub instrument. She sat up late into the night, working on the songs. At 9:30 I joined her for breakfast in her suite. She was eating lightly, a little fruit; she was trying to lose weight. And we went over the songs again, and again, and again, singing them together. I might be teaching her the songs but she was giving me a spectacular master class in what singing is all about.

The phone rang. I took the call. The public relations director of the hotel adked if Miss Vaughan would do some newspaper interviews. I discussed the question with Sass. Her answer was no. And I agreed with it. But I went to the p.r. office, for the sake of politeness, to deliver it, explaining that we just didn't have time for interviews. Would Miss Vaughan let them take some pictures on her way to rehearsal? Sass agreed at least to that. We went back to work. As we left for the Tonhalle, she paused for pictures.

Sass told me, sometime during those days in Düsseldorf, that there had been an effort to type-cast her, in her early career, as a blues singer. "And I am *not* and never have been a blues singer," she said. But she *is* a gospel singer. There is a great deal of the church in her work, as I was to discover.

We arrived at the Tonhalle for the afternoon's rehearsal. The television show was being directed by a Spanish director, Jose Montes Baquer, who has won many awards for his German TV work. But he, and these crews, were used to working with classical music, not with new music and jazz people. Someone complained that she was still holding sheet music in front of her. Of course she was! The woman was rehearsing and learning *the music!*

"Get her a teleprompter, damn it!" I finally said.

I do not remember who answered me. I remember only the icy superiority of the tone. "We do not use teleprompters in Germany." ("We" again.) Yes, and you can see it in the amateur quality of so much of their television.

Then they complained that the lights were glinting off her glasses. Wonderful. Let's make it impossible altogether for her to read. And they asked her to work closer to the front of the stage. "But I won't be able to see Lalo there," she said. "I have to see Lalo."

There was one particularly difficult passage, in *The Armaments Worker,* I think it was, that was giving her a lot of trouble. Frustrated, Shihab—who knew every note of those scores, having copied them—tried to show her how it went. Lalo tried singing it for her. But the problem was not entirely a musical one: it had a verbal and interpretive dimension comprehensible only to a singer. At last she nailed it, and we both grinned. "There!" she said triumphantly.

Later, in the tavern of the Novotel, I remarked to Art Farmer and the others, "What she's trying to do ain't exactly two choruses of *Dinah.*"

One evening in that tavern, Gigi reminisced about the three albums made by Francy Boland and the band without Klook. During a week of recording in Cologne, several of the musicians kept coming to Gigi for money. He found out why. Upstairs at the Cafe Campi, they had been playing poker with Frank Rosolino, and Frank was taking them all to the cleaners. Gigi described him laughing and doing a little dance, singing, *"Grazie mille, grazie mille,"* a thousand thanks—a folk song almost forgotten in Italy but apparently still known in America. We all laughed, remembering Frank, and then some of the faces clouded as we mused on how he ended, a suicide, like Ake Persson whom he had replaced. As for the Cafe Campi, it had, like London House in Chicago, long since become a Burger King.

We spent a lot of time in the evenings at the tavern in the Novotel; there was nothing much else to do in Neuss, out on the edge of Düsseldorf, a clean and sterile community of mostly new buildings. Everywhere we had gone I had been taken by the newness of things. You hardly ever encounter an old building in Düsseldorf. Only a few cities, such as Heidelberg, had escaped the almost total destruction.

A man in that tavern struck up a conversation with me. He said he was a Canadian now but he had been born here in Neuss. I asked him about the bombing, expressing my horror. He misinterpreted it. He said, in his slightly accented English, "Yes, I never see a school or a park named after Winston Churchill that I don't want to vomit." So much for German regret.

I was well aware of the wanton destruction of Dresden in the phosophorous and high-explosive bombing of February 15, 1945. It was a virtual museum of baroque architecture, one of the most beautiful cities of the world. It had no military value and it was crowded with refugees on that night, particularly old people and women and children. Dresden had, furthermore, a special meaning to me. It was at the Dresden Opera that Hugo Friedhofer's father and mother met, and it was in Dresden that, as a little boy, he sat out the San Francisco earthquake. No doubt the Dresden Opera had gone in that bombing. Some historians say that Churchill ordered its obliteration as a sobering demonstration to the approaching Russians of Allied air power. Whatever the reason for the attack, the destruction of Dresden stands as one of the atrocities of World War II. Yet, after Rotterdam and Warsaw and Coventry and Belsen, which I visited once, and Dachau and Treblinka and . . . "You started it. We finished it," I said and walked away.

My son Phil was sharing our hotel suite, which was on the second floor, overlooking the parking lot. One night some German businessmen, who had been drinking heavily in the bar earlier, were bidding their good nights before getting into cars. And suddenly we saw them snap up their arms in the Nazi salute and declare, "Heil Hitler!" Phil had worked for some time in rock and rhythm-and-blues groups in Los Angeles, and he has a way of speaking American ghetto slang with a French accent. He shouted a pungent example of it out the window at them.

And the next morning and afternoon Sass and I worked on the songs. They were beginning to take shape now, the melodies coming to soaring life in that great glorious voice of hers. Nonetheless, we were far from having this music truly together. Every once in a while—when, for example, the "classical" orchestra was having difficulties over a phrase with some hint of jazz inflection— Lalo would look at me, sitting there on the stage beside Sass, and raise his eyebrows ever so slightly in an expression that said, "We are in deep trouble." My admiration for him grew and grew. He is not only a fine composer but, I realized, has developed into a fine conductor, in which direction his career seemed to be taking him. He was the very soul of patience, control, and professionalism during those difficult days.

I had several serious altercations with Gigi. I thought I was coming to hate him. A year later I realized that, on the contrary, I was coming to love him. "The cat's creative," Shihab said, when we were reminiscing about those days. "Nobody else comes up with projects like that." But in the tension of the time, we clashed constantly.

And then we ran out of time. Ready or not, the day of the concert was upon us. We held a final press conference during which Gigi and I and Lalo answered questions about the project. One of the reporters asked if any of us had met the Pope.

There was a last dress rehearsal that afternoon, Saturday, June 30, 1984. I had come to perceive that at the heart of the magnificent talent that is Sarah Vaughan there is a very young girl. And that girl would soon be absolutely alone. When she hit that stage tonight, there would nothing that I or anyone else could do to help her.

The musicians took a long break for dinner. Then in their tuxedoes they emerged from the Novotel to climb into the hired cars which, one by one, pulled out for the Tonhalle. I remained with Sass in her suite at the Steinbergen Park Hotel. In another room of the hotel, as he donned his own tuxedo, Lalo said gloomily to Donna, "I have been in difficult situations, but not like this."

With Harry Adesso I escorted Sass to the concert. The audience and the orchestra assembled. Lalo raised a baton. Benard Ighner, tall and erect and very handsome, sang his song *Everything Must Change.* I looked at the program book we had put together in Milan, whose cover read: *Sarah Vaughan Sings John Paul II, 'One World One Peace.'* For a day or two, Francy and I had been calling it One World in Pieces. Then Lalo and the orchestra performed a Mozart work which he had programmed in place of a contemporary composition that would have cost precious rehearsal time. In the row in front of me, Sante Palumbo and Tito Fontana listened in rapture. Tito leaned over the back of his seat and said to me, "I never thought I would live to hear Sarah Vaughan sing my music."

Benard Ighner returned to the stage along with the choral group from England. Lalo raised the baton again. The chorus began *a capella.* The high strings joined them. Benard sang *The Mystery of Man.* Then Sass came out, resplendent in a gown of bright salmon-colored chiffon, the breast shining silver with a pattern of paillettes. I held my breath. Still looking at her music, and camera crews be damned, she sang *The Actor,* and sang it exquisitely. She went on to *Girl Disappointed in Love.* I got up and walked to the back of the auditorium. She got through that one too. During the next instrumental interlude, I went out to the bar. I couldn't bear to be in there watching her; I couldn't bear to be out here not watching her, either. I went back into the hall. She was singing *The Madeleine.* I felt as if I were watching through a powerful telescope a far-away friend skiing down a dangerous mountain slope whose every twist, rock, tree and precipice I knew only too well. *Go, lady, go,* I was thinking as she made her way through the curves of those songs. The chorus from England sang the first half of *The Black.* Francy and I had designed it that way, so that it would be what it was meant to be, a white statement of brotherhood rather than a black statement of racism, and Benard replied to them in its latter half. Sass went into *The Children* and *The Armaments Worker.* Once or twice she stumbled, but with those incredible ears of hers, she recovered, and did a swift skate through the changes until she was out of trouble.

The worst was over. The remaining song was *Let It Live,* the song I had written with Lalo to close the concert. This was home terrain to her, a gospel song. You could sense her relief. Bobby Scott played some wonderful gospel piano behind her. And then it was over. Or almost. The audience roared applause.

Gigi brought us all onstage, Sante and Tito and me in tuxes, and Francy, who had been working with Hirschmann and Nat Peck in the control room, in a red shirt and a camel-colored suede windbreaker. Still the audience applauded. No encore had been prepared. So Sass sang *Let It Live* again. And the audience demanded that she do it again. She sang it a third time. The lyrics were printed in the program and this time the audience sang it with her.

At last they let her go, and themselves dispersed. Backstage, the musicians congratulated her. Tito, glowing, expressed his admiration in his uncertain English. "Unbelievable," I told her. "Just unbelievable."

She gave a saucy toss of her head and grinned, as if to say, "Oh, it was nothing," and then said in a conspiratorial half-whisper to Janet and me, "Let's get outta here, I'm starved." So was I. We had eaten nothing before the concert. She changed into jeans and an old shirt and we left, just the three of us.

On the night of Lalo's arrival and birthdate, Gigi had given a little party at an excellent Hungarian restaurant that I thought I could find again. It was in what the people of Düsseldorf are pleased to call the Old Town, though there is nothing old about it. The architecture is traditional but all the buildings are postwar, and the area looks like a Disney simulation of German streets. We got into the car Gigi had hired for her, a Jaguar, and told the driver, Willie, where to go. As the car approached Old Town, crowds of drunken revelers brought it to a halt. A huge bull of a woman loomed up in front of it, her stance unsteady, her eyes glazed, her mouth in a snarl. "Let me outta here, I'll *kill* her!" Sass said, venting in one phrase all the fear and tension of these

last days. Thus began one of those hours when even the most trivial incongruity or witticism sets off another round of helpless
laughter.

We walked through the streets of the Old Town, from which
automobiles are barred. The crushing Saturday night crowds were
drunk and dangerous. You could feel the violence that seethed
below the surface. Sass walked between Janet and me, and the sul-
len faces told us all we wanted to know about what these young
Teutons thought of the black lady on their street. Three of them
blocked our path. Janet slapped one of them on the arm, saying,
"Get out of our way!" Surprisingly, they did. I learned later that
this atmosphere is common in Germany on Saturday nights. Gigi
told me, "They do not tell you in the books, but on Kristallnacht
. . ." the Night of Broken Glass, when Hitler's punks poured
through the streets smashing the windows of Jewish shops and
homes and dragging out the proprietors and residents to beat
them senseless or to death " . . . those people were all drunk."

We found the restaurant without further incident and consumed among other things a goulash soup that made your eyes
water. We laughed and laughed at I know not what. Sass said the
songs had been wonderful, the musicians had been wonderful,
Lalo had been wonderful.

"The singer wasn't bad either," I said, and we laughed some
more. We laughed until our weariness overcame us, and we
decided it was time for some sleep. Then, just as we were about to
leave, the owners of the place, both Hungarian, came out to intro-
duce themselves. They had recognized her when we arrived. And
they brought her a little cake, on the top of which was a tiny American flag. The three of us were very touched. At last I paid the
check, and we headed for the door. As we passed a private dining
room, Gigi yelled, "Sarah! Gene! Janet!" And there he was, with a
gang of our people, including Paolo. They insisted we stop long
enough for a glass of wine.

A quartet of Hungarian violinists entered the room and stood
around us, playing to Sass—I think they too recognized her. Or
else the owners had sent them to serenade her. They were superb

players, virtuosi in their idiom, and she was, as I was, flabbergasted by their musicianship. When they had gone, Gigi said, "And you know, they work for almost nothing."

It was one of the best straight lines I ever heard, and I could not resist it. "Most of us," I said, "do." I thought Sass would strangle with laughter.

The next day Gigi paid all the musicians in an impromptu office in the basement of the Novotel and the remarkable orchestra he had created for this one project ceased to exist as Art and Ed and all the rest bade farewells in the lobby and left. Janet and I were planning to go to Paris the next day. My son Phil said he was leaving now. "Wait, we'll come with you tomorrow," I said.

"No way, I'm getting out of here now. I don't like the atmosphere." Janet and I lingered in the tavern with Francy that evening. Suddenly we heard our concert on the sound system. Gigi entered. He had given the barmaid a freshly minted cassette of it to play. We listened, amazed that the concert had ever really happened, and already feeling a sadness that the adventure was over. At least I thought it was over.

Janet and I spent a few days in Paris, then flew home to California. I wanted nothing so much as rest. We had been back only two days when Gigi called from Cologne. Sass had heard the tapes and wanted to overdub some of the material. Could I come back to Germany to help in whatever way might be needed? I caught a Lufthansa flight from Los Angeles. I had still never seen Cologne, except from a train window. Now I was going to.

It was different from Düsseldorf, only a few miles away. It had culture, atmosphere, and charm. Paolo Campi doesn't care for Düsseldorf. He says it isn't a real city—not like Cologne. Francy came up from Geneva; then Sass and Harry Adesso arrived. The session had been scheduled at Wolfgang Hirschmann's excellent studio on the outskirts.

As I had anticipated, there was a good deal of leakage on the tapes, particularly through the string mikes. Even with the voice track turned off, you could hear Sass's voice hollowly in the distance. It was going to be necessary for her to cover her own voice while improving on her performances. Further, since there were flaws in the vocal track on *The Mystery of Man,* she would have to overdub that one too, covering up not herself but Benard Ighner.

And yet she grinned at me and said, "Now I *really* know these songs. I've been studying them for two weeks."

Wolfgang set her up with a stool and headphones in a darkened studio. She asked that I stay with her. I stood behind her as she sang. Sometimes in difficult passages she held my arm, or I held onto her hand. And I heard something that night that perhaps no one else has ever heard: a private concert by an unaccompanied Sarah Vaughan. She could hear the orchestra in the headphones, but I couldn't. I heard that voice totally naked.

Years ago Big Nick Nicholas told Sahib Shihab, "You should listen to Sarah Vaughan records if only for the way she uses vibrato." She is unique.

Jazz singers are inclined to show off technique and musicianship with an intent of impressing an audience—and musicians. One may indeed be impressed, but I am seldom moved by such singers.

Sarah Vaughan does neither of these things, though no singer in the world can skate—or ski, if you will—through the changes with more musicianship than she can. Sass doesn't use the voice like a horn simply in terms of her ability to bend and invent new lines, although she sometimes does that too. She creates emotion by tone color. Jazz instrumentalists from the beginning have used a variety of devices to impart vocal qualities to their playing, including plunger and bucket and harmon mutes in trumpets, false fingerings on saxophones, and all sorts of glissandi. An opera soprano in a duet with a flute affects an instrumental sound. But Sass emulates instrumental sounds that themselves in turn emulate vocal sounds.

Why music has the emotional effects it does is unknown. But any composer knows that straight mutes in French horns create a harsh and even nervous sound, while open horns can summon up effects of distant dignity. Tremolo strings can set up a suspenseful sensation. And while twentieth-century musical theory has tended to argue against inherent meaning in music, every working composer knows quite well that certain sounds evoke certain emotions. Sass evokes emotion not by imitation of speech patterns in the reading of a lyric but by coloring the sounds in a throat over which she has an almost supernatural control. She shapes one word in one of the songs in a way that amazes me more now than it did in the studio that night. There is a phrase in *The Mystery of Man,* "in traces of cities unknown lost in sand." The coloration she puts on the word "lost" is the most lost sound you've ever heard.

And so it went all evening. She matched her own voice on the tapes, and improved on her performance, creating an album that is a mixture of concert and studio performance. And then, about two or three in the morning, we all knew it was finished. This time the recording really was finished. Gigi, Harry, Francy, and Hirschmann went to summon cars. Sass was sitting on a chair, I on a box, alone in the dim-lit studio like the two last roses of summer.

She said something to the effect that this material must have been as hard to write as it had been to learn. I told her these were in fact the first lyrics I'd written in four years. "One of the last songs before this was written for you, *The Days Have No Names,* for that movie. After that, I wrote one or two more with Roger Kellaway and just quit."

"Why?"

"There seemed to be no point in writing literate songs in the age of rock and roll. And besides, I had come to just loathe the music business."

She sat in pensive quiet for a moment. Then she said, "I was starting to dislike it quite a bit myself. Maybe behind this project I'll get to like it again."

The cars came. Gigi and I took Sarah and Harry back to their hotel. I gave her a big hug and a kiss on each cheek. "See you at home," I said.

The next morning Gigi and Francy and I caught a flight to the transfer point, Frankfurt. Gigi's was the first flight to leave. "Give me a kiss," he said. And I did, on each cheek, and hugged him.

Long after this—two years after it—when the album was receiving rave reviews around the world, the critic Helen Oakley Dance called what Gigi had accomplished "Herculean." And she was right. I can think of no one else in the world who could have pulled that project together. I wasn't aware of the size of it then. We were all too close to it. And we were just plain tired.

Gigi took off for Milan. Francy and I wandered around the airport, the largest in the world. It is full of restaurants and boutiques and hard-core pornography shops, stores in a chain of them that you find all over Germany, called Dr. Sex.

We entered a quick-food restaurant and had something to eat, then a couple of beers. I felt forlorn in leaving him.

We had always been meticulous in sharing the costs of lunches and drinks but I was now out of German money, so Francy paid our bill. His flight was announced. I walked him to the departure gate. "I owe you ten dollars," I said. "Next time, I'll buy you lunch. A hamburger."

"*Oui, et un mauvais,*" he said. Yes, and a lousy one. We shook hands, almost shyly, and then he went through the gate. Thus I became the last one to leave. An hour later, they called my flight. When we were well up in the air, I sat back to think about all the wonderful people I had come to know through Gigi, above all Francy and Sahib. Sahib was back in Copenhagen. He did not know, and certainly I didn't, that in little more than a year he would come home to America to be lecturer and director of the jazz band at Rutgers University.

After a few hours, I found myself looking down on Arctic ice floes and then the Canadian tundra, the sunlight to the south crackling off countless lakes like sheets of steel. I thought of all the life down there, the fish in those lakes, and the Arctic foxes and hares, and of what Glenn Gould called the Idea of North. It is in the lyric I wrote to close the concert. Though I was looking at that landscape far below, I could still see Sass standing there at concert's end, her voice one moment the child who needs our protection and in the next the great earth mother who protects us all, in her vast dignity and joy, singing it.

There is life in shadowed caverns
where the great blue dolphin goes,
in the forests and the deserts,
in the wind and in the snows,
and it's all the precious cargo
of our fragile spaceship Earth,
and its countless voices cry,
O let us live.

In the roaring soaring cities,
in the mills and in the mines,
in the ice fields and the rice fields,
people work and live their lives,
and they strive to raise their children,
hoping somehow they'll survive.
Is it all that much to ask?
O let them live.

The miracle
is that we're here at all.
In the timeless night,
we are a fragment of light.
This miracle
may never come again.
The planet is alive,
let it live.

It's a hundred million light years
to the farthest fringe of space,
and there may be nothing out there
even like the human race.
We may be all alone then
on our tiny island home.
And the planet is alive.
Let it live.

Yet even that was not the most vivid moment in all the events since Gigi first had mentioned the project to me more than two years earlier. The most vivid moment came in Sass's hotel suite just before the concert. She was dressing in her bedroom while I looked out a window at this thriving modern city built out of ruins.

When she came out of the room, I said, "I was thinking about that interview I did with you at the Brant Inn. I didn't know what to ask and you didn't know what to answer. I probably said something equivalent to, 'Have you met the Pope?' That was so long ago. We were so young."

"And afraid of nothing."

"Except each other."

She went back into the bedroom, then came out and said, "I'm ready."

"You look wonderful."

And my friend, with whom I had worked so hard in these last days, looked at me and said, "I love you, Gene."

I put my arms around her and held her as if by that to dispel some of the fear we were feeling, and I said, "Yeah, and I'm still in awe of you, lady. Come on, let's go show them how it's done."

And she did.